Georgia

A Guide to Backcountry Travel & Adventure

Georgia

A Guide to Backcountry Travel & Adventure

Jeff Samsel

out there press
asheville, north carolina

Georgia:
A Guide to Backcountry Travel & Adventure

Library of Congress Catalog Card Number: 99–61543
ISBN   0–9648584–9–5

Cover photo: Jeff Samsel
Author photo: Travis Pruitt

Cover design: James Bannon

Out There Press
P.O. Box 1173
Asheville, NC 28802
out_there@earthlink.net

Manufactured in the United States of America

10 9 8 7 6 5 4 3 2 1

To Denise, my wife and best friend. Without her constant encouragement and long hours at home with two small children while I was out doing research, this book would not have been possible.

Contents

Maps

Map Legend

.... Hiking Trail

.... Gated Road

.... Mountain Biking Trail

.... Developed Campground

.... Primitive Campground

.... Backcountry Camping Area

.... Group Campground

.... Shelter

.... Boat Ramp

.... Interstate

.... U.S. Highway

.... State Highway

.... Secondary Road

.... Forest Service Road

.... Ranger Station/Park Office

.... Other Building

.... State Border

.... Forest/Park Boundary

Acknowledgments

Sincere thanks go out to all the people who have helped along the way, many unknowingly, by providing answers and directions. I have discovered that the staffs of state parks, national forest districts, national wildlife refuges and various other natural areas take tremendous pride in the lands they help manage and are eager to share their favorite places. Thank you also to folks at the U.S. Forest Service, Georgia Department of Industry, Trade and Tourism, State Parks Division and Wildlife Resources Division for various forms of assistance along the way. My thanks to all who have worked to ensure the preservation of so many of Georgia's finest areas—and to those who continue with such efforts. Thanks to Jim, for giving me the opportunity to write this. Thanks to Travis, for keeping me company on trails and in streams. Thank you, Denise, for persevering, and for encouraging me to do the same. Most of all, I thank God for His masterful creation.

Series Preface

Out There Press was started in 1994 with a single idea: to create guidebooks for outdoor travel and adventure that are as comprehensive and easy-to-use as possible. While there were plenty of other outdoor guides already available, we found that most focused on either a single region or a single activity. If you're like us, though, you're a generalist rather than a specialist when it comes to the outdoors. One weekend you might backpack deep into mountainous backcountry with a fly rod and reel in search of brook trout in remote headwater creeks. The next you might decide to kayak across a sound and set up camp on a deserted barrier island. The one after that...well, you get the point.

Each book in the *Guide to Backcountry Travel & Adventure* series covers an entire state, end to end, up and down. If there's a significant parcel of land where you can hike, camp, mountain bike, paddle, or fish, it's included. And all the information you need to decide where to go and how to get there is included too. Important facts like precise directions, location of trailheads, boat launches, and campground opening and closing dates. What we leave out of each guide may be as important as what we put in, too. It seems to us that "adventure" travel ought to be primarily about discovery and the unpredictable. About *not* knowing what's around every corner, down every river, or up every trail. Put simply, these guides are tools to get you there, not highly descriptive, colorful travelogues meant to bring the outdoor experience into your living room.

As you use this guide, keep in mind that things change. All the information included was accurate as of the time the book went to press. And while odds are very good that the lake we suggest for a paddling trip will still be there as you read this, the trail that once skirted its shoreline or the campground that overlooked it may have been rerouted or closed. Which brings us to a final request: if on your travels you notice that some of the information in the book is inaccurate, please drop us a line and let us know. One other thing: all our books are written by avid outdoor enthusiasts, who spend months in the backcountry pursuing their passions and gathering information so we can publish the most accurate guides possible. See ya out there.

Asheville
1998

Abbreviations

4WD	four wheel drive
AT	Appalachian Trail
CCC	Civilian Conservation Corps
E	east
ft	foot/feet
FS	Forest Service
hr	hour
jct	junction
I	interstate
L	left
mi	mile/s
mtn	mountain
N	north
NBP	national battlefield park
NF	national forest
NP	national park
NPS	National Park Service
NRA	national recreation area
NS	national seashore
NWR	national wildlife refuge
ORV	off road vehicle
R	right
RD	ranger district
rec	recreation
RS	ranger station
RV	recreational vehicle
S	south
SA	Scenic Area
SF	state forest
SP	state park
SR	secondary road
SRA	state recreation area
USFS	United States Forest Service
USGS	United States Geological Survey
W	west
WMA	Wildlife Management Area

Introduction

Although best known as "the Peach State," Georgia's official nickname is "the State of Adventure," and from the standpoint of the backcountry traveler, the moniker fits. From the Blue Ridge Mountains, where the Appalachian Trail officially begins its 2,000-mile route, to the Golden Isles, a string of barrier islands with isolated beaches and dense maritime forests, there are wild and remote places to play all across the state. Georgia's natural offerings are tremendously diverse, and wildflower-rich hardwood coves on northern slopes of high mountains don't look like they belong in same state as slash pine/palmetto sandhill communities of the Coastal Plain. The variety of landscapes creates an equally broad range of opportunities for backcountry travelers. A paddler, for example, can spend one weekend taking on Class IV and V rapids on the Chattooga National Wild & Scenic River, the next float-fishing for shoal bass between easy rapids on the Flint River; and the next paddling the dark, mysterious waters of Okefenokee Swamp. While seasons are distinct, except along the coast, winter is mostly mild and short-lived throughout Georgia, and most activities remain possible year round.

Georgia is the largest state east of the Mississippi River, covering 58,910 square miles and extending 315 miles from north to south. The state is divided into three distinct regions: the mountains, the Piedmont and the Coastal Plain. The mountain region makes up only a small part of the state, but contains the largest areas of backcountry. In the Chattahoochee National Forest and a handful of state parks, there are hundreds of miles of trails to hike and ride and thousands of miles of streams to fish and paddle. The Piedmont is the most developed part of the state, and its backcountry areas are much more scattered. Most are found in state parks, many of which either border a major lake or river or center around some unique natural feature or area of historical significance. The Coastal Plain, the largest region in the state, also has Georgia's most varied geography: sandhills, blackwater rivers surrounded by extensive bottoms, major swamps, tidal rivers, marshes and barrier islands. Backcountry areas range from state parks similar to those found in the Piedmont to completely undeveloped islands that can be reached only by boat.

Georgia is the southernmost of the original 13 colonies. It was settled by the British in 1733 and became a state in 1788. European history goes even farther back, however, as the Spanish occupied parts of Georgia as early as the 1500s. Indians have inhabited Georgia for centuries, but almost all human impact on the landscape has occured over the past 200 years. Nearly the entire state has been timbered at least once, and much of it has also been farmed extensively. Over the past few decades, suburban sprawl has had the largest impact, especially across the Piedmont.

Climate & Weather

Most of Georgia lies within North America's warm temperate subtropical zone, with the mountains lying within the cool temperate zone. Seasons are clearly defined, except along the coast, but none are extreme. July highs average 85° or so in the mountains, but are closer to 95° along the coast. Average January highs range from 45° in the mountains to nearly 65° along the coast. Except at the highest elevations, average snowfall is less than 2 inches per year statewide, and along the coast it is less than 0.5 inches per year. Statewide, annual precipitation ranges from less than 45 inches in parts of the upper Coastal Plain to more than 70 inches per year in the northeastern corner of the state. Late-winter cold fronts bring the most moisture to the northern part of the state, while summer thunderstorms create a second precipitation peak across the entire state. Tropical systems create a surge in rainfall during late summer and early fall some years.

The Backcountry

Approximately 1.5 million acres are covered in this guidebook. These lands include federal, state, local and private holdings. Although management objectives differ in the various jurisdictions, outdoor recreation is an important goal at all the areas covered. Among the areas are national forests, national wildlife refuges, national park service holdings, state parks, and a mix of other types of lands, including a private preserve.

National Forests

In terms of acreage, national forests easily account for the largest percentage of public lands open to outdoor recreation in Georgia. There are two national forests in the state, the Chattahoochee NF and the Oconee NF. The Chattahoochee NF stretches across the mountainous northern part of the state and covers approximately 750,000 acres. The Oconee NF, located in the Piedmont, covers 115,000 acres. The acreage is spread over a vast area with much private land intermingled among dozens of tracts. The forests are managed for a variety of purposes, which sometimes compete with one another. In addition to outdoor recreation, the best known and most controversial management objective is timber extraction. Conservationists and companies that make their profits selling the public forests' resources continue to battle in the courts and other public forums.

The Chattahoochee NF is divided into five ranger districts. The Oconee NF is managed as a single ranger district. All areas offer outstanding opportunities for outdoor recreation. Individual locations covered range from developed recreation areas that offer facilities such as swimming beaches on small lakes, bath houses and picnic grounds to designated wildernesses where the only signs of human presence are the primitive hiking trails. For additional information contact the Chattahoochee-Oconee National Forests, 1755 Cleveland Highway, Gainesville, GA 30501.

National Parks

While Georgia has no actual national parks, three areas covered in this guidebook are administered by the National Park Service: Kennesaw Mountain National Battlefield Park, Chattahoochee River National Recreation Area, and Cumberland Island National Seashore. Kennesaw Mountain is managed primarily to preserve and interpret a Civil War battlefield and its earthworks, but good hiking opportunities are available. Chattahoochee River NRA, which is comprised of numerous tracts, is managed with outdoor recreation as a primary objective, and facilities are very good for accessing the river and lands around it. Outdoor recreation and preservation of natural and historical resources are both important objectives at Cumberland Island.

State Parks

34 state parks are covered in this book. Parks not covered are generally small and offer little backcountry opportunity. One small park that is included, Stephen C. Foster State Park, covers only 80 acres, but is a primary access point to the Okefenokee Swamp. Other state parks included range from 280 acres to 10,000 acres. Many state parks are heavily developed, with facilities well suited for family vacations. A few of Georgia's state parks are quite primitive. Most parks have often been developed along a river or lake or around some outstanding natural feature, and many offer very good opportunities for backcountry adventure. Almost all

parks have hiking trails and campgrounds, and some offer backcountry camping along hiking trails. Many offer opportunities for fishing and paddling. A few have trails developed for mountain biking.

A $2 daily or $25 annual Georgia ParkPass is required for all Georgia state parks, except on Wednesdays, when the parking fee is waived. Georgia state parks are managed by the State Parks Division of the Georgia Department of Natural Resources. For information contact Georgia State Parks and Historic Sites, 1352 Floyd Tower East, 205 Butler Street, S.E., Atlanta, GA 30334; 404/656-3530.

National Wildlife Refuges

As their name suggests, national wildlife refuges are managed primarily to provide habitat to wildlife. Low-impact recreation that does not conflict with these goals is permitted on refuges. Some opportunity exists for all major activities covered in this guidebook on one or more of the refuges. Chances to observe wildlife while hiking or canoeing are outstanding. National wildlife refuges covered include Okefenokee NWR, Piedmont NWR, Banks Lake NWR and the Savannah Coastal Refuges. The Savannah Coastal Refuges include 7 separate refuges in South Carolina and Georgia, 3 of which offer enough public access in Georgia to be covered in individual chapters.

Other Natural Areas

Other areas covered include quite a mix. Under state ownership there is one natural area, one wildlife management area, and one conservation area covered. Most tracts designated as state "natural areas" are managed primarily to protect a particular, unique natural feature or ecosystem, with little opportunity for any public recreation. Georgia WMAs are managed primarily for hunting, and most offer limited opportunity or limited value as backcountry destinations. Smithgall Woods/Dukes Creek is Georgia's only designated conservation area. Also covered is Melon Bluff, a private preserve that has an extensive trail system.

Long Trails

From the summit of Springer Mountain, the *Appalachian Trail* follows the eastern ridge of the Blue Ridge 75 mi through GA to Bly Mountain, just across the NC border. The entire section of the trail in Georgia stays on or near the main ridge, with average elevations around 3,000 ft. The terrain is some of the most rugged in the state, and the trail cuts through several designated wilderness areas. Other long trails include the 35.5-mi *Duncan Ridge Trail*, which begins and ends at the *AT* and follows the longest spur off the Blue Ridge in Georgia; and the *Benton MacKaye Trail*, which runs 75 mi through Georgia. The *Pinhoti Trail*, when completed, will run approximately 120 mi in Georgia, and most of it will be open to hiking, mountain biking and horseback riding.

Long trails are not broken out as separate chapters but covered under individual areas they run through. All of the *AT* and *Duncan Ridge Trail* are covered. Portions of the *Benton McKaye Trail* are not included because the route runs through significant sections of private land and shares much of its route through public lands with other existing trails. The *Pinhoti Trail* is covered in areas where it crosses public land and where trail work is underway, which is primarily on the Armuchee RD of the Chattahoochee NF.

Backcountry Travel

At face value, backcountry travel does not appear to require any specialized knowledge. In the most basic sense, it's no more than walking in the woods. While there's an element of truth to that, it's also true that every year dozens of adventurers get themselves into situations from which they have to be rescued by others. These operations risk lives and cost considerable amounts of money. In addition to these well-publicized misadventures, there are the more mundane mishaps that endanger outdoor enthusiasts and the natural world they value. Although each of the five activities featured in this book requires at least some specialized knowledge and preparation unique to it, what follows is a basic outline of helpful information and potential hazards common to all backcountry pursuits.

How much preparation you need to do before setting out on your trip and how much you need to bring in the way of supplies will of course depend on a number of factors, including time of year, location, length of trip, and planned activities. Short, summertime hikes on popular, well-marked state park trails require little more than the clothes on your back and a water bottle. Longer trips and even short wintertime outings require more preparation and more supplies. The items on the first list below should be included on all but very short hikes on well-marked, heavily traveled trails. Items from both lists should be included on longer trips, especially if plans call for at least one night in the backcountry.

The 10 Essentials

Topographic Map   Compass
Warm Clothing   Adequate Food
Flashlight   Fire Starter & Matches
First Aid Kid   Water
Knife   Whistle

10 More Essentials

Insect Repellent   Sunscreen
Sunglasses   Rain Gear
Hat With Brim   Hiking Boots
Camera   50–100 ft Nylon Cord
Backpack or Daypack   Tent

Clothing

During the past quarter-century, a revolution in outdoor clothing has occurred with the invention of waterproof/breathable materials such as Gore-Tex and synthetic fabrics that wick moisture away from the skin. Utilizing these technologies, clothing is now made for the most extreme climatic conditions, from the sub-zero temperatures of the poles and the planet's highest peaks to the hot humid soup of the tropical rain forests. Fortunately, Georgia's climate is pleasantly distinct from these two extremes. For much of the year, in fact, shorts and a T-shirt are about all you'll need to be comfortable outdoors. During colder months, of course, more specialized clothing is required, and raingear should always accompany any trip of more than a couple hours.

In outfitting yourself for hiking or backpacking, there are two points to keep in mind: 1) Hiking boots are the single most important piece of equipment; and 2) Clothing should keep you comfortable and dry under the worst weather conditions you're likely to encounter. This means carrying raingear on almost every outing. In the mountains especially, but even along the coast, storms can come out of nowhere, materializing from blue skies in a matter of hours. The majority of backcountry tragedies involve hypothermia, the condition that results when the body's core temperature drops below a critical level. Wet clothes, fatigue, and cool or cold temperatures are usually the main culprits. In general, avoid wearing cotton during the cool months. Cotton retains moisture and is extremely slow to dry, which means that if you're wearing jeans and a sweatshirt and get caught out in a rainstorm, you can expect to stay wet until you change clothes. In winter, wearing the right clothes can mean the difference between misery (not to mention frostbite) and comfort. The appendix at the back of this book lists outdoor stores in the state. They can help you outfit yourself so that your next outing will be an enjoyable one.

Water

It's no longer safe to assume that water taken from rivers, lakes and streams is safe to drink. Regardless of how clear the water of a cool mountain creek may look, odds are good that it contains bacteria and viruses. Giardia, a microscopic organism, has become the number one culprit in illness resulting from drinking untreated water. If you're going to drink surface water, you'll need to treat it first. There are currently 3 main methods of treatment. The oldest, and probably safest, is to boil the water for several minutes (some sources recommend 10 minutes). This is the method usually recommended by park and forest rangers. Another method, increasingly popular with backpackers, is to filter the water through a portable water filter. Many different models are available. Most cost between $50 and $150 and weigh less than 20 ounces. If you choose this method, be sure to buy a filter that eliminates organisms as small as 0.5 microns. One that also eliminates bacteria is preferable to one that doesn't. The third method is to treat the water with iodine tablets. The tablets impart a taste to the water that many find unpleasant. This is probably the least effective method, particularly if the water is cold.

Hypothermia

Hypothermia is the condition that results when the body's core temperature drops below normal. If untreated, it is fatal. Symptoms include disorientation, lack of coordination, slurred speech, uncontrollable shivering and fatigue. To treat a victim, change him into warm, dry clothes, give him warm drinks, and put him in a sleeping bag. Building a fire can also help. In most cases of hypothermia, a combination of cold temperatures and wet clothes are responsible. The best way to prevent the condition is to be prepared. Bring clothes that will keep you dry and warm during the worst weather you might encounter.

Snakes, Alligators and Insects

Six species of poisonous snake inhabit Georgia. The timber rattlesnake (called a canebrake rattlesnake in South Georgia) is the only poisonous snake whose range covers the entire state. However, the pygmy rattlesnake, copperhead, cottonmouth and coral snake can each be found across more than half the state. The eastern diamondback rattlesnake is found only in the lower Coastal Plain, but many coastal areas have large diamondback populations. There is little reason to fear snakes, as they are nonaggressive unless threatened. The greatest danger is in stepping on one or placing a careless hand on one without realizing it. When hiking, always step onto logs, before stepping over them, and be aware of where you put your hands and feet. Snakebite kits, in almost all instances, cause more harm than good. If bitten by a poisonous snake, get to a hospital as quickly as possible.

Alligators are found in approximately half of Georgia's counties and are abundant in river swamps. They are seldom aggressive to humans but are potentially dangerous and should be respected. Precautions are little more than common sense. Never approach or feed an alligator (not only dangerous but illegal), and don't wade or swim in waters inhabited by large alligators.

Although insects are generally less dangerous than snakes and alligators, they can turn an otherwise pleasant trip into a maddening ritual of swatting and itching. Biting insects, including ticks, are most prevalent in the coastal region. Yellow jackets are common along many mountain trails. Good repellent, including tick repellent on clothes in the Piedmont and on the coast, should be considered essential equipment. Checking for ticks frequently is also necessary during the summer.

Bears

Black bears inhabit the mountain and coastal regions of Georgia. Their numbers are modest and the odds of seeing one of these shy creatures are actually quite low. Black bears are not naturally aggressive toward humans, and they should not be feared. Instances of bear attacks on people are almost always the result of the bear having been acclimatized to people from food or garbage, a camper sleeping with food in his tent in bear country, or a bear being threatened. If you're camping in bear country, be sure to store all food in a manner so that bears (or other animals) cannot get at it. If no food storage container is available, suspend the food between the limbs of two trees at least 10 ft off the ground and 5 ft from the nearest tree branch. Do not under any circumstances sleep with food in your tent.

Getting Lost

If you become lost while in the backcountry, the most important thing to do is to avoid panicking. Wherever you are, stop. Relax a minute or two. Try to remember how you got where you are. If you-re on a trail, backtrack and look for familiar landmarks. If it's getting dark or you're injured or exhausted, don't move. The universal distress signal is three of anything—shouts, whistles, flashes of light (a mirror works for this). If you've left or lost the trail, follow a creek drainage downstream. Eventually it will lead to a road or trail. The best way to avoid getting lost is always to carry a topo map and compass and to know how to use them. Also, be sure to leave plans of your trip with a friend or relative. Give them specific locations so they'll know where to send rescuers if you don't return on time.

Hunting

Hunting is a popular outdoor activity in Georgia. White-tailed deer, wild turkeys, black bears, wild boars and various small game species are all hunted in the state. Hunting is permitted on national forests, wildlife management areas, and some national wildlife refuges and state parks. During spring turkey seasons and fall/winter gun hunting seasons, the dates and lengths of which vary quite a bit from area to area, it's a good idea to wear an item of blaze orange that can be seen from all directions in the woods. Heavily hunted areas with short, concentrated gun seasons are best avoided during gun hunts, and some such areas are closed to other activities during hunts. Hunting regulations booklets, which include seasons and license information, are available at all license outlets, which include many country stores and most stores where sporting goods are sold.

The No-Trace Ethic

The no-trace ethic is neatly summarized in the oft-quoted phrase, "Leave only footprints, take only photographs." Where once the untraveled portions of the country were true wildernesses, unvisited regions where the principal dangers were to the traveler, today the situation is often reversed. When we speak of wilderness now, we mean a designated area protected by law from development and set aside for natural resource protection and backcountry recreation. The greatest dangers are to the wilderness, not to those who visit. Far from the mysteries and dangers that the word wilderness conjures, these places too often show abundant signs of human presence. Littering is of course inexcusable anywhere. But other, less obtrusive signs of human impact also diminish the quality of a trip into the backcountry—and of the backcountry itself.

Campfires are among these unsightly blemishes. Although the appeal of an open fire is undeniable, so too is its impact. Fire rings and the tramped-down, scarred earth that inevitably spreads around them remind us that we are not in the wilds, but are merely following the footsteps of many others. Whenever possible, a portable camp-stove is preferable. It may lack the visceral, romantic appeal of an open fire, but it preserves the resources that are unfortunately jeopardized by our numbers. If you do build a campfire, keep it small and contained within an already existing fire ring. If no fire ring exists, build your fire on soil cleared of vegetation; a fire ring is not necesary. When you break camp, make sure the fire is completely extinguished, scatter fire remnants, and return the surrounding area to a natural state.

In choosing a campsite, it's best to select a site that already exists, but has not deteriorated into an obviously overused state.

Minimize impact in making camp. Do not alter the site by digging trenches or creating log benches. When you break camp, return the area to a natural state by scattering leaves, twigs and other forest debris over the area.

To dispose of human waste, dig a hole six inches deep at least 100 feet from trails, campsites and water sources. After use, fill the hole in with soil and lightly tramp it down. Toilet paper should be burned or packed out. Anything you bring with you into the backcountry should be packed out. When hiking avoid using shortcuts on switchbacks.

Using This Book

This guidebook has two main purposes: 1) To catalog and describe all the major backcountry areas in Georgia open to the public for recreation; and 2) to provide all the information you need to decide where to go, how to get there once you do decide, and to know what to expect when you arrive. The book is divided into various backcountry areas covered in three main sections—the Mountains, the Piedmont, and the Coastal Plain. Within each section areas are organized geographically, from north to south and from west to east, with a few minor exceptions. The layout is intended to make it easy to locate an area geographically and to enable you to plan trips where you want to visit more than one area.

Each listing begins with a description of the backcountry area. Information such as size, location, major natural features, outdoor recreation potential, and open dates is included here. The main purpose of these descriptions, however, is to convey a general sense of the area—whether it's an isolated, roadless wilderness, a busy recreational lake, or a remote barrier island where water is scarce and mosquitoes abundant. Also included is the nearest town or city and the direction in which it lies.

A number of the areas have accompanying maps. These maps are intended to give a very general overview of the area. They are for illustration purposes only and should not be used for navigation or backcountry travel.

contact: Each entry includes the address, phone number and internet address of the administrative office that manages the area. This is your best source for additional information. If you have questions about local conditions or are uncertain about opening dates or times, this is the number to call. For all areas where there's a main listing followed by sublistings (i.e. national forest ranger districts) the contact information is listed only once, under the main heading.

getting there: Directions to each area are from either a nearby town or city or from a major highway. All directions given in the book were checked first hand, not simply estimated from maps. Because odometer readings vary, you should start looking for turns several tenths of a mile before they're indicated. In general, there are four major highway types in GA: interstate, US highway, GA highway and forest road.

A good road map is necessary to locate the starting point of the directions. If you do a lot of travel into remote areas, DeLorme's *Georgia Atlas & Gazateer* is an excellent investment. It's a 72-page atlas with large-scale maps that are particularly useful for finding and navigating backroads. You can buy it at many outdoor stores or bookstores or order one over the internet at www.delorme.com.

topography: This section is intended to give a rough idea of the type of terrain you can expect to encounter. Major geographical features—rivers, lakes mountains, forest cover—are described, and high and low elevations are given for mountain areas. Trail users will find this section useful in determining the general profile and level of difficulty to expect on the trails. **maps:** A good topographic map should be considered essential equipment for backcountry travel. This book is designed to be used with a map and compass. Maps listed under this heading are only those that have a large enough scale to be useable as topo maps for backcountry navigation. There are four types of topo maps that cover the backcountry areas described in this book: The 7.5-minute series published by the USGS, maps published by the USFS, a map published by the Appalachian Trail Conference; and navigational charts published by the NOAA. USGS topo maps are listed for every area covered in he book. For areas where other maps are available, those are also listed. The list of outdoor stores at the back of this book indicates which stores sell the USGS topo maps. They are also available by mail from the USGS, Distribution Branch, Box 25286, Denver Federal Center, Denver, CO 80225; 800/435-7627.

starting out: The primary purpose of this section is to indicate what you can or must do, once at an area, before heading out into the backcountry. Facilities such as restrooms, water, pay phones, etc. that are located in the area are always mentioned here. Also included is any on-site source of information, such as a ranger station, visitor center or park office. If you need to obtain a permit or pay a fee, that's indicated as well. The end of this section lists important restrictions, such as rules against alcohol use and pet regulations. Don't assume that because something isn't included it's allowed. Complete lists of regulations are available from the various administrative contacts.

activities: This guidebook describes Georgia's backcountry in terms of five major outdoor activities: hiking, camping, fishing, canoeing/kayaking, and mountain biking. These activities are listed in a rough sort of order, starting with the one that is most popular at a given area and working in descending order. Although many areas are suitable for other outdoor activities, such as rock climbing, horseback riding, nature study and photography, only those five are listed under this heading.

hiking: There are more than 1,000 miles of hiking trails in Georgia, with the largest concentration of trails in the mountain region. Descriptions under this heading are intended to give a general idea of hiking opportunities and conditions in each of the areas. Individual trails are commonly mentioned, but detailed descriptions of individual trails are generally not given. An attempt has been made to indicate trail mileage, conditions, allowed uses, location of trailheads, level of difficulty and any improvements, particularly bridges across rivers or creeks. Mileages have been taken from administrative sources and in some instances have been rounded off to the nearest half-mile. There are a number of good trail guides available for different parts of the state.

camping: Camping has been divided into four main categories: developed campgrounds (sometimes called car campgrounds), primitive camping areas that are accessible by car, group camping areas (usually called pioneer camps in state parks), and backcountry camping. Dates for campground openings and closings should be considered estimates, as they vary from year to year depending on the weather and in some instances, funding for their operation. Fees were accurate as of winter 1998.

fishing: Fishing in Georgia includes trout fishing in mountain streams and a few high-country lakes, river and lake fishing for a host of species throughout the state, and saltwater fishing in coastal rivers, bays and the open ocean. Species found in Georgia's 4,000 mi of trout streams include brook trout, rainbow trout and brown trout. Of these, only brook trout are native, but many mountain streams support naturally reproducing populations of wild rainbows and browns. Wild and stocked waters are not clearly delineated in Georgia, and some fish are stocked in many areas that support natural reproduction. Largemouth bass are the most commonly sought after species in Georgia's lakes and rivers, but spotted bass, crappie, bream, catfish, striped bass, hybrid bass and white bass also get their share of fishing pressure. Many Piedmont rivers also have redeye bass or shoal bass, which are similar to smallmouth bass in appearance and behavior. Among the most popular inshore saltwater species are spotted seatrout, red drum, flounder, sheepshead, spot, bluefish, cobia and Spanish mackerel. A fishing license is required for freshwater and saltwater fishing in Georgia, and a trout stamp is required for fishing designated trout waters. Licenses are available at many country stores and almost all sporting good outlets. Regulations booklets are also available at the same outlets.

Information in this section is primarily intended to list most of the major game species found in a particular body of water; to describe the most appropriate angling methods, whether from a boat, bank or by wading; and to describe access. Information for trout streams is more specific, and includes stream characteristics and in some cases, special regulations. Trout streams are described as year-round or seasonal. Year-round waters, as the name suggests, are open to fishing throughout the year. Seasonal waters are open from the last Saturday in March through the end of October.

canoeing/kayaking: Opportunities for paddling in Georgia include whitewater on mountain rivers, more placid moving rivers through much of the state and flatwater in lakes, coastal rivers, bays and the ocean. The intention of this section is to make you aware of the general conditions you can expect to encounter on a body of water and to indicate where access points are. Whitewater classifications, where given, are subjective. They are based on official sources, personal experience and common recognition within the paddling community. This section is not intended as a primer on paddling techniques. If you are inexperienced or uncertain about whether conditions on a body of water are within your capabilities, you should seek instruction or advice from a reputable outfitter or paddling school. Every year canoeists and kayakers become stranded or are seriously injured or killed because they put themselves in dangerous situations. The inevitable rescues cost money, risk lives and give the sport a bad name.

Paddling in winter requires specialized equipment. Because the human body cannot stand exposure to frigid water for any extended time, mishaps on winter paddling trips can quickly turn into disasters. No one should be canoeing or kayaking in cold weather without being fully prepared for the consequences of capsizing.

mountain biking: No section depicts more change than this one. Several trails in this book are brand new or still under development. Many not covered are being planned. Less than a decade ago almost all mountain biking in Georgia was done on dirt roads, often gated Forest Service roads, because few official routes existed. Today, largely because of cooperative efforts between the Southern Offroad Bicycle Association and various agencies such as the U.S. Forest Service, there are numerous outstanding routes, especially in the mountains. This section should be used in conjunction with the information provided under hiking, where the most trail information is given for routes open to mountain biking but used primarily as hiking trails. Information found under the mountain biking heading includes type of trail, whether single-track, gated Forest Service road, or road open to motor vehicles; traffic level; typical conditions; highlights; and difficulty level.

lodging: A select number of country inns, lodges, B&Bs and cabins have been included in this guide. Most have been chosen for their rustic atmosphere, attractiveness and the proximity to the backcountry areas featured. A single place is included for many of the backcountry areas featured, although many are without a lodging listing. Since this is first and foremost a guide to areas of undeveloped backcountry guide, no attempt was made to provide an exhaustive list of lodging options. The book's arrangement by geography should help you choose between several lodging options for a general region.

The Mountains

Mountains Region Key Map

1. Cloudland Canyon SP
2. Crockford-Pigeon Mtn WMA
3. Taylors Ridge Area
4. Johns Creek Area
5. Cohutta Wilderness
6. Cohutta Mountains—Northwest
7. Conasauga Lake Rec Area
8. Cohutta Mountains—East
9. Fort Mountain SP
10. Rich Mountain Wilderness
11. Lake Blue Ridge
12. Toccoa River
13. Blue Ridge WMA
14. Cooper Creek Area
15. Amicalola Falls SP
16. Lake Winfield Scott
17. Dockery Lake
18. Blood Mountain Area
19. DeSoto Falls Scenic Area
20. Dicks Creek Area
21. Brasstown Bald
22. Lake Chatuge

23. High Shoals Scenic Area
24. Swallow Creek WMA
25. Southern Nantahala Wilderness
26. Vogel SP
27. Smithgall Woods/Dukes Creek
28. Raven Cliffs/Dukes Creek Falls
29. Mark Trail Wilderness
30. Upper Chattahoochee River
31. Anna Ruby Falls Scenic Area
32. Tray Mountain Wilderness
33. Panther Creek Area
34. Lake Russell Area
35. Unicoi SP
36. Tallulah Lakes Area
37. Tallulah River Area
38. Stonewall Falls Loop Area
39. Warwoman Creek Watershed
40. West Fork Watershed
41. Chattooga Wild & Scenic River
42. Black Rock Mountain SP
43. Tallulah Gorge SP

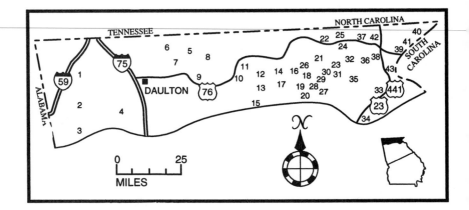

Weather & Climate Readings in Blairsville

Month	Avg High F°	Avg Low F°	Precipitation (Inches)	Snowfall (Inches)
Jan	47	23	5.2	2.3
Feb	51	25	5.2	1.7
Mar	59	33	6.2	1.0
Apr	68	41	4.7	0.4
May	75	49	4.7	0
Jun	81	57	4.3	0
Jul	84	61	4.9	0
Aug	83	60	4.4	0
Sep	78	54	4.2	0
Oct	69	41	4.0	0
Nov	60	34	4.5	0.2
Dec	51	26	4.8	0.5

Introduction

Georgia's mountain region forms a narrow band across the northern portion of the state, with the region's southern border following a line roughly from Summerville to Jasper to Toccoa. Although the physical area is small, relative to the size of the state, the mountains contain many of Georgia's most dramatic landscapes and some of its most expansive areas of backcountry. Georgia's mountains actually represent two distinct physiographic provinces. The northwestern mountains are part of the Ridge and Valley Province. Long, parallel ridges that lack distinctive peaks are separated by broad, flat valleys, most of which are covered by farms. From the Cohutta range east, the mountains are part of the Blue Ridge Province and have a more traditional Appalachian appearance. Of course, even Georgia's Blue Ridge is split, with the eastern Blue Ridge entering from North Carolina in northeast Georgia and running northeast to southwest. The western Blue Ridge, which is actually a series of mountain ranges, as opposed to a single, easily defined ridge, generally runs northwest to southeast, coming into the state from Tennessee. The mountain ranges join to form a V, with the apex at the summit of Springer Mountain, which is also the southern terminus of the *Appalachian Trail.*

Most of Georgia's highest peaks lie along the eastern Blue Ridge, although its loftiest single summit, 4,784-foot Brasstown Bald, sets just off the main ridge. The eastern slope of the Blue Ridge drops dramatically toward the Piedmont in most places, creating dozens of waterfalls in northeast Georgia. The state's highest waterfall, Amicalola Falls, plunges 729 feet and forms the centerpiece of a very popular state park. The Cohutta Wilderness, Georgia's most extensive individual backcountry with more than 37,000 acres under federal wilderness designation, sets along the western Blue Ridge.

The ridges and valleys of northwest Georgia, although not nearly as high as the Blue Ridge Mountains, are extremely rugged and are laced with caves, cut by canyons and bounded by cliffs. Lookout Mountain, the most westerly ridge, is a broad plateau that begins in Tennessee and runs South into Alabama, clipping Georgia along the way. The ridgetop is cut by Cloudland Canyon, which is close to 1,000 feet deep in places. Ridges to the east are much narrower.

Georgia's mountains epitomize the Southern Appalachian forest, which is not actually a forest type but a broad categorization that brings in the array of forest types that are prevalent throughout the

Southern Appalachian Mountains. Depending on elevations, orientations, drainages and soil make-up, the same mountain may support cove hardwood, oak/hickory, white pine/hemlock and mixed hardwood/pine forests, to name just a few. Broadly speaking, hardwoods are prevalent along northern slopes of Georgia mountains, while pines are more common on dryer southern slopes. Many mountain rivers are bounded by white pines and hemlocks and by tunnels of rhododendron and mountain laurel.

There are scattered old-growth tracts and individual trees that have somehow avoided the saw through the years, but almost all of Georgia's mountain region has been cut at least once. Some second-growth stands have matured into fabulous forests. Several yellow poplars in Sosbee Cove, an area last logged in the early 1900s, exceed 15 feet in diameter.

Black bears and ruffed grouse are favorite wildlife species in the mountain region. There are also plenty of white-tailed deer and wild turkeys. Woodland bird species, including handsome pileated woodpeckers, are abundant in Georgia's high country. The region's creeks, meanwhile, have a worldwide reputation for the number of salamander species they support.

The mountain region has extensive offerings for the backcountry adventurer, seen in the fact that half the chapters in this book detail areas located in the high country region. The Chattahoochee National Forest includes 749,455 acres of mountain land. Of that, 114,616 acres lie within 10 federally designated roadless wilderness areas. Beyond the national forest areas, half a dozen state parks, a wildlife management area and a state-owned and -managed conservation area are covered in the chapters that follow.

Opportunities abound in the mountains for all the activities covered in this guidebook. Hundreds of miles of hiking trails lace the mountain region, including the first (or last) 79 miles of the 2,000 mile *Appalachian Trail*. The Wild and Scenic Chattooga River is North Georgia's showcase paddling destination. Like a couple other rivers in the region, the Chattooga offers something for every paddler. The mountains have a few outstanding areas for riding mountain bikes, and opportunities are quickly expanding in this arena. Where no trails exist, hundreds of miles of gated Forest Service roads lend themselves to mountain bike riding. Hundreds of miles of tumbling trout streams, meanwhile, provide good opportunities for fishing. Both stocked and wild trout populations are present, with native brook trout still holding their ground in many small tributary streams. Opportunities for camping are too numerous and varied to even begin naming.

Cloudland Canyon State Park

For grandeur and drama, the views from the picnic area at Cloudland Canyon State Park rival any in Georgia. Cloudland Canyon, up to 1,000 feet deep, was carved into Lookout Mountain by Sitton Gulch Creek, a process that continues still. Cloudland Canyon actually consists of three gorges: Sitton Gulch, and tributary gorges formed by Daniel and Bear creeks. The state park, which was established in 1939, covers 2,219 acres along the edges of all three gorges. Although it has some resort-type development, including a pool, tennis courts and 16 cottages, its size is sufficient to accommodate such facilities and leave room for backcountry opportunities. The least developed areas are along the West Rim and up Bear Creek. Camping opportunities are outstanding and very diverse, with four different kinds of offerings that range from a backcountry loop to two developed car campgrounds. The park has 6.5 miles of day-use trails, with 1 trail following the West Rim of the canyon and the other leading to a pair of terrific waterfalls. The falls trail provides the only access to the canyon floor. The park has a large picnic area, with 75 picnic sites and 4 shelters; several of the sites offer views of the canyon. Deer, turkeys and squirrels are the most common wildlife species.

contact: Superintendent, Cloudland Canyon State Park, 122 Cloudland Canyon State Park Road, Rising Fawn, GA 30738; 706;657-4050; www.gastateparks.org.

getting there: From Trenton, Drive E on GA-136 8 mi to the park entrance on the L.

topography: The entire park sits atop Lookout Mtn, which the canyon cuts into. The canyon is cut by Sitton Gulch Creek and its 2 main tributaries, Daniel and Bear creeks. Although canyon walls are sheer and the hike down to the falls is steep, most of the park is spread out along the canyon's rim, with terrain that is flat to gently rolling. Most forests are mixed hardwoods and pines. Elevations range from 1,800 ft to 2,800 ft. **maps:** USGS Durham.

starting out: The park office, which serves as a visitor center, is open 8 AM to 5 PM daily. Maps and information are available inside, and restrooms, a pay phone and drink machines are there too. The park is open 7 AM to 10 PM.

Alcohol is prohibited in public areas. Pets must be on a leash of 6 ft or less.

activities: Camping, Hiking.

camping: Cloudland Canyon SP offers a variety of camping opportunities, beginning with backcountry camping at 11 sites well spaced along a 2.5-mi loop trail. Each site consists of a clearing with a picnic table, fire ring and pit privy. The trail begins behind a locked gate in an area separated from other park facilities. The terrain is mostly flat and the mixed forest is dense. The backcountry loop is open year round. A permit is required, and reservations are available. Rates are available through the reservations line.

For tent campers who prefer modern restrooms and the convenience of having a car nearby, the park has a walk-in camping loop with 30 sites. Sites are up to 0.5 mi away from a single parking area and restroom facility that has flush toilets and hot showers. The sites are modern, with a picnic table, tent pad, fire ring/grill, and lantern post. They do not have water or electricity. They are average sized and offer average isolation in a mixed pine/hardwood forest. The campground is closed during winter (specific dates vary). Sites cost $8/night.

The park also has 2 fully developed campgrounds, with 73 campsites in all. The West Rim Campground is very nice, with large sites that are well spaced and offer good privacy in a dense mixed forest on rolling terrain. Some sites are built up, like decks, and the restroom buildings look like log cabins. The East Rim Campground, located near the picnic area, is much less attractive. The sites are small and close together, and the pine forest is very open. All sites have a picnic table, tent pad, lantern post, fire ring/grill, water and electricity. Restrooms have hot showers, flush toilets, and laundry facilities. The campgrounds are open year round. Sites cost $13/night for tents, $15/night for RVs.

Finally, there are 4 pioneer camping areas, each of which can accommodate up to 25 campers. Pioneer sites are simply forest clearings, each with a 3-sided shelter, fire ring, picnic table and pit toilet. Pioneer sites cost $25/night and are available year round. To make reservations for any kind of camping, call 800/864-7275. Minimum stays may be required for reservations.

hiking: 2 day-use trails share a common trailhead, near the picnic area, and can be combined for a 6.5 mi hike. The trails share a path for a short distance before the *Waterfall Trail* splits off to the R and begins its descent into the canyon. The steep trail, which follows a step-and-boardwalk system most of the way, splits inside the canyon, with 1 fork leading to each waterfall. Both falls are on Daniel Creek and are very scenic, and the trail leads right up to the plunge pool beneath each. The round-trip hike that visits both waterfalls is 1.5 mi. The *West Rim Trail* crosses Daniel Creek by bridge in the shallow upper end of its gorge, winding down to the creek and then climbing to follow the opposite rim. Much of the hike is along the edge of the canyon, providing outstanding overviews. The *Waterfall Trail* is blue blazed initially, but looses its blazes once the step systems begin. It is easy to follow and an easy walk down. The hike out is strenuous but short. The yellow-blazed *West Rim Trail* is well marked and easy to follow. Walking is generally easy, with a couple moderate stretches.

lodging: The park has 16 2- and 3-bedroom cottages divided into 2 areas. All are fully furnished, including linens and kitchenware, and have heating, air conditioning, fireplaces and screen porches or decks. Cabins 1–5 are close the East Rim Campground and the picnic area. The area can be congested, but the setting is very nice since the cabins overlook the canyon rim. The remainder of the cabins are in a row on the West Rim side of the park. These are more isolated from park activity, and connector trails lead to the West Rim Trail. Cottages cost $65 to $95/night. For reservations, call 800/864-7275.

Crockford-Pigeon Mountain WMA

Pigeon Mountain gets its name from extinct passenger pigeons, which roosted by the thousand—some say million—on the mountain during the 1800s. The first half of the WMA's name honors Jack Crockford, a Georgia pioneer in wildlife biology. The Crockford-Pigeon Mountain WMA encompasses 15,527 acres atop the mountain and along its edges. High cliffs, unusual rock formation, crystalline springs, countless miles of caves and clear ponds are just some of the area's highlights. Two spectacular areas that are popular with backcountry adventurers are Rocktown, a vast area of massive sandstone boulders, and the

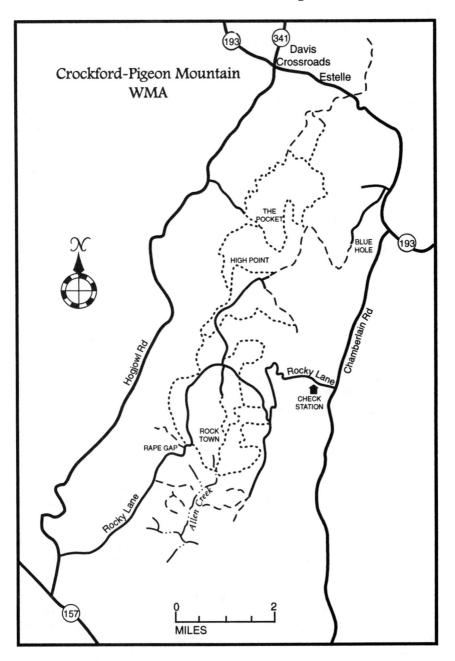

Pocket, a valley bounded by steep ridges on three sides. Although wildlife management remains the primary management focus, the Crockford-Pigeon Mountain WMA probably attracts a more diverse group of recreational users than any other single area in Georgia. In addition to mountain biking, hiking, camping and fishing, the WMA also offer opportunities for hunting, horseback riding, rock climbing, caving and hang gliding. Nearly the entire trail system, which includes more than 40 miles of blazed routes, is open to hikers, mountain bikers, and equestrians. Primitive camping is permitted in most areas. The Crockford-Pigeon Mountain WMA is a no-frills area, and a WMA brochure stresses that the area is not a park. Roads, through generally passable by passenger vehicle, are often steep and always very rough. Beyond deer and wild turkeys, both abundant on the WMA, bats and golden eagles are among the wildlife species that make use of the Pigeon Mountain's unique habitats.

LaFayette (NE) is the nearest town.

contact: Department of Natural Resources, Wildlife Resources Division, Region 1 Office, 2492 Floyd Springs, Rd, Armuchee, GA 30105; 706/205-6042; www.georgia.org/dnr/wild

getting there: From the jct of US-27 and GA-193 in LaFayette, Drive W on GA-193 (official designation is GA-193 N) 2.8 mi to Chamberlain Rd and turn L. Drive 3.6 mi to Rocky Lane, on the R, which leads into the WMA. Turns are marked with signs for the WMA.

topography: Pigeon Mtn is a major spur off Lookout Mtn, which runs SW to NE and extends from the N-to-S-running Lookout Mtn like the thumb of a mitten. A plateau, the mountain is generally level on top, but its sides drop off dramatically. There are numerous cliffs, caves and unusual rock formations. Forests include hardwood stands and mixed hardwood/pine forests. Top elevation is at 2,329 ft at High Point. The valley is approximately 1,500 ft below. **maps:** USGS Cedar Grove, Estelle, Dougherty Gap.

starting   out: The check station building, just inside the WMA entrance on the L, serves as an information center and office. Brochures and trail maps are available. Information posted might include standard area rules, special regulations in effect at the time, hunt date schedules, and areas of interesting wildlife sightings during recent days. Although the office is sometimes used, it generally is neither staffed nor open.

Alcohol is prohibited except in established camps. WMA quiet hours are 10 PM to 7 AM. Check specific regulations regarding caving, rock climbing, horseback riding and hang gliding.

activities: Mountain Biking, Hiking, Camping, Fishing.

mountain biking: The WMA has one of the best collections of routes for riding mountain bikes anywhere in GA. Options are so extensive, in fact, that an entire guidebook could be devoted just to riding here. 9 trails, ranging from 0.6 mi to 13.2 mi and totaling 42.5 mi, are open to mountain biking. The only trail closed to bikes on the entire WMA is the 1-mi trail to Rocktown. Several trails are interconnected, creating dozens of different possible routes. Biking is also permitted on more than 15 mi of roads through the WMA. The road system links the trails to make many loops possible, and some of the roads are significantly rougher than mountain biking trails in other areas. The whole gamut of terrain and trail types are represented. There are creek crossings, boulderfields, woodland trails and routes over open rock, to list just a few. In general, the easiest routes are those that stay atop the mountain, where much of the terrain is fairly flat. Routes that climb from the Pocket—and even Rocky Lane, the main access road—are grueling, as they gain well over 1,000 ft. All trailheads are clearly marked and routes are blazed, with six different colors used in the trail-marking system. The WMA brochure lists trails, their lengths and the colors of their blazes. An area map shows all trails and distinguishes them by blaze colors. Biking is not permitted off designated trails and roads or during any firearms deer hunt. Biking is also not permitted before 10 AM on days of archery hunts. Trails are designated for multi-use and are popular with equestrians, so bikers should respect other trail users.

hiking: The entire 42.5-mi trail system is open to hiking, but heavy equestrian and mountain bike use tends to limit the popularity of hiking on most WMA routes. The *Rocktown Trail*, open to foot traffic only, is by far the most popular hiking trail. The route itself is only about 1 mi long, but any backcountry enthusiast could spend hours in Rocktown, which the trail leads into. Rocktown is a vast area of massive undisturbed sandstone boulders and rock formations. The reddish rocks come in every imaginable shape. There are places to climb, passages to squeeze through and countless rocks to simply marvel at. The other area used regularly by hikers is the Pocket. Like another area of the same name, just a few ridges over in the Chattahoochee NF, the Pocket is a low, flat area with high ridges wrapped around it. 3 trails—South Pocket, North Pocket and a section of the West Brow—combine to create a long and difficult but fabulous loop hike. The loop climbs to the ridge, follows it around to High Point, which is in fact the highest point on Pigeon Mtn, and circles back down to the Pocket. The 9.3-mi loop is blue blazed all the way, with the West Brow portion blazed both blue and white. Many hikers come primarily to see the Pocket and the wildflower area that is maintained there, hiking a modest distance up one side or the other and then returning by the same route.

camping: Backcountry camping is permitted throughout the WMA, except in the Rocktown, within 100 yards of the Blue Hole or the Pocket Wildflower area, or in wildlife clearings or plantings. All camping is primitive, with no facilities. A minimum impact approach is expected. Small fires, using wood from dead and downed trees only, are permitted in existing fire areas. Camping is permitted year round. There are no fees. Primitive group camps are in the Estelle and Sawmill areas. Again, there are no facilities, but these areas have been opened up to accommodate groups. All camping is on a first-come, first-served basis.

fishing: Half a dozen small ponds and 2 trout streams provide limited opportunities for fishing at Crockford-Pigeon Mtn. The ponds, which are clear and rocky, have populations of bream, bass and catfish. They are not actively managed and offer anglers varying levels of success. All except Sawmill Pond are open to fishing, with no special regulations, unless posted at the site. Sawmill Pond is open only to kids 16 and under. Almost all fishing is from the banks, and fishing pressure is typically light.

2 streams that tumble off the mountain, Allen and Duck creeks, are designated as trout waters. The Allen Creek watershed is seasonal, while the Duck Creek watershed is open year round. Both streams offer only limited amounts of access on public lands and marginal habitat, especially during summer. Allen Creek, in fact, offers almost no habitat some summers, nearly drying up. Neither stream offers more than 1 mi of fishable waters and both are steep and overgrown. Allen Creek is accessible only by trail.

Armuchee Ranger District

Chattahoochee National Forest

Separated by many miles from the rest the Chattahoochee National Forest, the Armuchee Ranger District is quite different in character from the other five districts. Its mountains are not part of the Blue Ridge. Long, narrow ridges, they are actually more closely associated with Cumberland Plateau. Although not nearly as tall as the mountains farther east, the Armuchee Ridges are often steep-sided and rugged, with waterfalls tumbling off them and mountain laurel shrouding the creeks that drain them. Armuchee is by far the smallest of the six districts, totaling just under 65,000 acres, and there are no vast backcountry areas. A strip of Forest Service holdings does extend more than 25 miles along Taylor Ridge, but in most places the strip is quite narrow. Five hiking trails on the Armuchee District total 16.4 miles and lend themselves well to day-hikes. All facilities are in the Johns Mountain area, where there are three recreation areas—Keown Falls, the Pocket and Hidden Creek. There are campgrounds at the Pocket and Hidden Creek. A few small streams and one small lake provide limited opportunities for fishing. Deer and wild turkey populations are sizable on the Armuchee District, and grouse can sometimes be seen high on the ridges.

Mountain bikers use various FS roads on the district, but a long, multi-use trail that will greatly increase biking opportunities is being developed. The *Georgia Pinhoiti Trail*, which will eventually connect the *Alabama Pinhoiti Trail* with the *Benton McKaye Trail* in the Cohutta Mountains, will run 60 mi across the Armuchee District, with some portions following public roads, gated forest service roads or existing trails. Much of the route will be newly established trail, however, and 49 mi of it will be open to hiking, mountain biking and horseback riding. The route was laid out in early 1999, with parking areas in place off GA-136 and GA-100, but portions of the trail were still in the development stage. The trail enters the forest near High Point, at the south end of Taylor Ridge. From High Point to US-27, the trail is fully developed and open, as are scattered other sections along the way.

Dalton (NE), Calhoun (SE), Summerville (SW) and LaFayette (NW) are the nearest towns.

contact: Armuchee Ranger District, U.S. Forest Service, P.O. Box 465, LaFayette, GA 30728; 706/638-1085; www.fs.fed.us/conf/.

getting there: GA-136 and Pocket Rd are the major access roads for the Armuchee RD. The district RS is located 3 mi E of LaFayette on GA-136.

topography: The Armuchee RD is characterized by long, narrow ridges, which run parallel and are separated by flat valleys. The ridges run NE to SW. Taylor Ridge and Johns Mtn are the most prominent individual ridges. Prevalent forest types include mixed pine/hardwood forests and hardwood stands. Elevations range from 700 to 1,800 ft. **maps:** See below under individual areas.

starting out: The district RS, open weekdays from 8 AM to 4:30 PM, has numerous brochures, and answers to questions are available. Annual parking permits, NF maps and trail guides may be purchased.

activities: Hiking, Camping, Fishing, Mountain Biking.

hiking: 5 trails, ranging from 1.8 to 6.2 mi and totaling 16.9 mi, provide a good mix of opportunities for day-hikes. 2 routes follow ridgetops, 1 leads to a set of waterfalls, and 2 wind through networks of seasonal branches at the heads of creeks. All trails are blazed and relatively easy to follow. Access to 3 of the routes requires additional walking along gated roads when rec areas are closed. The *Pinhoiti Trail*, once completed, will roughly quadruple the total mi of developed trail, most of which will be open to mountain biking and horseback riding, as well as to hiking. Sections of the trail, which are blazed frequently with white rectangles and marked occasionally with turkey tracks on small plastic squares, are in place and open.

camping: Backcountry camping is permitted anywhere on NF land, except where posted as prohibited. There are, however, no wilderness areas or other expansive areas of backcountry. Developed camping areas are at the Pocket and Hidden Creek. The latter is the less developed and more isolated of the two.

fishing: Fishing is possible in a couple small seasonal trout streams and at Pilchers Pond, a 3-acre walk-in pond that requires a hike of a mile or so to access. Fishing in the pond is for bass, bream and catfish.

mountain biking: Mountain biking is permitted on gated or ungated FS roads, but until recently there have been no established trails for mountain biking. The *Pinhoiti Trail*, when completed, will offer 49 mi of multi-use trail on the Armuchee District.

Taylors Ridge Area

The skinniest backcountry in Georgia, this strip of national forest land surrounds Taylors Ridge for more than 25 miles, with no portion of it more than two miles across. Most of the tract, in fact, is less than one mile across, encompassing little more than the forested ridge. Valleys on both sides are made up mostly of farmland. The Taylors Ridge area has no facilities or improvements, except for 2 hiking trails and a section of the new *Pinhoiti Trail* under construction. When completed, the *Pinhoiti Trail* will add more than 10 mi of trail for hiking, mountain biking and horseback riding to the Taylors Ridge area. The entire backcountry is open for camping, but most gets very little use because it's accessible only by hiking or mountain biking on gated roads or following the trail-less ridgetop. Although the backcountry is narrow, mountainsides that drop sharply on both sides of the ridge make this area seem much more remote than it is. The entire forest falls under general forest designation, so some logging takes place. The forested ridges, with agricultural fields beside them, create good habitat for deer and turkeys.

LaFayette (W) and Summerville (W) are the nearest towns.

getting there: From LaFayette, drive E on GA-186 7 mi to the top of Taylors Ridge. Just past the crest, the road bends L, and there is a pair of gated FS roads on the R. The lower road is the beginning of the *Taylors Ridge Trail*. Ponder Creek Rd, which leads to the trailhead for the *Chickamauga Creek Trail*, is 2 mi past this point on the L. Once on Ponder Creek Rd drive 0.6 mi and fork R onto FS-219. Follow FS-219 1.8 mi to its end at a small parking area. The road is rough in places and fords Ponder Creek, but it is manageable in a passenger vehicle.

topography: Taylors Ridge is a long narrow ridge that runs N to S and NE to SW from Tennessee to the town of Holland, GA, SE of Summerville. The ridge, which has top elevations near 1,550 ft, drops off sharply to the W and alternates between spur ridges and creek drainages to the E. Toward the N end of the district, the ridge crosses the Tennessee Valley Divide. Forests are dominated by hardwoods around creek drains. Pure hardwood, mixed hardwood/pine, and pure pine stands can all be found on the ridge. **maps:** USGS Catlett, Nickajack Gap, Summerville, Subligna, Trion, Tunnel Hill.

starting out: Except the parking area for the *Pinhoiti Trail* and the *Chickamauga Creek Trail*, there are no facilities in the Taylors Ridge area. Pets must be on a leash.

activities: Hiking/Mountain Biking, Camping.

hiking/mountain biking: There are 2 established hiking trails in the Taylors Ridge area; 1 atop the ridge and 1 in the valley below. The 2.4-mi *Taylors Ridge Trail* begins just E of the ridgetop, using gated FS-217 as its initial route, and then climbs away from the road to the crest, which it follows for most of its route. The *Chickamauga Creek Trail* is a very diverse 6.2-mi loop. It begins by crisscrossing a network of small intermittent streams that form Ponder Creek's headwaters and then crosses the Tennessee Valley Divide to a similar network of streams that join to form Chickamauga Creek. The return trip is along Dicks Ridge, a spur of Taylors Ridge. Both trails are white blazed and easy to follow. Hiking is generally easy, but with some moderate slopes. Many creek crossings along the *Chickamauga Creek Trail* have no footbridges, but most require nothing more than a long step, and many branches are often dry. These trails are open to foot traffic only.

The *Pinhoiti Trail*, when completed, will run more than 10 mi along Dicks Ridge, from High Point to Hammond Gap before turning E across private property to climb Strawberry Mtn. The southern half of the route was completed by early 1999. The route begins with a climb from the valley to the ridge, but from there it is mostly level. Much of the Taylors Ridge section follows FS roads or logging roads, so it is a broad, gravel track, Other sections, created with hand tools, are single-track. The trail is blazed frequently with white rectangles, and marked occasionally with plastic squares that display the trail's symbol, a turkey track.

camping: Backcountry camping is permitted throughout the NF, except where posted as prohibited. At present, none of Taylors Ridge is closed. The *Pinhoiti Trail*, when completed, will create access to much of this backcountry. As it stands, various FS roads provide plenty of opportunity to reach the remote portions of the ridge for camping. There are no developed campgrounds on Taylors Ridge.

Johns Creek Area

Bounded by Johns Mountain to the west and Horn Mountain to the east, the Johns Creek Valley runs through the heart of the section of the Armuchee Ranger District that is most developed for recreational use. There are three hiking trails, two campgrounds, a pond and a trout stream, plus a large picnic area. Major attractions are Johns Mountain, Keown Falls and the Pocket. Johns Mountain has a hiking trail that loops along its ridge and a fantastic vista of ridges and valleys to the west from the trailhead parking lot. Keown Falls actually includes two waterfalls of 25 and 50 feet. Along with a hiking trail that ascends Johns Mountain to the falls, there is a small picnic area. The Pocket, not to be confused with another Northwest Georgia area that shares the same name, is a flat, U-shaped valley between Horn Mountain and a short spur ridge. Dozens of tiny spring-fed streams rise within the Pocket, crisscrossing the entire area. The branches eventually join to form a major tributary of Johns Creek, which flows lazily through the campground and a large picnic area. Johns Creek itself is a nice tumbling trout stream that even has a handicapped accessible fishing pier on it. Unfortunately, most of the creek runs through private property, except in its upper reaches, where it is too small to provide much recreational value. The entire Johns Creek area includes parcels of private land interspersed with public holdings, but private lands remain undeveloped and most consist of farmland or timberland. Deer, turkeys and various woodland type songbirds are the most commonly seen wildlife species.

Calhoun (SE) and LaFayatte (NW) are the nearest towns.

getting there: From LaFayatte, drive E on GA-136 13.5 mi to Pocket Rd and turn R. Pilchers Pond and the FS roads that access the *Johns Mountain Trail*, Keown Falls and the Pocket are all off Pocket Rd. The parking area for Pilchers Pond is at 3.8 mi on the L. FS-208 to *Johns Mountain Trail* is at 4 mi on the R. FS-702 to Keown Falls is at 5 mi on the L. Entry roads into the Pocket are at 7.1 mi on the L. The Pocket has 2 entries, less than 0.1 mi apart. The first leads to the campground and the second to the day-use area. Hidden Creek is most easily accessed from Calhoun. Drive W on GA-156 7.5 mi to Everett Springs Rd and turn R. Drive 1.9 mi and turn R at a brown sign for Hidden Creek (this is Rock Creek Rd, but there is no street sign.) Drive 3.3 mi to FS-955 on the R, which leads to the campground.

topography: Johns Mtn, Johns Creek and Horn Mtn, all oriented NE to SW, are the major geographical features. Prevalent forest types include diverse mixed hardwood stands and forests of mixed hardwoods and pines. Elevations range from 700 to 1,808 ft **maps:** USGS Sugar Valley, Plainville, Villanow.

starting out: There are restrooms and water fountain at the Pocket Rec Area and pit toilets at the Hidden Creek and Keown Falls rec areas. Beyond that, the only facilities are information boards and picnic tables. The Pocket and Keown Falls are open from Apr 1 to mid-Nov. A $2 daily or $30 annual parking fee is required at the Pocket and Keown Falls. Pets must be kept on a leash of 6 ft or less.

activities: Hiking, Camping, Fishing.

hiking: 3 trails, each quite different from the others, provide good opportunities for hiking in the Johns Mtn area. The *Johns Mountain Trail* and *Keown Falls Trail*, both loops, provide access to a common deck overlooking lower Keown Falls and can therefore be hiked together, for a total hike of 5.3 mi. The 3.5-mi *Johns Mountain Trail* begins at the lookout at the top of the mtn and winds along both sides of the ridge. The 1.8-mi *Keown Falls Trail* begins at the base of the mountain and climbs through a moist forest along a small, tumbling stream to the falls and the cliffs that surround them. The waterfalls can disappear completely during dry spells, so a sign at the trailhead tells whether they are running. The *Pocket Trail* is a 2.5 mi-loop that crosses numerous seeps and springs by footbridges as it circles through hardwood forests in the shadows of Horn Mtn. The first portion of the trail has interpretive signs, and a cut-off route allows for a 0.5-mi nature hike along the interpretive portion.

The *Johns Mountain* and *Pocket* trails are white blazed. The *Keown Falls* trail is unblazed, but it is bordered by rocks through its initial portion and follows the only practical route as it climbs toward the falls. The *Pocket Trail* is easy to walk. The other 2 include moderate grades. All trails are located in seasonally closed areas, but hikers are permitted to park outside of gates (giving care not to block the way) and walk in. The *Johns Mountain Trail* parking area is a more than 2 mi from the gate, however, and at the top of the mtn. A more interesting way to access this trail during winter is by the *Keown Falls Trail.*

camping: Backcountry camping is permitted anywhere on NF land, except where posted as prohibited. Areas closed to camping include the picnic and parking areas at Keown Falls and the Pocket.

There are 2 campgrounds in this part of the forest. The Pocket Campground has 27 sites, each with a picnic table, tent pad, lantern post and fire ring/grill. Sites are spread out along the main creek and among the network of branches that join to form it. The forest is made up of mostly hardwoods and is fairly open. Restrooms have flush toilets and hot showers. Sites are available on a first-come, first-serve basis and fill up most summer weekends. Camping costs $8/night. The campground is open from Apr 1 to mid-Nov.

Hidden Creek Campground is more remote and gets much less use, having no other facilities immediately adjacent to it. 16 sites are set in an isolated cove of mature hardwoods. The campground is surrounded by steep ridges. Dry Branch, an intermittent stream, cuts through the campground and gives the area its name as it "hides" during dry periods. Sites are quite simple, each with rock fire ring and lantern post. They are medium sized and well spaced. Water pumps and pit toilets are in the campground. It's open from May to Oct, and is rarely full. Camping costs $8/night.

fishing: Some fishing is possible in the Johns Creek area, but opportunities are limited. The Pilchers Pond Fishing Area is a 3-acre walk-in fishing pond. The pond has bass, bream and catfish. All fishing is from the banks, and bank access is good. Trout fishing is possible in Johns Creek and in the branch that runs through the Pocket. Both streams are seasonal and almost completely dependent on the hatchery truck for their trout. Johns Creek is actually a very attractive stream of medium size where it runs beside Pocket Road, but most of this section is through posted private land. Just S of the Pocket, there is a handicapped-accessible fishing platform over a deep pool in the creek.

Cohutta Ranger District

Chattahoochee National Forest

High ridges and deep valleys characterize the Cohutta Ranger District, 35,268 acres of which lie within the largest national forest wilderness east of the Mississippi River. The district covers 107,635 acres in Murray, Fannin and Gilmer counties, almost all within the Cohutta Mountains. The Cohutta Wilderness, although laced with trails and fairly heavily traveled, contains Georgia's two most pristine major rivers, the Conasauga and the Jacks. Even outside the designated wilderness, the district contains extensive areas of fabulous backcountry, accessible only by rough roads that wind from gap to gap. Conasauga Lake and Barnes Creek are the only developed recreation areas, but several semi-developed camping areas or trail access areas are scattered across the district. The district also has numerous ATV and ORV routes, but they are sufficiently isolated from most backcountry areas that they remain non-intrusive. Opportunities for hiking, camping, fishing and mountain biking are all extensive, and horseback riding is popular on those trails where it is permitted. The Cohutta Mountains support deer and turkeys and some of Georgia's best populations of bears, boar and grouse.

Chatsworth (W) and Ellijay (E) are the nearest towns.

contact: Cohutta Ranger District, Chattahoochee National Forest, 401 Old Ellijay Rd, Chatsworth, GA 30705; (706) 695-6736; www.fs.fed.us/conf/.

getting there: US-411, GA-52, US-76 and GA-5 form a loop around most of the Cohutta RD, but almost all direct access to any part of the district is up a mountain by a gravel FS road. The district RS is located in Chatsworth, at the jct of US-411 and GA-52 W.

topography: The crest of Georgia's western Blue Ridge runs S to N through the eastern portion of the Cohutta RD. The Cohutta range runs basically parallel to the W of the Blue Ridge, although portions run E to W. The entire district is an unending series of high ridges with numerous peak and gaps divided by deep valleys. Streams run off the Cohuttas in several directions, with the Conasauga and Jacks rivers and Mountaintown, Holly and Mill creeks all major drainages. The Southern Appalachian forest is very diverse, with elevations that range from 950 to 4,150 ft, but oak/hickory and mixed hardwood/pine forests are dominant. **maps:** See below under individual areas.

starting out: The district RS, open M–F from 8 AM to 4:30 PM, offers free brochures and sells trail guides, FS topo maps of the Cohutta Wilderness and annual parking permits for fee areas.

activities: Hiking, Camping, Fishing, Mountain Biking.

hiking: Hiking trails range from the interpretive *Songbird Trail*, a short, easy trail well suited for family groups, to the 16.7-mi *Jacks River Trail*, which is entirely within the wilderness and fords the river 40 times. All but a few trails are at least moderate in difficulty, and many are strenuous. There are more than 85 mi of trail in the wilderness, with most routes leading to or connecting the *Jacks River* and *Conasauga River* trails. More than 45 mi of trail are open to hiking outside the wilderness, although several are multi-use routes and more popular with mountain bikers or horseback riders than hikers.

camping: Backcountry camping is permitted throughout the NF, except where posted as prohibited. However, ground flat enough to camp on is somewhat rare in the Cohuttas. Most camping within the wilderness is along the two main rivers. Outside the wilderness, a developed campground at Conasauga Lake and several semi-developed campgrounds and undeveloped hunt camps provide a good range of opportunities.

fishing: Trout fishing is outstanding in the Cohutta RD. The Conasauga and Jack rivers alone provide more then 30 mi of wild trout waters, and numerous other streams on the district offer fine trout fishing. Most streams contain only wild trout, with some high-elevation branches holding native brook trout, but scattered stream stretches along the edges of the district receive stocked trout. Conasauga Lake is also stocked with trout through spring and summer, and it carries a good natural population of bass and bream. Fishing for bass and bream is also possible on Murrays Lake and Peeples Lake, both of which are quite small.

mountain biking: Although mountain bikes are not permitted in the wilderness, 35.8 mi of multi-use trail open to mountain biking are available on trails scattered across the district. Various routes course creek gorges, cross streams and lead to terrific mountain vistas. All routes include technical and/or strenuous sections. Several mi of ATV and ORV trail are also listed as open to mountain biking, but these get little use by non-motorized bikes. FS-roads that connect with trails are often used to form longer loops or add variety to a ride.

lodging: The Cohutta Lodge & Restaurant (706/695-9601) sets high in the Cohutta Mountains at the edge of the NF. Its 2-tiered porch offers great vistas. An old English-style lodge, the Cohutta Lodge also has a fully equipped honeymoon cottage tucked away in the woods. Lodge rooms cost $69 to $89/night. The cottage begins at $169/night.

Cohutta Wilderness

Unlike most of Georgia's wilderness areas, which straddle mountaintops, the Cohutta wilderness surrounds the deep valleys of the Conasauga and Jacks rivers, so most trails go down into the wilderness, instead of up. The Conasauga is Georgia's most pristine major river, with its entire headwaters within the 37,042-acre federally mandated roadless wilderness, and the Jacks come in as a close second. The Jacks is best known for Jacks River Falls, a powerful 60-foot main-river drop near the midpoint of the river's run through the wilderness. The rivers, which have a clarity that rivals that of streams in the western U.S., run a combined 30-plus miles through the wilderness, not including many miles of tumbling tributaries. The rivers eventually join forces in Tennessee, outside the wilderness. A little bit of the Cohutta Wilderness actually spills into Tennessee as the boundary between it and Tennessee's Big Frog Wilderness are defined by the Tennessee Valley Divide, not the state line. Hiking and camping are popular within the wilderness, as is horseback riding on trails where it is permitted. Trout fishing, although some of the best in Georgia, is not that popular. The vast wilderness supports good wildlife populations, with bears and boars in the mix.

Chatsworth (SW) is the nearest major town.

getting there: FS-17, FS-68, FS-22, FS 64 and FS-22 connect all access points along the edge of the wilderness, and the best

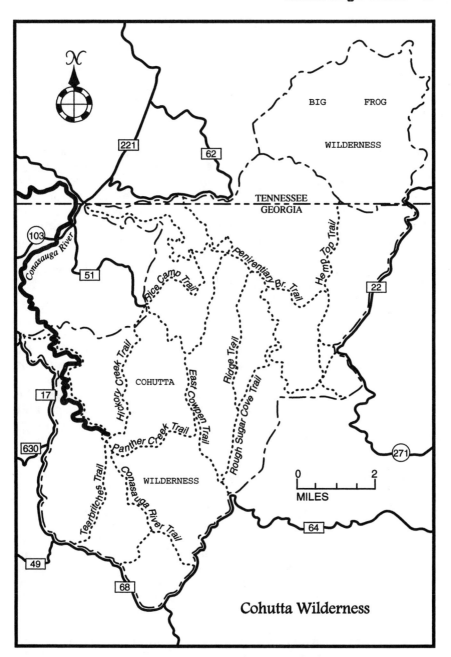

Cohutta Wilderness

approach varies enormously according to the area a person wants to explore. At Three Forks Mtn, access is possible to either the Conasauga or the Jacks watershed. From Blue Ridge, drive N on GA-5 3.9 mi to Old Highway 2 on the L. Turn L and drive 10.8 mi to Watson Gap. Turn L onto FS-64 and drive 8.9 mi to Three Forks. Betty Gap, where the *Conasauga River Trail* begins, is 3.9 mi past Three Forks.

topography: The Conasauga and Jacks rivers flow S to N through the wilderness and are separated by Cohutta Mtn and Hickory Ridge and bounded to the E by Georgia's western Blue Ridge. The mountains are covered with dark rich soils, and forest types are diverse. Oak/hickory and oak/pine, cove hardwood and white pine/hemlock forests are all common. The highest elevation is in the TN portion, atop Frogtown Mtn at 4,224 ft. The highest peak in the Georgia portion is Cowpen Mtn at 4,149 ft, while the lowest elevation is in Alculsy Valley at 950 ft. **maps:** USGS Hemptop, Tennga, Dyer Gap, Epworth, Crandall, Caney Creek (TN), Ducktown (TN); USFS Cohutta and Big Frog Wilderness.

starting out: 10 access points along the edge of the wilderness have parking areas and information boards. A $2 daily or $30 annual parking fee is required at Three Forks and the Hickory Creek trailhead. Pets must be on a leash. Some roads are subject to winter closures when driving conditions become dangerous. The area around Bray Field, a major trail jct along the Conasauga, and around Jacks River Falls, can get crowded during the warm months, especially on weekends.

activities: Hiking, Fishing, Camping.

hiking: A vast network of interconnected trails provides good opportunities to explore all parts of the Cohutta Wilderness. Most trails follow or lead to the Conasauga or Jacks rivers, but some stay high on ridges, never winding down to the rivers. Small waterfalls on feeders, mountain overviews, diverse forest types and outstanding wildflower displays and spectacular scenery along the rivers are among the highlights of the trails. Trail length varies from 1.4 mi to 15.7 mi, and the 15 trails total more than 85 mi.

Trailheads, which are scattered around the edge of the wilderness and at interior junctures, are well marked. Most trails are blazed, although infrequently. Many trails follow old roadbeds or railroad grades and are easy to follow, except around some stream crossings. Crossings are unimproved, with many wet fords, and a walking staff is strongly recommended for crossings on the *Conasauga River* and *Jacks River* trails. Caution is also advised if heavy rains have occurred or are predicted as the rivers are steep sided and can rise very quickly. Horseback riding is permitted on some trails.

fishing: Both the Conasauga and the Jacks offer excellent fishing for wild rainbow and brown trout, plus brook trout in their extreme headwaters. No trout have been stocked since the 1960s. The fish are abundant but extremely finicky in ultra clear water. Fly-fishing is the most popular approach to both rivers, which together offer more than 30 mi of fishable waters, with access by wading. Both rivers offer a good mix of riffles, runs and deep plunge pools and are plenty open for casting. Depending on how small a stream an anger is willing to crawl up, numerous tributaries also offer good fishing within the wilderness. The Conasauga River watershed is open year round, with only artificial lures permitted from Nov 1 through the end of Mar. The Jacks River watershed is seasonal. Access is by the *Conasauga River Trail* and *Jacks River Trail*, which closely follow their respective rivers through most of the wilderness, and by various shorter trails that connect with the main routes.

camping: Backcountry camping is permitted throughout the wilderness, except on the trails themselves or at trailheads, with no permits required or designated sites, and backpacking is quite popular. Trip registration forms are available at some trailheads and are recommended but not mandatory. No-trace camping is strongly encouraged. It's important to hang packs, as the wilderness supports a large bear population.

lodging: The Ivy Inn Bed & Breakfast (706/517-0526; www.bbonline.com/ga/ivyinn/) is a large country farmhouse built in 1908, with a rocking chair front porch and a screened back porch. Located in Eton, 10 mi or so from the edge of the wilderness, the inn has 3 upstairs guest rooms, each with private bath, telephone, television and individual temperature controls. A full country breakfast and evening desert are served, fresh coffee is always on, and bicycles are available to guests. Rooms cost $65-$75/night.

Cohutta Mountains—Northwest

Often overlooked for nearby Lake Conasauga and the Cohutta Wilderness, the northwestern quadrant of the Cohutta Ranger District is somewhat nondescript. There are no signature rivers, waterfalls or high peaks, and no developed recreation areas to concentrate the attention of explorers. The most popular area is really best known for its lack of drama. Unlike upstream in the wilderness, the Conasauga is flat and gentle as it flows through the Alaculsy Valley. Like the rest of the Cohuttas, the northwestern mountains are characterized by high peaks and deep valleys. There are trails and primitive camping areas, but facilities are very scarce, and access points are spread throughout the region. Forest service roads follow major ridges and provide access to various areas, but extensive tracts have no roads or trails penetrating them. Such areas are only seen by backcountry travelers equipped with a compass, quads and plenty of endurance. In terms of developed trails, mountain bikers enjoy two outstanding routes in this area, one of which runs part of its course through Tennessee. Hikers, too, can use these trails, plus one very short loop around Murrays Lake. Murrays Lake also offers nice primitive campsites and the finest fishing prospects in this part of the forest. Large wildlife species include bears, boar, grouse, deer and turkeys.

Crandall (W) and Cisco (W) are the nearest towns.

getting there: From Cisco, Drive E on Old GA-2. FS-17 forks R off Old GA-2 and provides access to the *Sumac Creek Trail* and Murrays Lake. Going straight on Old GA-2, it is 7.9 mi from Cisco to Cottonwood Patch, which is the where *Iron Mountain Trail* begins.

topography: Although this area has no outstanding geographic features, steep slopes and deep valleys characterize the landscape. Mountainsides are heavily forested, with hardwoods prevalent on N slopes and a mixture of hardwoods and pines on S slopes. Mill Creek, Sumac Creek and a short section of the Conasauga River are the major waterways. Elevations range from 950 to 3,105 ft. **maps:** USGS Tennega, Crandall.

starting out: There are no facilities, except scattered information boards and pit toilets at campgrounds. There is a $3 daily or $30 annual parking fee at the *Sumac Creek* and *Iron Mountain* trailheads.

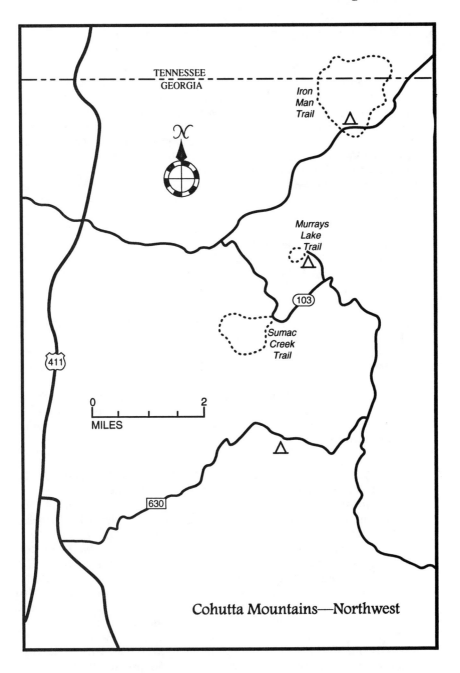

TENNESSEE
GEORGIA

*Iron
Man
Trail*

*Murrays
Lake
Trail*

103

*Sumac
Creek
Trail*

0   2
MILES

411

630

Cohutta Mountains—Northwest

activities: Hiking, Mountain Biking, Fishing, Camping.

mountain biking: Bikers have 2 great rides to pick from on the W site of the Cohuttas. Iron Mountain and Sumac Creek trails are 12- and 12.5-mi loops, respectively, each with tough climbs, fast downhills, plenty of single-track and outstanding views. Both routes are also well maintained and easily followed. The *Iron Mountain Trail*, which begins along the Conasauga River in Alaculsy Valley, runs part of its route though Tennessee, where a spur off the main trail leads to a tower that offers fabulous views. The route begins and ends with fun river crossings. These can be avoided as river levels necessitate by using an easily recognizable alternative starting point across the river. The *Sumac Creek Trail* runs part of its course on a road open to vehicular traffic, but most of the trail is single track or rough old fire roads. A portion of the trail alternates between the top of a narrow ridge and the side of Sumac Creek, far below. Trails are open to mtn biking, horseback riding and hiking.

hiking: The *Iron Mountain* and *Sumac Creek* trails are both open to hiking, and both trails go through some outstanding terrain. Both routes get enough use from bikers and horseback riders, however, to detract from their appeal as hiking trails. The *Murrays Lake Trail* is a nice, easy walk around a very pretty lake, but it is only 0.7 mi long. The trail is not blazed but is marked at its trailhead and is easy to follow. This area also offers good opportunities for serious backcountry exploration, away from any trail, with compass and quad.

fishing: The streams in this area don't offer nearly the same quality of trout fishing that other parts of the Cohutta RD are famous for. In fact, most streams are too small to offer much fishing at all. The Conasauga River flows about 1 mi across public land in Alaculsy Valley before hitting the Tennessee border, but this stretch is of marginal quality as trout waters, and small redeye bass are the main sport fish. The lower Conasauga is accessible from the banks or by wading at Cottonwood Patch. Mill Creek, a fabulous-looking small to medium-sized stream that rises on Grassy Mtn and tumbles W toward Crandall, has some trout it in, but again the water gets a little warm for trout, and redeyes predominate. FS-630 parallels the creek, but most access is by wading, as the creek is often well below the road at the bottom of a gorge. Murrays Lake offers good prospects for bass and bream. While the lake is small, covering only 4 acres, boating is the best fishing approach because Murrays Lake's banks are densely forested. There is a primitive boat ramp.

camping: Backcountry camping is permitted anywhere on FS land, except where posted as prohibited. There are no developed campgrounds N of Lake Conasauga, but there are 3 established primitive camping areas. The nicest is Murrays Lake, which has 5 simple sites along a short trail that goes around the 4-acre mountain lake. The sites, none of which are very far from the parking area, simply consist of a clearing for a tent and a fire ring. Camping is free and permitted year round. Cottonwood Patch in Alaculsy Valley and Hickory Creek Gap, near Mill Creek, have only pit toilets and open areas for tents. Sites are not formally defined, but several sites with fire rings have been established through regular use. The Cottonwood Patch camping area is just an open field, but it is riverside to the Conasauga. Hickory Gap is isolated and attractive, and suitable sites are set among a forest dominated by hemlocks. Both areas are open year round. Camping costs $3/night.

Lake Conasauga Recreation Area

At 3,150 feet, Lake Conasauga is the highest lake in Georgia. It also ranks among the clearest, and its 19 acres are surrounded by a dense evergreen forest dominated by white pines and hemlocks. The lake, which is close to the summit of Grassy Mountain, was built by Civilian Conservation Corps crews and opened to the public in the 1940s. The Lake Conasauga Recreation Area is the most popular single spot in the Cohutta Ranger District. There is a lakefront picnic area, a designated swimming area, a developed campground, a boat ramp and 3 hiking trails. Lake Conasauga is quite popular with fishermen and offers good prospects for catching bass, bream and trout. 350 acres around the lake are included in the Lake Conasauga Songbird Management Area. The area is actively managed for songbird use, primarily by the cutting of selected plots to encourage new growth of seed- and fruit-bearing plants. Creating open-area habitat beside woodland tracts has attracted well over 100 bird species to the area. A few of the mammals that frequent the area are deer, bears and bobcats.

Chatsworth (E) is the nearest town.

getting there: From the jct US-411 and Holly Creek Rd in Eton, marked by a sign for the Lake Conasauga Rec Area, drive E on Holly Creek Rd, which eventually becomes FS-18, 10.3 mi to FS-68. Turn L and drive 6 mi to a T-intersection. Turn L to stay on FS-68 and drive 4.5 mi to the camping area entrance or 5.4 mi to the day-use area entrance, both on the R.

topography: Lake Conasauga impounds a small tributary of Mill Creek, near the top of Grassy Mtn. A white/pine hemlock forest with a dense understory of rhododendron and laurel surrounds the lake and area creeks. Mixed hardwoods are prevalent in surrounding forests. Elevations range from 3,682 ft atop the mountain to the lake's full-pool elevation of 3,150 ft. **maps:** USGS Crandall

starting out: There are restrooms with flush toilets, a water fountain and an information board in the day-use area. A $2 daily or $30 annual parking fee is required. The rec area is open from mid-Apr to Oct. During closed season, hikers or fishermen may still park outside the day-use area gate (taking care to not block the route) and walk into the area. All pets must be kept on a leash of 6 ft or less.

activities: Hiking, Fishing, Camping.

hiking: Although the setting is high in the rugged Cohutta Mountains, the 3 short trails at Lake Conasauga provide fairly easy hiking. The *Grassy Mountain Tower Trail*, the longest of the routes at 2 mi, is also the most challenging as it makes the final climb from the lake to the mountaintop. Even so, however, most grades are easy to moderate and no climbs are sustained. Wildflowers are abundant along the way, but the tower is the trail's high point, in more ways than one. The *Lake Conasauga Trail*, a 1.2-mi loop around the lake, and the *Songbird Trail*, a 1.5-mi loop through the Songbird Management Area, are both easy hikes. The lake trail passes picnic and camping areas that can be crowded, but it also winds through tunnels of rhododendron beside the lake and crosses a few scenic branches on footbridges. The *Songbird Trail*, in interpretive route with numerous signs detailing the area's management philosophy, passes several new-growth openings that are sometimes alive with the birds the trail is named for. The trails are not blazed, but they are well marked at their trailheads and easy to follow. Both the *Grassy Mountain Tower Trail* and *Songbird Trail* have directional signs along the way. The *Grassy Mountain Tower* and *Conasauga Lake* trails begin at the picnic area. The *Songbird Trail* begins at the overflow campground, which is just past the turn-in for the day-use area on the R.

An additional hiking option in the Lake Conasauga area, although it does not begin from the rec area, is the *Emory Creek Trail*, a 3.2-mi (1-way) route from the headwaters of Emory Creek to its confluence with Holly Creek. There are 2 waterfalls along the way. The trail is accessible at Ball Field, 1 mi E of Lake Conasauga, or off FS-18, 3 mi W of its jct with FS-68. The trail is unblazed and in places tough to follow as it fords the stream several times. The farthest downstream crossing, which is actually across Holly Creek, requires getting wet at most water levels and can be dangerous during high water.

fishing: Conasauga Lake offers good fishing for bass and bream throughout the year, and trout are stocked through spring and summer. The best cover, especially for the bass, lies several feet below the surface, where numerous tall stumps surround old creek channels in some of the coves. Fishing is popular from the banks and from boats. While the banks are forested, the picnic area and numerous small openings around the lake provide plenty of places to cast from. Boats are restricted to electric motors. Fishing is permitted year 'round, and a trout stamp is not required as long as any trout caught are immediately released.

camping: 35 campsites in 2 loops are all convenient to the lake but few are right beside the water. Sites are medium sized to large but privacy is only average, as the forest of white pines and hemlocks is quite open. Each site has a picnic table, fire ring/grill, and tent pad. Restrooms have flush toilets and cold showers. Water is also available between sites. The campground is open from mid-Apr to Oct, and sites are often full on weekends from the beginning of summer through the end of the season. Camping costs $8/night.

An overflow campground, located just past the day-use area entry on the R, has 6 fairly large campsites in a flat, open forest of cove hardwoods and hemlocks. Each site has a picnic table, tent pad and fire ring. There are pit toilets. Camping is permitted year round and costs $5/night. Camping is not permitted in the rec area, except at designated sites, but it is permitted throughout most of the NF. There is a primitive camping area at Ball Field, 1 mi E of Lake Conasauga. Pit toilets are the only facilities at this site, which is a large grassy field. There are also a couple hunt camps quite close to the lake, which are simply areas that have had the understory cleared to create room for tents. The hunt camps have no facilities, but they are free.

Cohutta Mountains—East

One needs not spend multiple days backpacking in the Cohutta Wilderness to get a sense of the overall bigness of the region or experience the remoteness of a rugged backcountry. Even from the main forest service routes that follow ridges through the eastern portion of the Cohutta Ranger District, there is a backcountry feel, as densely forested mountainside drop off sharply on both sides of long, winding, rough gravel tracks. There are no specific outstanding features to define this area, and facilities, which are quite limited, are widely dispersed. The eastern Cohuttas do have some outstanding trails, most of which are open to hiking, mountain biking and horseback riding. Mountain bikers commonly combine the trails with the gravel roads they begin at to create loops that suit their riding preferences. Most of the best trout waters in the Cohuttas lie within the wilderness, but one gem of a stream, Mountaintown Creek, flows away from the wilderness. The only designated camping areas on the east side of the Cohuttas are a tiny semi-developed campground and a small, primitive camping area with no designated sites. That said, tens of thousand of acres are open to camping, mostly within a vast, rugged backcountry that is not accessible by road or by trail. There is a scenic picnic area on Barnes Creek, beside a small waterfall. Bears, boar, bobcats, deer and turkeys are among the wildlife species that make use of the Cohutta Mountains.

Blue Ridge (E) and Ellijay (SE) are the nearest towns.

getting there: Most of the E side is best accessed from Blue Ridge. Drive N on GA-5 3.9 mi to Old GA-2 on the L. Drive 10.8 mi to the 4-way jct with FS-22 (R), a private road (straight) and FS-64 (L). FS-64 is the main access road through the E side of the ranger district and provides direct or indirect access to all trailheads and campgrounds.

topography: The western Blue Ridge splits the E side of the Cohutta RD, running SE to NW to Watson Gap, where to turns S to N through the edge of the wilderness. Like the rest of the Cohutta RD, the E side is made up of high ridges divided by deep valleys.

Major watersheds are Mountaintown Creek, Fightingtown Creek and the South Fork of the Jacks River, which flow S, E and NW, respectively. Forest types are diverse, with oak/hickory, mixed hardwood/pine and white pine/hemlock forests all common. Elevations range from 1,760 to 3,580 ft. **maps:** USGS Hemp Top, Dyer Gap, Epworth, Cashes Valley.

starting out: There are no facilities in this area beyond scattered information boards and pit toilets at the Jacks River Campground. Barnes Creek is a designated rec area, but it's only a picnic area, offering no special access for backcountry adventure. A $2 daily or $30 annual parking fee is required at Barnes Creek and the *Bear Creek* and *Mountaintown Creek* trailheads. Pets must be kept on a leash.

activities: Hiking/Mountain Biking, Fishing, Camping.

mountain biking/hiking: Except for portions of the *Benton McKaye Trail*, all the trails in this part of the NF are designated for multi-use and open to hiking, mountain biking and horseback riding. The 70-mi *Benton McKaye Trail* cuts 7 mi across the Cohutta RD, but part of that uses the *South Fork Trail*, part uses FS roads, and part uses existing trails in the Cohutta Wilderness. That leaves only a couple mi of the trail, with its white diamond blazes, open to hiking alone. Multi-use trails include *Mountaintown Creek*, *Bear Creek* and *South Fork*. Mountain bikers probably make the heaviest use of *Bear Creek*, but all 3 routes attract all types of users. The 5.6-mi *Mountaintown Creek Trail* is accessible only at one end, so hiking or riding the entire length requires an 11.2-mi round-trip. Most hikers either backpack or only go halfway. The trail is steep and rough, with numerous stream crossings. Huge maples, white oaks and hemlocks, a boulder-strewn gorge and countless cascades provide plenty of reward for the effort, however. The *Bear Creek Trail* is best known for the Gennett Poplar, an immense old growth yellow poplar about 1 mi into the route. Most hikers use only this easy section of trail, returning after seeing the biggest tree in the forest. Mountain bikers will combine the 6.7-mi double loop with various spurs, the *Mountaintown Creek Trail* or FS roads to create an assortment of long and difficult loops. The *Bear Creek Trail* includes steep climbs, technical single-track and multiple stream crossings—it's an extremely fun trail for experienced riders. The *South Fork Trail* is by far the easiest route in this area. Following the South Fork of the Jacks River through grassy meadows and hardwood forests, this easy to moderate trail offers great opportunities for seeing wildlife.

Except for the *Benton McKaye Trail*, none of the routes are consistently blazed. All are signed at trailheads. The *South Fork* and *Mountaintown Creek* trails are directly accessible off FS-64. The *South Fork Trail* begins 4.2 mi S of Watson Gap. The *Mountaintown Creek Trail* is 9.1 mi S of Watson Gap. The *Bear Creek Trail* has multiple access points, but the main trailhead provides a direct route to the Gennett Poplar. From Ellijay, Drive W on GA-52 5 mi to Gates Chapel Rd on the R. Drive 4.6 mi to FS 241 and drive 2 mi to the trailhead parking area at the end of the road.

fishing: Several streams flow off the Blue Ridge on the E side of the Cohutta RD, but most are too small to provide decent fishing prospects. Mountaintown Creek is the exception, and it is a noteworthy one. The stream is small and access requires considerable effort, but fishing is good for wild rainbows and browns. Private land blocks access from the lower end, even to the section of the creek that's on public land. Therefore, fishermen must hike the 5.6-mi *Mountaintown Creek Trail* down through the river's headwaters to reach fishable waters. The trail doesn't hit the main creek until the final couple mi, and the lower stream corridor is somewhat flat. The best approach, by far, is an overnighter. The best waters are upstream of the jct of the trail and the stream. 3 or 4 mi of Mountaintown Creek, plus some of its tributary waters, are large enough to fish. The stream never gets large on the NF, but there is sufficient open water for casting. Only artificial lures are permitted on Mountaintown Creek, and fly fishing is by far the most popular approach. The stream is open year round.

camping: Camping is permitted anywhere on NF land, except where posted as prohibited, and the area has vast sections of rugged backcountry for campers to pick from. The toughest part, in most instances, is finding an area flat enough to set up a tent. There are nice campsites along Mountaintown Creek, as well as a semi-developed campground on the E side of the district. The Jacks River Campground has 5 simple sites in an open field along the river's W Fork. Each site has a picnic table, fire ring/grill and lantern post. There are pit toilets. The sites cost $5/night. There is a primitive camping area along Bear Creek, which has no facilities or established campsites and costs $2/night. Several hunt camps are similar to Bear Creek in their offerings, except they are free.

lodging: Sanctuary Cove (706/632-6645) is a 2-bedroom cottage located of Old GA-2, just outside the NF border. The cottage is tucked away in the woods and has private stream access and hiking trails around it. It is fully furnished, with linens and kitchenware, and has a fireplace and a covered deck with a swing. Rates begin at $50/night.

Fort Mountain State Park

Named for a mysterious stone wall located near its summit, Fort Mountain is a prominent peak at the southern end of the Cohutta Mountains. No one is actually certain of the origin of the wall, which is 855 feet long and up to six feet high. The most widely accepted theory says an Indian tribe built the wall around 500 AD, either as a fortification against attacks from other tribes or for religious purposes. Fort Mountain State Park surrounds two major peaks atop the mountain and totals 3,428 acres. The park was partly developed in the 1930s by Civilian Conservation Corps workers. Among their projects was construction of a 40-foot stone lookout tower atop the mountain that remains open to the public. Day-use facilities are concentrated in a cove around a 17 acre lake and include a beach, a large picnic area, a couple short trails, and a miniature golf course. Despite these developments, much of the park consists of a backcountry characterized by steep slopes, rock outcrops, waterfalls, boulderfields and forests of many different types. Fort Mountain has an outstanding trail system for hiking and mountain biking, with backcountry campsites scattered along the longest hiking trail. There is also a large, developed campground, and the lake provides good fishing prospects. Fort Mountain, like the rest of the Cohutta Mountains, has a sizable bear population. Deer and turkeys are also abundant.

Chatsworth (W) is the nearest town.

contact: Superintendent, Fort Mountain State Park, 181 Fort Mountain Park Rd, Chatsworth GA 30705; 706/695-2621; www.gastateparks.org.

getting there: From downtown Chatsworth, drive E on GA-52 7.1 mi to the park entrance on the L.

topography: The park surrounds 2 high peaks on Fort Mtn. The mountain is part of the Cohutta Range. The picnic area is set in a cove at approximately 2,400 ft, but outside that area, most of the park's terrain is very steep—sometimes vertical. With elevations ranging from 1,730 ft to 2,840 ft and slopes oriented in many directions, habitat types are broadly varied, among them mixed upland forests, Virginia pine stands, hardwood forests, rhododendron thickets and rock outcrop communities. **maps:** USGS Crandall.

starting out: The park office, which also serves as a visitor center, is open daily from 8 AM to 5 PM. Maps and information are available inside. Restrooms, a pay phone, water fountain and drink machine are also there. The park is open from 7 AM to 10 PM.

Alcoholic beverages are prohibited in public areas. Pets must be on a leash of 6 ft or less.

activities: Hiking, Camping, Mountain Biking, Fishing.

hiking: 5 hiking trails that total just over 14 mi provide a great opportunity to explore the park on foot. The trails provide access to many of Fort Mountain's most prominent features, including the rock wall and stone tower, the lake, an old gold mine and several outstanding vistas. The shortest walk is the *Nature Trail*, a 0.7-mi loop, although parts of this interpretive walk are fairly demanding. This easiest trail is the 1.1-mi *Lake Loop*. The longest trail, which makes up more than half the total trail mileage, is the 8.2-mi *Gahuti Backcountry Trail*, which forms a loop around the park's main day-use areas and connects with the area around the rock wall and tower. The *Gahuti Trail* has 4 backcountry campsites beside it, but it is also makes a very nice, long day hike. The *Old Fort Trails*, generally counted as a single route, actually consist of 3 trails at the top of the mtn that total 1.8 mi. From the parking area, the *Old Fort Loop* is 1.3 mi. The *Stone Wall Trail* parallels the wall for 0.3 mi. And a 0.5-mi shortcut route goes straight up the ridge, across the wall and to the tower and observation platform. All trails in the park are well maintained, clearly marked at trailheads, and frequently blazed. Blazes are color coded and colors are listed on a trail map available at the visitor center. Except for the lake loop, all trails are moderate to difficult.

camping: Backcountry camping is permitted at 4 sites along the 8.2-mi *Gahuti Backcountry Trail.* Each of the sites, which are well spread along the loop, consist of nothing more than a clearing large enough for 2 tents. Because the trail is accessible from several points in the park, no site requires a walk of more than a couple mi to reach. Backcountry camping costs $5/person, per night. Reservations can be made for specific sites, and only 1 group is permitted per site.

The park's developed campground includes 70 tent/RV sites on 2 loops. Both loops are set in hilly, hardwood-dominated forests. Sites are average sized and provide average privacy. Each site has a picnic table, lantern post, tent pad, fire/ring grill, water and electricity. Restrooms have flush toilets, hot showers and laundry facilities. There are also 4 walk-in campsites and 6 walk-in Squirrel's Nest platforms. The walk-in campsites are on a hillside and are well isolated form each other and from the rest of the sites on that loop. They don't have electricity, but water is available from a hand pump. Squirrel's Nest sites are elevated camping platforms with no other facilities. The campground is open year round. Camping costs $14/night for tents, $16/night for RVs. Walk-in sites and Squirrel's Nest sites cost $8/night.

3 pioneer sites, well isolated from the rest of the park, are set in a mixed hardwood/pine forest. The sites, which require a walk of a few hundred ft to get to, have pit toilets, 3-sided shelters, and fire rings. The understory has been cleared for tents. Each site can accommodate 15 to 25 campers and costs $25/night.

mountain biking: The park has an outstanding network of mountain biking trails, just opened in fall 1998. Routes range from a short, simple ride around the lake to a long and demanding loop that covers an elevation range exceeding 1,000 ft. There is something for every rider on the park's 4 trails. The *Lake Loop, Gold Mine Loop, Cool Spring Loop,* and *East West Loop* are best suited for beginning, intermediate, advanced and expert riders, respectively. The 13-mi *East West Loop* circles well down the mtn from the park's main developed areas to remote sections of backcountry that are accessible in no other way, some actually beyond the park's boundaries. It passes talc mines and unnamed waterfalls on tiny streams. The route includes very steep ascents and descents but is all double-track as it follows an old mining road. The 7-mi *Cool Springs Loop* is highlighted by a screaming, technical downhill through 11 switchbacks and extensive boulderfields. The route includes a portion of the *East West Loop* and uses the road to the *Cool Springs Overlook* to complete its loop. The 6.3-mi *Gold Mine Loop* uses park roads part of the way and then parallels a portion of the *Gahuti Backcountry Trail*. It has some fun ascents and descents, but they are neither steep nor sustained. It passes the remnants of an old gold mine. The 1.1-mi *Lake Loop* is the same trail open to hiking. Trails follow old road systems and are mostly double track. All trails are well marked with brown metal posts. The park office has trail descriptions and free topo maps with all routes marked on them. All riders must possess a $2 special-use permit (separate from ParkPass). Foot traffic is permitted on mountain biking trails.

fishing: A 17-acre spring-fed lake that is the center of the park's day-use area offers good fishing prospects. The deep, clear lake has bass, bream and catfish, and all three species get their share of attention. Fallen trees around the lake's shore provide the best cover. Most fishing is done from the bank. The lake's shoreline is wooded, but there are many openings large enough to cast from. The *Lake Loop* provides access all the way around the lake. Fishing is not permitted from the beach or pedal-boat dock. Fishing boats are available for rent during the summer. Private boats are not permitted on the lake.

lodging: The park has 15 cottages, 10 of which are grouped together on a scenic hilltop, overlooking much of the park but isolated from most activity. The 2- and 3-bedroom cottages are fully equipped, with linens and complete kitchen furnishings. Each has central heating and air, a fireplace, and a picnic table and grill. Cottages cost $50 to $90/night, with a 2-night minimum stay required for reservations. There is a 5-night minimum Jun–Aug. For reservations, call 800/864-7275.

Toccoa Ranger District

Chattahoochee National Forest

The summit of Springer Mountain, in addition to being the southern terminus of the *Appalachian Trail*, is the meeting point of Georgia's eastern and western Blue Ridge. The mountain top is in the heart of the Blue Ridge Wildlife Management Area and of the

147,017-acre Toccoa Ranger District. District boundaries are difficult to describe because they are formed by a combination of highways, ridges, and private land borders. To the east, the district takes in most of the Coopers Creek and Blue Ridge WMA areas. Rich Mountain is the most westerly tract. The district has a few small recreation areas and a designated wilderness of nearly 10,000 acres, but most of it consists of open backcountry coursed only by long trails and rough forest service roads. Ridges on each side are distinctive, with those to the west of Springer rounded, less rocky and more fertile than those to the east. The district includes a lot of high-mountain terrain, plus land around the namesake Toccoa River and Blue Ridge Lake. Good opportunities exist for hiking, mountain biking, fishing, camping and canoeing /kayaking. Offerings are especially good for overnight excursions, by canoe, by 1 of 3 long hiking trails, or within the rugged, untrailed backcountry of the Rich Mountain Wilderness. Wildlife includes bears, deer, turkeys and grouse.

Blue Ridge (NW), Blairsville (NE), Dahlonega (SE) and Ellijay (W) are the nearest towns.

contact: Toccoa Ranger District, Chattahoochee National Forest, 6050 Appalachian Highway, Blue Ridge, GA 30513; 706/632-3031; www.fs.fed.us/conf/.

getting there: GA-60, GA-52 and US-76 circle the RD, providing indirect access to all areas. An array of county and FS roads complete the routes to various access points. The RS is located 3 mi E of Blue Ridge on the S side of US-76.

topography: the Blue Ridge forms a V in Georgia, the bottom of which is centered in the Toccoa RD, with the E and W ridges extending NE and NW respectively from Springer Mtn. Creeks that rise in the Rich Mountains and on the Blue Ridge WMA flow into numerous watersheds. The Toccoa is the largest river to flow a significant distance across the district. Terrain is almost invariably steep. Southern Appalachian forests, with all their usual variety, are found throughout the district. **maps:** See below under individual areas.

starting out: The district RS is open weekdays 8 AM to 5 PM, Sa 9 AM to 5 PM. Some free maps and information are available. Forest maps, trail guides and annual parking permits are sold.

activities: Hiking, Mountain Biking, Fishing, Camping, Canoeing /Kayaking.

hiking: Most hiking opportunities are on long trails. The *Appalachian Trail* stays on the Toccoa RD for 12.2 mi from Springer Mtn to Justus Mtn. The *Duncan Ridge Trail*, which begins and ends on the *AT*, is 35.5 mi long. The 2 routes can be combined for a 60-mi loop, most of which is within the Toccoa RD. Also, the *Benton McKaye Trail*, which covers 78 mi in GA, begins atop Springer Mtn and runs several mi on the district. Because the trail shares parts of its route with the *AT*, *Duncan Ridge Trail* and various roads, and it winds on and off public lands, a measurement of mileage on the district is difficult to draw and would not be particularly useful. Sections of all the long routes can be hiked for day-trips or short overnighters. Most terrain is moderate to difficult. The only 2 short trails on the district are the 0.9-mi *Stanley Gap Trail*, which is the main access into the Rich Mountain Wilderness, and the 1.2-mi *Eyes on Wildlife Trail*, which begins in the Cooper Creek Scenic Area. 4 other trails that total 7.4 mi are in the Cooper Creek area; they're covered in the Cooper Creek chapter of this section. The trails are actually on the Brasstown District, but the scenic area and recreation areas on the creek are split by the district border.

mountain biking: There are 2 outstanding areas for riding mountain bikes on the Toccoa RD. The *Aska Trails*, a network of hiking/biking routes between Rich Mtn and Lake Blue Ridge, offer 17 mi of moderate to difficult trail that can be ridden in many different ways. Mountain biking is the most popular use of this trail network, which includes a 1,700-ft elevation range. A second system of trails still in development is the Bull Mountain Area of the Blue Ridge WMA. These trails, which will cover more than 50 mi when completed, are also open to equestrian use. Parking lots are in place and many mi of trails have been even opened, but much remains to be done in terms of trail building, marking, mapping, etc. Trails include single-track and old fire roads, but they also include some established FS roads, both open and gated. Completed sections, including Bull Mtn and Turners Creek, have quickly become popular.

fishing: The Toccoa RD offers very good and widely varied opportunities for anglers. Numerous outstanding wild trout streams rise high along the Blue Ridge, with browns, rainbows and brookies all present in different streams. Some streams, like

Noontootla and Jones creeks, are well known for their wild trout populations. Many others are tiny and remote and don't draw much attention. Cooper Creek, Rock Creek and the Toccoa River, on the other hand, are a few of the most popular stocked trout streams anywhere in the mountains. The lower Toccoa River also produces smallmouth bass and walleyes, and Blue Ridge Lake offers more of the same, plus jumbo-sized bream and white bass.

camping: Backcountry camping is permitted anywhere on NF land, unless posted as prohibited. The *AT* and *Duncan Ridge Trail* provide the most practical access into the backcountry on the Toccoa RD. The most remote areas for camping are in the Rich Mountains, both in the designated wilderness and on the northern slope, which, while not designated as backcountry, is rugged and undeveloped. Canoe camping is possible along the Toccoa River. Lake Blue Ridge and Coopers Creek each have 2 developed campgrounds, and the Blue Ridge WMA has one. In some heavily traveled areas on the Blue Ridge WMA, camping is restricted to designated sites, which are very simple and linked with no facilities or formal campground.

canoeing/kayaking: The Toccoa RD's namesake river has a 17-mi canoe trail along it, with 7 access points detailed in a brochure available at the RS. The scenery is terrific and the trail is suitable for beginning or intermediate paddlers. Canoe camping trips are also possible. Lake Blue Ridge, which the Toccoa backs into, makes a nice flatwater paddling destination amid steep-sided hardwood coves. The lakes get some motorboat traffic, but not enough to be problematic on most days.

lodging: The Mountain Top Lodge (800/526-9754; 706/864-6848) is a cedar lodge with a large front porch and deck that sits atop a mtn among oaks, pines and abundant dogwoods. The lodge, which is near Dahlonega, has 13 guest rooms, all with private baths. Some have fireplaces and oversized hot tubs. The lodge is open year round. Rooms cost $60/ to $135/night, including a full country breakfast.

Rich Mountain Wilderness Area

Part of Georgia's western Blue Ridge, the Rich Mountains are similar in character to the better known Cohuttas, which lie to their N and W. Soils are dark and rich, supporting lush forests and abundant wildflowers. There are no singularly outstanding features, like a major waterfall, isolated mountain peak, major cliff or deep gorge. Instead, the beauty is broadcast, with outstanding views from the ridgetop, pockets of old-growth forest, rock outcrops, boulderfields and streams tumbling over numerous small, isolated waterfalls. The main ridge that the backcountry centers around is commonly referred to simply as Rich Mountain, but the highest peak on the ridge is actually Big Bald at 4,081 feet. Although 9,476 acres in the Rich Mountains fall under wilderness designation, the wilderness itself really cannot be looked at apart from the adjoining non-wilderness backcountry, which is also undeveloped and covers the botanically rich northern slopes of the mountain. With the exception of a single, short hiking trail, all travel along the steep slopes into the backcountry of the Rich Mountains is by unofficial and often rugged routes. Within the backcountry, there are opportunities for camping and trout fishing. The Rich Mountains are home to sizable populations of turkey, deer and bear.

Blue Ridge (N) and Ellijay (W) are the nearest towns.

getting there: From Blue Ridge, drive S on Aska Rd 8.1 mi to Stanley Gap Rd on the R, marked with a brown sign for Rich Mtn WMA. Stanley Gap Rd, which begins paved but soon becomes gravel, runs along the S side of Rich Mtn. The best access to the Wilderness is by the *Stanley Gap Trail*, which begins at a small pull-off 3.5 mi from Aska Rd.

topography: The main ridge of Rich Mountains runs NE to SW. Terrain is steep throughout the area, and mountainsides are densely forested. Hardwoods dominate the N slope, while S slopes are covered with mixed pine/hardwood forests. Creeks are lined with hemlock and white pines, plus dense thickets of mountain laurel and rhododendron. Elevations range from 2,400 to 4,081 ft; **maps:** USGS Blue Ridge, Tickanetley.

starting out: There are no facilities at Rich Mtn. Nearest supplies are in Blue Ridge. Pets must be kept on a leash, except for hunting.

activities: Camping, Hiking, Fishing.

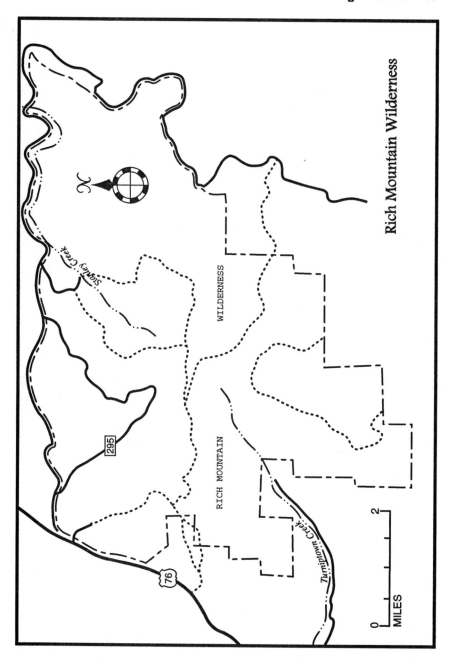

Rich Mountain Wilderness

camping: Backcountry camping is permitted anywhere on NF land, if not posted as prohibited. A couple open areas near Stanley Gap Rd are used for camping. Most sites are accessible only by foot, however, usually without the benefit of a trail to follow. Beyond access, the biggest limitation backcountry campers face is trying to find a flat spot that's large enough to set up a tent on.

hiking: The *Stanley Creek Trail*, the only maintained trail in the area, also serves as the main approach to the wilderness. The 0.9-mi, white-blazed trail follows Stanley Creek for most of its length as it climbs 200 ft to Brownlow Gap at the edge of the wilderness. From there all travel is pure backcountry exploration. There are unofficial trails, mostly across the ridgetop and along old fire roads and logging roads, but no trails are mapped out or maintained in the Rich Mountain Wilderness. The non-wilderness northern slope has a few gated roads that can be used to penetrate the backcountry. Quads and a compass are essential for any hiking beyond the *Stanley Creek Trail*. The forest is dense, and routes can be confusing.

fishing: Stanley Creek is the largest of several streams that tumble off Rich Mtn. Even it is quite small, however, so anglers have to contend with very tight quarters. The mountain terrain creates a lot of drops and pools large enough to fish in even the very small streams. All trout in the creeks are wild. Most are rainbows, but there are some brook trout in N slope tributaries. Only artificial lures may be used on Stanley Creek, which is a seasonal fishery. Streams in the Ellijay and Cartecay River watersheds are open year round.

Lake Blue Ridge

Fed by the Toccoa River, which tumbles freely from high in the Blue Ridge Mountains, Lake Blue Ridge is clear, cool and deep. A very scenic lake that is popular with fishermen, Blue Ridge covers 3,290 acres. Land surrounding the lake includes scattered private holdings, but much of the shoreline is within the National Forest. Most of that land is undeveloped, with little access, except by water, but the Lake Blue Ridge and Morganton Point recreation areas each has a boat ramp, picnic grounds and campground. Lake Blue Ridge also has a short, lakeside hiking trail. A separate set of trails, which are centered up the ridge from the lake's upper end, are designated for multi-use but are used primarily by mountain bikers. Deer and turkeys, through less abundant than around Piedmont lakes, are sometimes spotted around Lake Blue Ridge, and on occasion a bear will roam into a campground in search of food.

Blue Ridge (W) and Morganton (E) are the nearest towns.

getting there: Old US-76, between Blue Ridge and Morganton, crosses Blue Ridge Dam, wraps around the lake's north shore and provides access to 2 rec areas, a forest service boat ramp and a private marina. To get to Lake Blue Ridge Rec Area from the town of Blue Ridge, drive W on Old US-76 1.5 mi to Dry Branch Rd on the R. Turn R and drive 2.5 mi into the area. Morganton Point is accessed directly out of Morganton, off Old US-76. The road into the rec area is marked with a brown sign.

topography: As its name would suggest, Lake Blue Ridge is tucked away in the mtns. Its upper end is steeper-sided than the lower end. Banks forested with hardwoods rise steeply from the lake, which is typically clear and emerald colored. Green Mtn, which borders the upper end of the lake, is 2,557 ft at its peak. The lake's full-pool surface elevation is 1,690 ft. **maps:** USGS Blue Ridge, Mineral Bluff, Wilscott.

starting out: A $2 daily or $30 annual parking fee is required for day-use at both rec areas, the trailhead for the Aska trails and at Lakewood Landing. Swimming is not permitted in the vicinity of the boat ramps. Dogs must be on a leash throughout the area. Morganton Point has a swimming beach; no animals are permitted on the beach, except seeing-eye dogs. Lake Blue Ridge is drawn down 30 ft or more each winter for flood control during which time only boat ramps at Morganton Point and Blue Ridge Marina can be used.

activities: Fishing, Camping, Mountain Biking, Canoeing/Kayaking, Hiking.

fishing: Smallmouth bass and walleyes are the main attractions on Lake Blue Ridge, but big white bass and bluegills also provide good fishing. Rocky points, fallen trees and man-made fish attractors offer some of the lake's best cover, and fish tend to hold deeper than they do in most Georgia reservoirs because of the lake's clear water. Limited bank fishing is possible, especially around the 2 rec areas and off Aska Rd up the Toccoa River arm, but most fishermen work Blue Ridge from boats.

camping: Primitive camping is allowed on NF land, except where noted as prohibited, and boat-camping is possible on Lake Blue Ridge. Flat ground is scarce around the lakeshore, however, and some land is privately owned. Campers should be aware of public/private land boundaries before leaving the boat.

The Lake Blue Ridge Rec Area campground has 58 sites split on 2 loops, 1 of which winds close to the lake and has several sites that are either on the water or offer views of it from just up the ridge. The campground is hilly and forested. The Morganton Point Rec Area campground, as the name suggests, is located on a long point. The campground is forested, primarily with hardwoods. 6 walk-in sites are larger than the rest and offer the nicest seclusion.

Most sites through both campgrounds are fairly small, but nicely secluded. Each site has a gravel tent pad, picnic table, fire ring/grill and lantern post. Lake Blue Ridge has pit toilets. Morganton Point has flush toilets and hot showers. Sites cost $8/night or $10 for lakeside sites. Water is available in scattered locations through both campgrounds. The campgrounds are open from mid-Apr through Oct.

mountain   biking: 17 mi of multi-use trails near the lake's headwaters offer a good variety of riding opportunities with grades that range from moderate to difficult. Several routes extend from Deep Gap, the central parking area, with some going up the mountain and others going down to the lake. Individual trails are as short as 2.5 mi, but all are interconnected, making various loops possible. The total elevation difference encountered across the entire trail system is 1,700 ft. The trails, which combine single track and old fire roads, are well blazed, with different colors and configurations of blazes, according to the trail. Routes and blazes are detailed at an information board at the parking area. The trailhead parking area is located on Aska Rd, 4.5 mi S of Old US-76 in Blue Ridge, just past the gap, and is well marked.

canoeing/kayaking: Limited development, modest boat traffic, clear water, and steep-sided coves fed by tumbling streams make Blue Ridge a delightful flatwater paddling destination. The winter drawdown doesn't hurt this lake's scenic value in most places, as it exposes rocky bluff-like banks instead of mud flats. There are boat ramps at both rec areas.

hiking: Hiking is permitted on the Aska Trails, but the popularity of the routes with mountain bikers keeps foot traffic to a minimum and makes the trails somewhat unappealing for hiking. The *Blue Ridge Lake Trail*, an easy 0.6-mi loop that begins and ends at the picnic area at the Blue Ridge Lake Rec Area, offers nice views of the lake and forest. The blue-blazed trail is fairly level and well suited for family excursions.

Toccoa River

Rising high along the Blue Ridge, the Toccoa River runs through a narrow strip of mostly private land in its upper reaches. By the time it reaches Deep Hole, the first significant public access point and the single most popular spot along the river, the Toccoa is big water, plenty big enough for paddling at almost any water level. From Deep Hole the river flows 20 miles through a combination of public and private lands before emptying into Lake Blue Ridge. Downstream of the lake, the Toccoa leaves the national forest for good as it flows northward toward the Tennessee line. At the border it changes names, and soon after its character changes also. The placid Toccoa become the crashing Ocoee, made famous by paddling events at the Centennial Olympic Games. From Deep Hole to just upstream of Lake Blue Ridge is the *Toccoa Canoe Trail*, with access possible at several points. The river is generally quite mild, with plenty of easy shoals and only a couple strings of moderate rapids. The surrounding land is mostly field or forest, with some unobtrusive riverside houses along the way. Beyond fine paddling prospects, the Toccoa offers good fishing for trout and for smallmouth bass and walleyes in its lower reaches. There is a developed campground at Deep Hole, and backcountry camping is possible in scattered places along the river's route.

Blue Ridge (N) and Morganton (N) are the nearest towns.

getting there: From Morganton, Drive S on GA-60 14.6 mi to the Deep Hole Rec Area on the R, which is the uppermost major access point. The canoe trail ends near Shallowford Bridge, off Aska Rd. From Blue Ridge, drive S on Aska Rd 9 mi to the bridge on the L. There are several public access points in between. All are accessible by crossing Shallowford Bridge and turning R, or by various county and FS roads off GA-60.

topography: The Toccoa River rises high on the Blue Ridge and flows northward toward the Tennessee River. From Deep Hole to Lake Blue Ridge, the Toccoa River is large and, for the most part, gentle. The valley is generally broad, although in places mountains rise quickly from the river's edge. There are white pine/hemlock forests along the river's upper end, but forested banks along the canoe trail consist mostly of hardwood forests and mixed hardwood/pine forests. The river elevation is 1,690 ft at Lake Blue Ridge. The surrounding mountains rise to approximately 2,800 ft. **maps:** USGS Blue Ridge, Wilscot, Noontootlah.

starting out: The only facilities are at Deep Hole, which has restrooms and information boards. A $2 daily or $30 annual parking fee is required. The Toccoa River winds on and off public land. River users should be careful to never use private land as an access point or camping area without permission. The Toccoa RS can provide a canoe trail map that shows 7 boating access points, all either on public land or along a public road where a right-of-way allows access. A Chattahoochee NF map shows approximate public/private land boundaries.

activities: Canoeing/Kayaking, Fishing, Camping, Hiking.

canoeing/kayaking: The entire *Toccoa River Canoe Trail* is suitable for intermediate paddlers, and much of the route lends itself to beginners. With 7 access points along 17 mi of river, numerous trip options exist. A developed canoe launch is at Deep Hole; other access points listed on the USFS *Toccoa River Canoe Trail* brochure are simply areas where there is public access and a road is within reasonable carrying distance from the river. Class I shoals ripple the surface all along the canoe trail, but actual rapids are infrequent. The only significant rapids, which still do not exceed Class II—except at flood stage—are between Margeret and Butt Bridge, near the mid-point of the canoe trail, and right before the final take-out, off Aska Rd. The river is scenic, with mostly wooded banks along the canoe trail. Rhododendron and mountain laurel are abundant, and their blossoms peak in late May to early June.

fishing: Trout fishing is good along the Toccoa, with some natural reproduction occurring but most fish coming from the hatchery. The river's size allows it to carry some fish through multiple seasons, so there are some big fish in the mix. Deep Hole is a popular bank-fishing area. As the name suggests, there is a large, deep hole where the river wraps around the rec area. A handicapped-accessible fishing platform stretches out over the hole. The river is stocked heavily and often at Deep Hole. Downstream, much of the river is best fished from a canoe. There are scattered public access points, but the Toccoa is a large river that is generally too deep to wade. The amount of water a bank-fisherman can reach is severely limited in most areas. Good shoals for wading are found upstream of Shallowford Bridge. The area immediately upstream of the bridge is all private property, but NF land begins a couple hundred yards upstream, providing access to the shoals. Boundaries are clearly marked. The lower end of the river also yields smallmouth bass and walleyes. The Toccoa is a year-round trout stream.

camping: Backcountry camping is permitted on FS lands that border the river, so canoe-camping trips are possible. A topo map is important for figuring out before a trip which public land areas have enough flat land along them to offer good prospects as campsites. Roughly half the land from Deep Hole to the end of the canoe trail is privately owned, so being aware of and respecting boundaries is essential.

There is a small, developed campground at Deep Hole, with 8 sites on a riverside loop. A few of the sites are right on the river. The campsites, which vary in size, are nicely spaced. Each one has a picnic table, fire ring/grill, tent pad and lantern post. Restrooms have flush toilets but no showers. Water is available between sites. The campground is open from late Mar through the end of Oct. Because of the campground's small size and the area's popularity with fishermen and paddlers, Deep Hole is often full, even on weeknights, during the summer. Camping costs $8/night.

lodging: Toccoa River Lodging B&B (706/632-3137) sits atop a hill overlooking the river near Shallowford Bridge. The lodge has a commons area with a fireplace and TV, a large screened-in porch, and a private deck over the river. Rooms with private and shared baths are available. Rooms cost $61 to $75/night and include a full breakfast.

Blue Ridge Wildlife Management Area

Although at 3,782 feet Springer Mountain falls well short of being Georgia's loftiest peak, it easily ranks as our most famous mountain. Beyond forming the apex of Georgia's eastern and western Blue Ridge, Springer Mountain is the southern terminus of the 2,000-mile *Appalachian Trail*. Surrounding the mountain, especially to its north, is the 32,000-acre Blue Ridge Wildlife Management Area. Most of the WMA surrounds the Blue Ridge, so high elevations are prevalent. A vast network of FS roads—some open to public travel, some gated—provide access to most of the WMA. The routes are long and steep on rough gravel roads, however, and many areas are extremely remote, despite having roads connecting with them. Georgia's 2 longest trails begin atop Springer Mtn and together offer more than 35 miles of trail in this part of the national forest. A network of mountain biking trails is currently being developed, with some of it already in place. There are numerous streams to fish both for wild and stocked trout. Camping ranges from backpacking along the *AT* or *Benton McKaye Trail* to setting up camp at Frank Gross, a small developed campground on Rock Creek. Common wildlife include bear, deer, turkeys, squirrels and woodland songbirds.

Dahlonega (SE) is the nearest town.

getting there: A vast network of FS roads leads to various points within the WMA, and the best route varies markedly by destination. Nimblewill Church Rd, off GA-52, is a popular starting point that provides access to several main routes that cross the mountains within the WMA. From Dahlonega, drive W on GA-52 13.1 mi to Nimblewill Church Rd on the R, beside the abandoned Grizzle Store.

topography: The summit of Springer Mtn is the convergence of the E and W Blue Ridge in Georgia. The WMA takes in part of both ridges. Almost all terrain is steep and much of the WMA is located high in the mountains. Forests are diverse, but mixed hardwood and white pine/hemlock forests are well represented. Elevations range from 1,550 to 3,782 ft. **maps:** USGS Noontootla, Nimblewill, Campbell Mountain, Suches, Amicalola, Tickanetley, Campbell Mountain.

starting out: Facilities are limited to parking areas and information boards. A $2 daily or $30 annual parking fee is required at the Springer Mtn access area on FS-42. Parking fees will also be required at the Bull Mtn and Jake Mtn parking areas. Pet must be on a leash.

activities: Fishing, Hiking, Mountain Biking, Camping.

fishing: Trout fishermen find plenty of places to fish on the Blue Ridge WMA, with excellent variety in the offerings. Most streams are in the upper watersheds of the Toccoa and Etowah rivers. Several of them offer excellent prospects for wild trout. Among them are Noontootla and Jones creeks, both open to fishing with artificial lures only. On Noontootla, all trout under 16 inches must be released immediately. Noontootla, which reaches medium size by the end of its run across NF land, is the largest of the wild trout streams on the WMA. FS-58 parallels the creek from its headwaters near Winding Stairs Gap to the FS border.

Several remote trout streams, some containing wild brook trout, measure just a few feet across and are absolutely shrouded in rhododendron. The most intriguing thing about Jones Creek, which is quite small, is that it contains mostly brown trout. FS-77A, off FS-77 Winding Stairs Rd), crosses Jones Creek. Access from that point is by wading. Creeks through the WMA are generally surrounded by dense rhododendron and mtn laurel. They are steep, however, creating good pool habitat even in very small creeks. For anglers who prefer trout freshly stocked, Rock Creek runs right beside a federal fish hatchery and gets plenty of trout on a weekly basis during the season. Rock Creek Lake is also regularly stocked in spring and summer. Most fishing in Rock Creek and Rock Creek Lake is done from the banks, with bait. FS-69, accessible off GA-60 near Deep Hole, parallels Rock Creek and leads to Rock Creek Lake. The Noontootla Creek watershed is open year round. Most other streams on the WMA are listed as seasonal.

hiking: Most hiking in this area is on long trails, specifically the *Appalachian Trail* and the *Benton McKaye Trail*. Both begin their lengthy routes atop Springer Mtn and extend to GA-60, 20 mi for the *AT*, 17 for the *BMT*. Both routes cross the WMA border well before they reach GA-60 but remain on a block of NF land that is contiguous with WMA lands. The entire portion of the *Duncan Ridge Trail* that is W of GA-60 shares a single path with the

Benton McKaye Trail. Day hikes of various lengths are possible along both trails because numerous FS roads cross them in different places. Waterfalls, wonderful vistas, massive white pines, and hemlocks are just a few of the highlights along either trail. Both routes wind from mountaintops to gaps most of the way, occasionally dipping all the way down to a creek or river valley. Hiking on them is moderate to difficult. The *AT* is blazed with white rectangles, the *Benton McKaye Trail* with white diamond-shaped markers. The best access to either trail is from the Springer Mtn parking area, along FS-42. The *Benton McKaye Trail* also crosses FS-42, 2 mi farther up the road, but it is 1.7 mi to the mountaintop by that route, as opposed to 0.7 mi by the *AT*. Springer Mtn can also be approached from the S, using a 2.3 approach trail from Nimblewill Gap. Parking is free there, but the hike is longer and the area is more remote and probably less secure. Multi-use trails on the WMA are open to hiking, but regular use by horseback riders and mountain bikers make these routes pretty unappealing to hikers.

mountain biking: An extensive network of multi-use trails is being developed on the S side of the Blue Ridge WMA. When completed the interconnected routes will total more than 50 mi of trail and FS road. A parking area is already in place at Bull Mtn, as are several mi of trail, but a second lot at Jake Mtn and much of the trail system are still being developed. Routes have not yet been fully marked, measured or mapped. Those trails in place, including the 15-mi *Bull Mountain Trail* and the 7-mi *Turner Creek Trail* are open to hiking, mountain biking and horseback riding, with almost all users coming from the latter two groups. The trail system will include a mix of riding conditions, but routes are generally difficult and include steep slopes, technical single track, rocky areas and stream crossings. For experienced riders, these routes take on some rugged and beautiful terrain and are well worth exploring. A $2 daily or $30 annual parking fee will be required at the Bull Mtn and Jake Mtn parking lots. Mountain biking is not permitted on days of archery gun hunts or before 10 AM on days during archery hunting season. Season dates are posted at all information boards on the WMA.

camping: Backcountry camping is permitted anywhere on NF land, unless posted as prohibited. In some heavily used sections of the Blue Ridge WMA, including roadside areas adjacent to Nimblewill and Rock creeks, camping is restricted to established sites. Primitive sites laid out with landscaping ties have been scattered through these areas, which are clearly marked with signs. The best opportunities for backcountry camping are along the *Appalachian Trail* and the *Duncan Ridge Trail*. The only developed campground in the area, Frank Gross, is very primitive. Located on FS-69, 0.4 mi S of the Rock Creek hatchery, the campground has 9 sites in an open flat beside Rock Creek. Each site has a picnic table, lantern post and fire ring/grill. They are fairly large and laid out with landscaping ties. There are pit toilets and a pump for water. The campground is open from late Mar through the end of Oct. Camping costs $8/night.

Cooper Creek Area

Cooper Creek is one of those trout streams where an angler almost has to bring his own rock to stand on during the summer. A large parking area, easy access near a bridge, 2 campgrounds, a beautiful stream and very heavy, regular stocking somehow combine to attract a lot of anglers. The crowds stay concentrated around the parking area and the campgrounds, however, and Cooper Creek is far too nice to avoid because of the people. A major tributary of the Toccoa River, the creek sparkles as it tumbles gently between steep hillsides forested with huge hemlocks and white pines. Upstream of a forest service road bridge, 2 miles of the creek are surrounded by a scenic area, so designated for the virgin forest on both sides of the creek. There are several hiking trails well suited for day-hikes in the area, plus 20 miles of an arduous route, which follows the Duncan Ridge, parallel to Cooper Creek. Several miles upstream of the scenic area and the two recreation areas, FS-33 runs beside a much smaller and more intimate Cooper Creek. Wildlife in the area includes bear, deer, turkey and woodland songbirds.

Morganton (N) and Suches (S) are the nearest towns.

getting there: From Morganton, drive S on GA 60 14.6 mi to Cooper Creek Rd, marked with a brown sign for the Cooper Creek WMA, and turn L. The road will begin paved, turn gravel, return to pavement, and then turn gravel again, somewhere along the way becoming FS-4. Drive 5 mi to Mulky Campground on the L or 6 mi to FS-236 at Cooper Creek Campground. At FS-236 turn R and drive 0.5 m to the scenic area parking lot on the L, just past a bridge that crosses Cooper Creek.

topography: A major tributary of the Toccoa River, Cooper Creek flows E to W. Duncan Ridge, a long Blue Ridge spur, borders the creek immediately to the N. The Southern Appalachian forest that blankets the area is diverse. Within the scenic area, old-growth forest surrounds the creek on both sides and includes white /pine/hemlock forests at creekside and forests of mixed hardwoods that include massive poplars. Elevations range from 2,150 to 4,271. **maps:** USGS Mulky Gap.

starting out: There are no facilities, beyond a parking lot and information boards, for day-use areas. A $2 daily or $30 annual parking fee is required. The scenic area parking lot is closed form 10 PM to 7 AM. Pets must be kept on a leash, except for hunting.

activities: Fishing, Camping, Hiking.

fishing: Most trout fishing on Cooper Creek takes place right around the campground and scenic area and is done from the banks with bait or spinners. The creek is heavily stocked and gets extensive fishing pressure. Crowds are typically large enough, in fact, that any approach other than stationary fishing is impractical. One need not travel far upstream from the scenic area parking lot to get away from the crowds, though. There, fly fishing and wading with ultralight spinning gear are more popular. Trout are a mix of stocked and stream-bred fish. The creek crosses a small private tract just upstream of the scenic area, but most of its length, from its headwaters to just downstream of Mulky Campground, is on public lands. Through the scenic area the creek is medium size. The grade is moderate, with the creek tumbling just enough to create good holding areas. It is plenty open for casting. Coopers Creek is seasonal.

camping: Sections of the rec area and all of the scenic area are closed to camping because of potential for over-use, but backcountry camping is permitted where not posted as prohibited. The *Duncan Ridge Trail* follows the high ridge that borders Coopers Creek to the N for nearly 20 mi and provides the best opportunity for an extended trip into the backcountry. There are 2 campgrounds along the creek, Coopers Creek and Mulky. Coopers Creek Campground has 17 campsites, most of them along a riverside loop and a few in a more isolated area just uphill the creek. All sites offer average isolation or better and are average sized and nice. Each site has a picnic table, fire ring/grill, lantern post and tent pad. Mulky is located just down the creek on FS-4. 11 campsites are set directly along the road, just across from the creek. The sites are in field openings with some very close together and not very attractive, but they're quite convenient to the creek and are used almost exclusively by fishermen. Each site has at least a picnic table and a lantern post. Some also have a fire ring/grill and established tent pad. Both campgrounds have pit toilets and water available. They are open from late Mar through the end of Oct. Camping costs $8/night. Waterfront sites at Cooper Creek cost $10/night..

hiking: 5 trails that total 8.6 mi begin close to the parking area for the Cooper Creek Scenic Area. The 1.2-mi *Eyes on Wildlife Trail*, which begins directly across from FS-236, is well marked at its trailhead and appears newly created. It has been storm-ravaged, however, and was in bad need of maintenance in late 1998. Numerous downed trees made the loop trail difficult to walk, and sections were overgrown. The other short trails, which range in length from 0.4 to 3.4 mi, begin 0.1 mi N of the parking lot on FS-236. A sign with a color-coded map marks the beginning of the yellow-blazed *Yellow Mountain Trail*. The 2 shortest routes, *Cooper Creek Trail* and *Shope Gap Trail*, are accessible only from other trails. The orange-blazed *Mill Shoals Trail* begins just past the *Yellow Mountain Trail*. The trails are near Cooper Creek but none follow right beside it. The interconnected trails climb ridges and lead to several tumbling tributaries. They border the scenic area and offer peaks at least of the old-growth trees. All trails are moderate to difficult, with some fairly steep ascents mixed in. Although generally well blazed, the trail system has confusing sections.

The blue-blazed *Duncan Ridge Trail* runs 20.4 mi from GA-60 to its N terminus at Slaughter Gap on the *Appalachian Trail*. Nearly 15 mi of the trail form the N border of the Cooper Creek WMA, and most of the trail stays right on the ridge that the mountains N of the creek slope upward toward. The well-maintained trail is difficult, with a near continuous alternation between drops and climbs, some long and steep. The trail is accessible off GA-60, 11.6 mi S of Morganton, or off GA-180 at Wolfpen Gap, 3.1 mi W of US-19/129.

Amicalola Falls State Park

Plunging 729 feet, Amicalola Falls is the highest waterfall east of the Mississippi River and the centerpiece of a 2,059-acre state park. Along with its "tumbling waters," as the Cherokee word that Amicalola was derived from means, the park is also well known for one of its trails, the 8.3-mile approach to Springer Mountain, the southern terminus of the 2,150-mile *Appalachian Trail*. The park surrounds Little Amicalola Creek, both above and below the falls, and includes the steep ridges on both sides of the lower creek's gorge. While most visitors never get beyond the 0.3-mile trail to the face of the falls, the park has an excellent trail system that provides a good range of opportunities for hikers. One trail leads to the Len Foote Hike Inn, a lodge that is accessible only by a 5-mile hike. Opportunities for camping and trout fishing also exist in the park. Nice picnic sites are scattered along the creek below the falls. Deer and bear are sometimes seen, especially above the falls, where the park borders the Chattahoochee National Forest.

Dawsonville (S) and Dahlonega (E) are the nearest towns.

contact: Superintendent, Amicalola Falls State Park, 240 Amicalola Falls State Park Rd, Dawsonville, GA 30534; 706/265-4703; www.gastateparks.org.

getting there: From Dahlonega, drive W on GA-52 19 mi to the park entrance on the R.

topography: Amicalola Falls forms the head of a V-shaped gorge. Despite steep ridges and a broad range of elevations between 2,660 and 1,693 ft, the park has a surprising amount of fairly flat terrain above and below the falls. Forests are made up almost exclusively of hardwoods. Mountain laurel is abundant along the ridge sides. **maps:** USGS Amicalola.

starting out: The park visitor center and trading post, open 9 to 5 daily (closed for lunch), has interpretive displays and can provide information and maps. Restrooms, drink machines and a pay phone are available. Signs around the top of falls and all rim trails warn that crossing fences or straying off trails constitutes criminal trespass and that fatalities have occurred in these areas.

Alcoholic beverages are prohibited in public areas. Pets must be on a leash.

activities: Hiking, Fishing, Camping.

hiking: Though best known for just 2 trails, the 0.3-mi climb along Amicalola Creek to the base of the waterfall and the 8.3-mi approach trail to the *Appalachian Trail*, the park has 10 different trails that total 17 mi. A steep 1-mi route climbs the E ridge, leading to the top of the falls, and a network of short routes wind along the edge of the W ridge and ascend it. Other trails include a fitness trail and interpretive nature trail near the lodge and a fairly easy walk along the lower creek, through the picnic area. All trails are blazed, well maintained and easy to follow, and have signs with color-coded trail maps at all trail junctions and footbridges where needed. Most trails are moderate or moderate to strenuous. The *AT* approach trail and the trail to the Hike Inn are largely on NF land. Both are accessed from above the falls. Other trails, which are interconnected, can be accessed near the visitor center or from the parking area beside the reflection pool. A park brochure includes a trail map that lists colors of blazes.

fishing: 1 mi of Little Amicalola Creek, from the reflection pool to the park's S boundary, is stocked through spring and summer and open to fishing as a seasonal stream. Although small, the creek tumbles just enough to have nice pools for holding trout. Almost all fishing is done with bait or small spinners and from the banks. The creek cuts through the day-use area and is easy to access from the reflection pool to the visitor center.

camping: 20 medium-sized campsites are well-spaced along a hilly loop in a hardwood forest. Each site has a picnic table, tent pad, fire ring/grill and lantern post, plus water and electricity. Restrooms have flush toilets and hot showers, plus laundry facilities, a pay phone and drink machine. Sites cost $15/night for tents, $17 for RVs. The campground is open year round.

lodging: The Len Foote Hike Inn, opened in 1998, is Georgia's only backcountry inn. Rooms have bunk beds and electric lighting (no outlets), but no heat or air. Bath houses have composting toilets and hot showers. Stays include a hearty dinner and hot breakfast, served family style. A community room has a wood-burning stove and library. Rooms cost $55/person, double occupancy, $75/person, single occupancy, including meals.

The wood-shingle sided Amicalola Falls Lodge has a grand appearance as it sets atop the E ridge, overlooking the creek valley and surrounding mountains. The lodge lobby has a big fireplace, wood floors and huge picture windows. The lodge has 57 guest rooms with costs ranging from $59–199/night.

The park also has 14 cabins, with some along the lower creek and some up on the ridge, above the falls. 1-, 2- and 3-bedroom cabins are fully furnished, with rocking chair screen porches and grills. Cabins by the creek are more contemporary in design than those on the ridge, but all have brown wood siding and a natural appearance. Cabins cost $65–155/night. For lodging reservations, call 800/864-7275.

Brasstown Ranger District

Chattahoochee National Forest

Georgia's highest mountain, Brasstown Bald, and Blood Mountain, the highest point along the Peach State portion of the *Appalachian Trail*, are both part of the Brasstown Ranger District. Each mountaintop is the namesake and centerpiece of a wilderness area. The largest and least developed of the six ranger districts of the Chattahoochee National Forest, the Brasstown has more than 35,000 acres of federally designated wilderness, including all or parts of the Blood Mountain, Brasstown, Mark Trail, Southern Nantahala Wilderness and Tray Mountain areas. Beyond those areas designated as wilderness, large portions of this 157,504-acre district are included in large backcountry tracts with no facilities and limited access. Wildlife, including black bear, wild boar, white-tailed deer and wild turkey, is abundant on hardwood-dominated north slopes that are common through this district, the southeastern border of which follows the crest of the Blue Ridge much of the way.

All but the first 8.1 miles of Georgia's portion of the *Appalachian Trail*, plus a 6.4-mile section of the trail through the Raven Cliffs Wilderness, either runs through or follows the border of the Brasstown RD, as do more than more than half of the 35.5-mi *Duncan Ridge Trail* and numerous shorter routes. Backcountry camping opportunities are outstanding, and waters that offer good prospects for trout are scattered across the district. Lake Chatuge offers lake fishing, along with a good spot for canoeing and kayaking, while mountain biking is possible on Forest Service roads throughout the district.

Blairsville (N), Dahlonega (S) and Cleveland (S) are the nearest towns.

contact: Brasstown Ranger District, U.S. Forest Service, P.O. Box 9, Blairsville, GA 30512; 706/745-6928; www.fs.fed.us/conf/.

getting there: GA-60, GA-180, US-19/129 and US-76 are all major arteries through the Brasstown RD. The district RS is located 1.9 mi W of Blairsville on US-76.

topography: The Blue Ridge, which runs NE to SW along the edge of much of this district is the key defining feature, although the state's highest mtn, Brasstown Bald, rises apart from the ridge. Duncan Ridge, which runs E to W and is the longest spur off the Blue Ridge in GA, is also prominent in this district. North slopes, with botanically rich coves at high elevations, are common, although the Brasstown and Blood Mountain wildernesses surround their respective mountains within the district, allowing for a broad range of forest types including oak/hickory, hemlock /white pine and mixed hardwood/pine forests. The headwaters of several rivers, including the Toccoa, Nottely, Hiawassee and Chestatee, rise within this district. Elevations range from 1,550 to 4,784 ft. **maps:** See below under individual areas.

starting out: The district RS, open weekdays 7:30 to 4:30 and weekends 8:30 to 5:30, has some brochures and can provide answers to questions about the district. Annual parking permits, topographical maps of some wilderness areas, trail guides and USGS quads are available for purchase.

activities: Hiking, Fishing, Camping, Canoeing/Kayaking, Mountain Biking.

hiking: Not including the *Appalachian Trail* and *Duncan Ridge Trail*, which together extend more than 75 mi through the district, more than 55 mi of hiking trail are maintained within the Brasstown RD. The 2 long trails either follow or stay close to ridgetops most of the way, while the others offer a little bit of everything, from very short waterfall access spurs to long, difficult highcountry loops. Beyond maintained trails, many mi of old fire roads and ridgetop routes are used by backcountry hikers in areas that have no blazed paths through them.

fishing: Fishermen enjoy opportunities ranging from lake fishing for bass, hybrids and crappie on Lake Chatuge to trout fishing for native brookies in tiny headwater branches. Dicks, Waters and Cooper creeks are 3 of the best-known trout streams in the district, but several smaller creeks together provide a fair amount of opportunity to catch both stocked and wild trout. The Brasstown RD also has 2 small highcountry lakes, Dockery Lake and Lake Winfield Scott, which are stocked with trout through spring and summer.

camping: The district has only 4 developed campgrounds, at the Waters Creek, Chatuge Lake, Dockery Lake and Lake Winfield Scott rec areas. None or these are large, but opportunities for backcountry camping are outstanding with 5 wilderness areas, plus along significant sections of the *AT* and *Duncan Ridge Trail* that provide backpacking access. Backcountry camping is permitted throughout the NF, except where noted as prohibited.

canoeing/kayaking: Canoeing and kayaking on the Brasstown RD is limited to Chatuge Lake, a 7,050-acre mountain lake that straddles the NC/GA border.

mountain biking: The only trail open to mountain biking is the 5-mi *Davenport Trail*, a long-established ORV route that is generally flat and popular with 4-wheelers, two characteristics that make it unappealing to most mountain bikers. Almost all riding in this district is done on gated and ungated FS roads.

lodging: The Blueberry Inn (706/219-4024), a large 1920s farmhouse, looks over the mountains of the Brasstown RD—the best place to enjoy the view is from the inn's big wrap-around porch. A creek tumbles across the property, which also has a stocked pond, herb and perennial gardens and, of course, plenty of wild blueberries. 12 guest rooms, each with private bath, are furnished individually with family pieces and antiques. Rooms cost $85/night, except during fall, and include a full breakfast and complementary wine, iced tea and evening snack.

Lake Winfield Scott

An 18-acre lake at the head of Cooper Creek, Lake Winfield Scott sets high in the mountains but is nearly surrounded by higher peaks, the highest being those along the Blue Ridge, just east of the lake. Lake Winfield Scott actually sets along the western slope of Blood Mountain, and the small creeks that feed the lake rise as springs near the summit of the mountain. The lake is ultra clear and stays cool year round. Its banks are wooded and steep, but not too steep to walk along. Stocked with trout through spring and summer and offering outstanding scenery, Lake Winfield Scott is popular with fishermen and picnickers. The area also offers 2 nice camping areas and 3 hiking trails. The day-use area and campground are confined to a narrow corridor around the lake where the ground remains somewhat level. Deer, turkeys and bears use this area, and signs caution campers to keep food properly stored and to never feed bears.

Blairsville (N) is the nearest town.

getting there: From the traffic circle in Blairsville, Drive S on US-19/129 10.1 to GA-180 W. Turn R and drive 6.9 mi to the second sign for Lake Winfield Scott, on the L, which is the main entrance. This entrance is 0.6 mi past the lake and the first entrance, which leads to a small parking lot for day-users, but does not connect with the road to the campground or boat ramp.

topography: Fed by 2 small branches, Lake Winfield Scott is considered the head of Cooper Creek. The lake sets in a dip between 2 lesser ridges on the W slope of Blood Mtn. The forest is mixed, but hardwoods are dominant. The lake elevation is 2,940 ft. **maps:** USGS Neels Gap.

starting out: Lake Winfield Scott Rec Area has pit toilets and information boards at scattered parking areas. A $2 daily or $30 annual parking fee is required. Gas motors are prohibited on the lake, which has a primitive boat ramp. All pets must be on a leash.

activities: Fishing, Camping, Hiking.

fishing: Rainbow trout, stocked seasonally, are the main attraction to fishermen at Lake Winfield Scott, although the lake also supports a decent population of largemouth bass and plenty of bluegills. The trout population is largely dependent on stockings and the fish pretty well run out by early fall, but the lake is sufficiently large and deep to protect some trout, allowing for occasional catches through the offseason and annual catches of a few large fish that have been in the lake for a year or more. Most fishing is done from the bank, around which there is a loop trail, and from fishing platforms that stretch out over the water. Some fishermen do use small boats to work the lake. Lake Winfield Scott is open year round to fishing, and no trout stamp is required to fish for species other than trout, but no trout may be kept by any fisherman who does not possess a trout stamp.

camping: Camping around the lake is restricted to 26 sites in a designated campground, which is divided into 2 areas. The first camping area is along the main entry road, just before of the lake and on the R. The other is lakefront, in the back of the rec area, but its sites are generally smaller and less isolated than those in the first area. Both campgrounds are densely forest, with plenty of undergrowth to help provide privacy. Each site has a picnic table, tent pad, fire ring/grill and lantern post. Each area has a restroom with flush toilets and cold showers. Sites cost $8/night. Double sites cost $25. The campground is open from the beginning of May through Oct.

hiking: 2 blue-blazed *Appalachian Trail* approach trails climb moderately from Lake Winfield Scott to gaps along the Blue Ridge. Together with the 2.3-mi section of the *AT* that connects them, the trails make a terrific loop hike of 6 mi. A third trail, the 0.4-mi *Lake Winfield Scott Trail*, circles the lake and is a very easy trail that is used more by fishermen than by hikers. The 2 longer routes, the 2.7-mi *Slaughter Creek Trail* and the 1-mi *Jarred Gap Trail*, share a trailhead across from Lake Winfield Scott's boat ramp, but the paths soon split. Both trails follow old roadbed much of the way and are well maintained and marked. The *Slaughter Creek Trail* joins the *AT* 0.9 mi from the summit of Blood Mtn, which has outstanding views to the N and to the S.

Dockery Lake

Set in a cove, well up the southeastern slope of the Blue Ridge, 6-acre Dockery Lake is clear and cold. Although small, the recreation area that surrounds the lake provides good opportunities for backcountry adventure. Beyond offering a nice setting for a campground and picnic area, Dockery Lake supports a good seasonal trout fishery with easy bank access. Two hiking trails that begin in this area offer two very different hiking experiences. Bears, deer and wild turkeys all use the area, and bears, in fact, have visited campgrounds often enough that there are signs warning visitors not to feed them and to keep food properly stored.

Dahlonega (S) is the nearest town.

getting there: From GA-52 E and GA-60 at the N end of Dahlonega, drive N on GA-60 11.1 mi to Dockery Lake Rd (FS-654). Turn R on FS-654, which is one lane and winding, and drive 0.9 mi to the rec area.

topography: Built on an unnamed Waters Creek tributary, Dockery Lake sets at 2,388 ft in a cove that is bounded by Cedar Ridge to the S and SW and the Blue Ridge to the N and W. The forest is a mix of pines and hardwoods. **maps:** USGS Neels Gap; ATC Springer Mtn to Bly Gap

starting out: Dockery Lake has pit toilets at the picnic area parking lot, which is also the lot for fishing or hiking, plus an information board. A $2 daily or $30 annual parking fee is required. Pets must be on a leash.

activities: Fishing, Hiking, Camping.

fishing: Dockery Lake provides good put-and-take trout fishing through spring and summer, but by the time trout season closes at the end of Oct, stocking has long since ceased and most trout have been caught and taken home. Most fishing is done from the banks, with both bait and artificial offerings popular. A trail circles the lake and numerous spurs formed by fishermen lead to good open spots for casting all around the lake. A trout stamp is required for fishing Dockery Lake, even if fishermen are pursuing bream or other species, and the lake is considered seasonal waters.

hiking: The Dockery Lake Rec Area has two trails, with one that circles the lake and another that climbs away from it and connects with the *Appalachian Trail*. The *Lakeshore Trail* is 0.5 mi long, easy to hike, and true to its name, never straying far from the shores of the lake. The *Dockery Lake Trail*, which never actually runs beside Dockery Lake, is 3.0 mi long and moderate to strenuous, as it ascends toward its jct with the *AT* at Miller Gap. The trail runs beside and/or crosses a network of Waters Creek tributaries along the way to the gap, at 2,980 ft. The scenery changes regularly as the trail alternates between creeks and the ridges that divide them, making a trip up and down the trail a good day-hike. The trail is wide and well marked with blue blazes. The *Lakeshore Trail* is unblazed but easy to follow. Both trails are easy to find.

camping: The rec area's 11 campsites, although small and simple, are very nice. Stone walls form the sites, each of which has a tend pad, picnic table, lantern post, fire ring and stand-up grill. The mixed forest is dense and the terrain is hilly, providing nice isolation, but the lake is within sight. Pit toilets and pumped water are available. Sites cost $5/night. The campground is open from the beginning of May through near the end of Oct.

Blood Mountain Area

At 4,461 feet, the top of Blood Mountain is the highest point along Georgia's portion of the *Appalachian Trail* and the centerpiece of a 7,800-acre wilderness. Views from the summit, which is capped by a stone shelter built by Civilian Conservation Corps workers in the 1930s, are outstanding. The Blood Mountain Wilderness, established in 1991, is the most heavily traveled wilderness in the Chattahoochee National Forest because it is laced with trails and accessible by foot from several other areas, including Vogel State Park. The northern portion of the wilderness surrounds the summit, taking in all sides of the mountaintop, while the southern half is bordered to the northwest by the Blue Ridge to Woody Gap and is made up mostly of southeastern slopes. Along Blood Mountain's northern slope, just outside the wilderness, the 175-acre Sosbee Cove Scenic Area preserves one of the state's finest old-growth hardwood forests, with towering buckeyes, yellow poplars and richly varied wildflowers. Hiking is easily the most popular activity on Blood Mountain, but backcountry camping is also popular along trails throughout the wilderness. Deer, turkeys and bears all call Blood Mountain home, and grouse make good use of thickets at high elevations.

Blairsville (N), Cleveland (SE) and Dahlonega (S) are the nearest towns.

getting there: From the traffic circle in Blairsville, drive S on US-19/129 13 mi to the parking area for Blood Mountain hiking on the R or 13.5 mi to Neels Gap.

topography: The Blue Ridge runs E to W from Neels Gap to the top of Blood Mtn and then turns NE to SW to Woody Gap. At Slaughter Gap, Duncan Ridge, the longest spur ridge off Georgia's Blue Ridge, splits off from SE to NW. The terrain is invariably steep, but forest types vary enormously according to orientation, elevation and proximity of water. Northern hardwood coves are botanically rich, while southern slopes are often dominate by pines. Oak/hickory forests are common. The mountaintop is largely covered by rhododendron thickets broken by rock outcrops. Elevations within the wilderness range from 2,000 to 4,461 ft. **maps:** USGS Neels Gap; ATC Springer Mtn to Bly Gap.

starting out: The Walasi-Yi Center at Neels Gap, a native stone structure built in the 1930s by CCC workers, houses Mountain Crossings (706/745-6095), an outfitting store that has extensive backpacking supplies and is a terrific source of information about trails in the Blood Mountain area. Restrooms and pay phones are available. Parking for Blood Mountain exploration is 0.5 mi N of Neels Gap. Dogs must be kept on a leash in the NF.

activities: Hiking, Camping.

hiking: Opportunities for hikes on Blood Mountain hikes range from a leisurely stroll along 0.6 mi of easy footpaths through the wildflowers and fabulous trees of Sosbee Cove to a 10.7-mi, moderately strenuous hike along the *AT* from Neels Gap to Woody Gap. By far the most popular route is the 2.2-mi (one way) climb on the *Freeman Trail* to the summit of Blood Mountain to connect with the *AT*. The climb is moderate to strenuous, but stunning as it cuts through numerous forest types and beautiful boulderfields before climbing to outstanding vistas. The steepest sections have steps built of rocks and logs.

Counting trails or measuring mileage for this area is difficult because parts of the Blood Mountain area are not in the wilderness and parts of the wilderness are not on Blood Mountain. Also, the *Dockery Lake Trail*, *Duncan Ridge Trail*, *Slaughter Creek Trail*, *Bear Hair Gap Trail* and *Coosa Backcountry Trail* all run through the Blood Mountain Wilderness for part of their length, but each is more closely associated with another area and is detailed in another chapter. The *AT*, the *Byron Herbert Reece Access Trail* and the *Freeman Trail* total 13.2 mi within the wilderness, while portions of the other routes add another 6 or 7 mi. The *Sosbee Cove Trail*, outside the wilderness, is 0.6 mi. It is unblazed but easy to follow. Hiker parking for Blood Mtn is 0.5 mi N of Neels Gap at a marked lot, where the blue-blazed *Freeman Trail*, an *AT* spur, begins. All trails are interconnected, except the *Sosbee Cove Trail*, which is accessible off GA-180, 3 mi W of US-19/129.

camping: Camping is permitted throughout the wilderness, but flat land is limited and most water sources are unreliable. Campsites are more abundant throughout the S half of the wilderness than the N half, but the 2-room shelter atop Blood Mtn is a great place to camp, if it's available. Car-camping is possible around the hikers' parking lot 0.5 mi N of Neels Gap. All campfires and the gathering of firewood are banned within 300 ft of the *AT* from Neels Gap to Slaughter Gap, and that includes the fireplace in the Blood Mtn shelter.

DeSoto Falls Scenic Area

DeSoto Falls Scenic Area is a long, narrow, 650-acre tract along Frogtown Creek that is named for three separate waterfalls on the creek and its tributaries. The area gets its name from a piece of Spanish armor that is said to have been found near one of the falls by early settlers and believed to have been a remnant from Hernando DeSoto's expedition through Georgia in 1540. The uppermost set of falls, a long slide of more than 150 feet on the Frogtown Creek, is no longer accessible by trail. The middle and lower falls, both on tributaries, can be hiked to. The creek, which is a major tributary of the Chestatee River, has a picnic area and a campground beside it, plus a hiking trail running along it. Limited trout fishing is possible. Deer and squirrels are the most likely wildlife species to be encountered.

Blairsville (N), Dahlonega (SW) and Cleveland (SE) are the nearest towns.

getting there: From the traffic circle in Blairsville drive S on US-19/129 17.4 mi to the road into the SA on the R, which is marked with a sign.

topography: The entire scenic area is within the valley of Frogtown Creek, which rises on the SE slope of Blood Mtn, and flows S between Cedar and Hogpen mountains. White pine/hemlock forests are prevalent along the creek, with hardwoods more common up the ridges. Elevations range from 2,000 to 2,700 ft. **maps:** USGS Neels Gap

starting out: Pit toilets and an information board are available at the parking lot for day-use. A $2 daily or $30 annual parking fee is required. The entire area closes during the winter, generally from Nov through the end of Mar, but hikers are permitted to park at the gate and walk the extra 0.2 mi to the trailhead. All pets must be on a leash.

activities: Camping, Hiking, Fishing.

camping: 17 campsites are well spaced along a hilly loop in a mixed forest of pines and hardwoods that offers a diversity of settings. Some are up the hill and well isolated in dense woods; others are on a creekside flat among an open forest of white pines and hemlocks. Each site has a tent pad, picnic table, lantern post and fire/ring grill. The campground has restrooms with flush toilets and hot showers. Sites cost $7/night. The campground is open from early May through the end of Oct.

hiking: From a bridge that crosses Frogtown Creek near the campground, short hiking trails go upstream and downstream, each leading to a waterfall on a small feeder stream. Both falls are scenic and have nice observation platforms, but both are on tiny streams, so low water can leave them almost dry. The 0.25-mi trail to the lower falls is moderate. The 0.75-mi trail to the middle falls is easy. The same trail that leads to the middle falls used to continue 2 mi to an overview of the upper falls, but this section is now closed. Trails are unblazed but very easy to follow as they are heavily trodden. The trailhead is signed and easy to locate.

fishing: Frogtown Creek is stocked regularly through summer in the area around the campground and picnic area, but it is a small stream that doesn't get large numbers of fish. The stream is fairly flat here, and bait-fishing from the banks is common. Just upstream, the creek cuts through a steep-sided, narrow gorge that is lined with rhododendron, and all fishing for small, wild rainbow trout is by wading. The stream is large enough to fish for roughly 1 mi upstream from the campground.

Dicks Creek Area

A fairly large and scenic stream that tumbles over several impressive cascades and is very accessible by a Forest Service road which parallels the creek and crosses it several times, Dicks Creek is popular with campers and day-users. Fishermen enjoy the creek's heavily stocked pools, and picnickers come just to sit on creekside boulders or swim in the pools beneath the falls. Camping is popular both in a developed campground and at scattered primitive sites. Some fishermen also come to take on Waters Creek, a Dicks Creek tributary that has large but finicky trout and falls under special management. The upper end of the Dicks Creek watershed, high along the Blue Ridge, is a vast, undeveloped and lightly traveled backcountry. Deer, turkeys and bears all make good use of the Dicks Creek area, with bears most common at higher elevations.

Cleveland (SE) and Dahlonega (SW) are the nearest towns.

getting there: From Cleveland, drive N on US-129 11.4 mi to US-19 at Turners Corner. Turn L on US-19 and drive 0.6 mi to FS-34 on the R, well marked by a sign for the Waters Creek Campground. Turn R on FS-34, which is paved initially and passes several private holdings before reaching the Waters Creek Campground at 1 mi.

topography: Dicks Creek pulls from a large watershed that begins high on the Blue Ridge from Blood Mountain to Woody Gap, its tributaries divided by several spur ridges. The creek runs NW to SE through most of its course, perpendicular to the Blue Ridge. Dicks Creek's valley is sometimes broad, but steep slopes rise on both sides of it. White pines and hemlocks dominate the forest near the creek and its feeders, while deciduous forests are prevalent farther up the slopes. Elevations range from 1,550 to 2,600 ft. **maps:** USGS Neels Gap.

starting out: The Dicks Creek area has no facilities, except scattered information boards. A $2 daily or $30 annual parking fee is required for day use. While FS-34 parallels Dicks Creek for several miles, it is not maintained for private vehicles past the confluence of Waters Creek. Dogs must be on a leash at all times, except when used for hunting. This area is heavily used by hunters, so wearing bright colors is a good idea during late fall and winter.

activities: Fishing, Camping.

fishing: Dicks Creek is a heavily stocked trout stream that is also heavily fished, mostly from the banks, with bait. A medium to large stream, with huge pools beneath many steep drops through its lower end, the creek offers plenty of room for casting. Dicks Creek alternates between long, flat stretches and strings of drops, some of which are best characterized as waterfalls. The creek's large pools allow many fish to survive more than one season, resulting in some very large rainbows and browns being caught every year. The creek strays on and off posted private holdings through much of its course, so it's important that anglers be aware of private land boundaries. Upstream of Water Creek, Dicks Creek loses size with every tributary passed, but it remains large enough to fish for several miles. Dicks Creek is a seasonal trout stream

Waters Creek is reputed as one of Georgia's premier streams for big trout, having been managed as trophy trout waters for more than 20 years, but fishing quality is presently down from historical levels. Poaching, beavers and two powerful storms that downed hundreds of trees across the small stream have left big fish numbers down and fishing very difficult. That said, this creek still supports a good population of rainbows, browns and brookies, with trophy-caliber fish of all three species in the mix. Beyond being tough to access, with all the downed trees, Waters Creek is extremely technical, being small and very clear and possessing trout that have been caught and released many times before.

Waters Creek is only open to fishing on W, Sa and Su during trout season, from 6:30 AM to 6:30 PM. Fishermen, who must check in and out at a station near the mouth of the creek, must possess a WMA stamp, in addition to a fishing license and trout stamp. Only artificial lures with a single barbless hook no larger than size No. 6 may be possessed, and no net may exceed 2 ft in length. The daily limit is 1 trout; season limit is 3 trout. Brook trout must measure 18 inches, while brown or rainbow trout must measure 22 inches.

camping: Backcountry camping is permitted on FS land, except where expressly prohibited, and several primitive campsites in the Dicks Creek area are heavily used. No camping is permitted between FS-34 and the Dicks Creek for 2.5 mi upstream of the Waters Creek confluence.

The Waters Creek Campground, despite its name, is on the lower reaches of Dicks Creek. The campground has 8 sites, scattered along a creekside flat, each with a tend pad, picnic table, fire ring, stand-up grill and lantern post. The forest cover is sparse, but the sites offer good isolation because they are well spaced. Pit toilets are located across FS-34 and up a small hill. Sites cost $5/night. Signs warn fishermen not to park in the campground, unless they want to pay the $5 camping fee, instead of the $2 fee for parking along the road. The campground is open from the beginning of Apr through the end of Oct.

lodging: Lily Creek Lodge (706/864-6848 or 888/844-2694) sets in a wooded valley outside Dahlonega and is built in the style of a European Royal Hunting Lodge. 12 Guest rooms, each antique-decorated with a geographical or period theme, have separate entrances from common rooms and private baths. The sitting room has a huge arched stone fireplace. Gourmet continental breakfasts are served in the formal French dining room, on the deck or in the treehouse, which overlooks surrounding mountains. Rooms cost $85–135/night, including breakfast.

Brasstown Bald

Georgia's highest mountain at 4,784 feet, Brasstown Bald is the centerpiece of the 12,975-acre Brasstown Wilderness. The mountaintop, capped by a large, stone and concrete observation tower and visitor center, is not part of the designated wilderness, but most of the mountain does lie within the wilderness. Most visitors never enter the wilderness, parking in the big lot just below the summit and either walking the short but steep trail to the top or taking a shuttle bus up the final stretch to enjoy the fabulous view and the thrill of being at the highest point in the state. Grassy areas around the parking lot have picnic tables that overlook the Blue Ridge Mountains and are a popular stopping point. Three longer trails also start at the parking lot, however, all going down instead of up and providing good opportunities to hike and camp in the Brasstown Wilderness. Because the wilderness encircles the mountain and includes a broad range of elevations, habitat types vary enormously throughout the wilderness. Northern coves are moist and botanically rich. Southern slopes are generally arid and dominated by pines. The entire wilderness lies on the steep slopes of the mountain and is heavily forested, so access is almost exclusively by the 3 hiking trails. Wildlife species include deer, bear and grouse.

Blairsville (W) and Hiawassee (NE) are the nearest towns.

getting there: From the traffic circle in Blairsville, drive S on US 19/129 10.1 mi to GA-180 E. Turn L and drive 7.4 mi to the access road to Brasstown Bald on the L, which is clearly signed. Turn L and drive 2.6 mi to the parking lot, near the top of the mtn.

topography: Brasstown Bald's ridge, a spur off the Blue Ridge, runs roughly S to N, and the wilderness covers most of the mountain, save only the top and the road up it, which nevertheless are part of the NF. Almost all terrain is steep, but forest types vary notably, with northern hardwood, spruce/pine and mixed deciduous forests, plus heath balds and rhododendron thickets all present. Elevations range from 2,080 to 4,784 ft. **maps:** USGS Hiawassee, Jacks Gap

starting out: Though not actually part of the wilderness, the parking lot near the top of Brasstown Bald is the starting point for most exploration. All 4 trails begin here, and there are restrooms, a water fountain and information boards. A $2 daily or $30 annual parking fee is required. A very nice interpretive visitor center inside the tower that caps the mountain is open from 10 AM to 5:30 PM on weekends only, beginning in mid-Apr, and daily from Memorial Day weekend through the end of Oct. The summit can be reached by a 0.5-mi hike or by a shuttle, which a private concessionaire runs on the hour through the summer and fall.

activities: Hiking, Camping.

hiking: 3 of 4 hiking trails at Brasstown Bald go down the mountain from the main parking lot, all in different directions. Because they go down different sides of the mountain, these trails are markedly different in the forest types they course. A fourth trail climbs the final 0.5 mi to the summit and observation tower, which offers an outstanding 360-degree view of the mountains.

The trail to the top is paved and fairly easy to walk, despite being quite steep as it gains 500 ft. The trail has a few interpretive signs, plus benches along the way for walkers who need to catch their breath.

The 4 trails total 15.5 mi, and the 3 longer routes are similar to one another in length, ranging from 4.5 mi to 5.5 mi. All 3 trails are difficult, if hiked uphill. *Arkaquah Trail*, an unblazed route that descends a ridge on the N side of the mountain and then winds down to Trackrock Gap, is the easiest hike, going downhill, and the only Brasstown Bald trail that can be accessed by vehicle at both ends for a 1-way hike in either direction. The blue-blazed *Jacks Knob Trail* goes downhill initially, but its final 2 mi ascend to Chattahoochee Gap, in the Mark Trail Wilderness, where it dead-ends into the *Appalachian Trail*, 4.4 mi from the nearest road access. The *Wagon Train Trail*, which in fact is the route of an old wagon road, dead-ends into private property just outside the wilderness, so the only way to hike it is down the mtn and then back up it, making for a 10 mi, very difficult hike. The *Wagon Train Trail* is unblazed, but it is wide and easy to follow.

camping: Backcountry camping is permitted throughout the wilderness, but spots flat enough to set a tent on are somewhat limited. Some primitive sites off FS-292, just outside the wilderness on the S side of the mtn, are accessible by car or by a short walk. There are no developed car campgrounds.

lodging: Brasstown Valley Resort (800/379-9900 or 706/201-3205) is tucked away on 500 acres in the hardwood-forested valley of Brasstown Creek, which rises near the summit of the mountain. The lodge, through very large, is built among the trees, painted a muted green and accented with field stone to help it blend in with its surroundings. The great room centers around a 72-foot-high stone fireplace and has light fixtures fashioned from shed deer antlers. 102 guest rooms and suites are decorated with hand-crafted twig furniture and fixtures inspired by mountain artists. The lodge also has 8 log cottages. Room rates range from $149–250/night.

Chatuge Lake

Although bounded mostly by private land, Chatuge Lake (also commonly called Lake Chatuge) can be accessed by one Forest

Service recreation area in Georgia and provides good opportunities for fishing and flat-water paddling. The Chatuge Lake Recreation Area also has a campground and a short hiking trail. The lake, which covers 7,050 acres on the Hiwassee River, straddles the Georgia/North Carolina border; its acreage is fairly evenly split between the two states. While Chatuge lies within 10 miles of Georgia's highest peak, the mountains that rise directly from its banks are modest in height and the lake contains extensive flats for a high country lake, especially through the Georgia portion. Parts of the lake are quite deep, and its waters are usually clear. While most of Chatuge Lake is developed, a lot of homesites remain wooded, with the houses built well up the banks from the lake.

Hiawassee, which the SE portion of the lake wraps around, is the nearest town.

getting there: From Hiawassee drive W on US-76 2 mi to GA-288 and turn L. Drive 0.9 mi to the Chatuge Lake Rec Area on the L.

topography: The Georgia portion of Chatuge Lake is largely riverine, consisting of the Hiwassee River and the flats that surround it. The lake begins to open up near the NC border, however, as the embayments of several major tributaries surround the main channel. The banks rise modestly around most of the lake. Lake elevation at full pool is 1927 ft. **maps:** USGS Hiawassee, Macedonia.

starting out: The Chatuge Lake Rec Area consists of a boat ramp and campground. A $2 daily or $30 annual parking fee is required. Pets must be on a leash. Chatuge Lake is typically drawn way down through the winter for flood-control purposes, leaving much of the lake's upper end high and dry.

activities: Fishing, Camping, Canoeing/Kayaking, Hiking.

fishing: Once Georgia's best smallmouth bass lake, Chatuge is now primarily a spotted bass lake, with smallmouths making up less than 5 percent of the black bass catch in recent years. The non-native spots do offer very good fishing, however, especially around bluffs and rocky points. Flats adjacent to Georgia's portion of the main channel sometimes yield good largemouth fishing. Other popular fish on the lake include white bass, hybrids, walleyes and crappie. The rec area offers limited opportunity for bank-fishing, but most anglers work Chatuge from boats. The lake has numerous fish attractors in it. A reciprocal agreement between GA and NC allows anglers properly licensed by either state to fish the entire lake by boat. Bank-fishing anglers must be licensed for the state they are standing in.

camping: Camping is restricted to a car campground in the rec area, which has 31 sites. A hilly road winds through the campground, forming a loop across a point that extends into Chatuge Lake. Each site has a picnic table, lantern post and grill, but they vary considerably in size and spacing. A young mixed forest generally provides decent privacy, but some sites are quite close together. The campground has both pit toilets and a restroom that has flush toilets and cold showers. Water is available between sites. Sites cost $6/night. Lakefront sites cost $8. The campground is open from May 1 through Oct.

kayaking/canoeing: Although generally not too obtrusive, extensive development around Lake Chatuge makes it only a decent destination for kayaking or canoeing. On summer weekends the lake also gets too much traffic from pleasure boaters for enjoyable paddling. The hills that rise from the lake, along with nearby mountain ranges make for nice scenery however, and numerous coves and islands make Chatuge an interesting lake to explore by canoe or kayak early or late in the day or the season. A boat ramp is located in the rec area.

hiking: The 1.2-mi *Lake Chatuge Trail* encircles the campground. The trail provides little separation from campground activity, but it does offer nice views of the lake as it stays quite close to the water most of the way. Walking is generally easy, suitable for families, with no sustained climbs. The trail, which is a loop, begins near the boat ramp and is easy to find and follow.

lodging: The Fieldstone Inn (706/896-2262 or 800/545-3408) is, as the name suggests, constructed of field stone. A 66-room inn on the banks of Lake Chatuge, the Fieldstone combines a rugged appearance with plush Victorian decor. The inn also has a restaurant and marina. Trails through the property wind through gardens and down to the lake. Rooms cost $99–124/night.

High Shoals Scenic Area

Dropping more than 100 feet over a series of steep ledges, High Shoals Falls is the centerpiece of the 170-acre High Shoals Scenic Area. Five falls actually break up High Shoals Creek through this stretch, but three are difficult to see and dangerous to seek. Blue Hole Falls, next largest to High Shoals and easily viewed from a platform at its base, is striking for its drop but even more so for the deep plunge-pool the falls is named for. Although quite small, this creekside scenic area is a great backcountry, coursed by a good trail, and is ideal for a day-hike, a short overnight backpacking trip or a small-stream fishing adventure. The scenic area centers around the creek and its falls, but it is part of a much broader backcountry along the western slope of Tray Mountain. Deer, bear, wild hogs and turkeys all use this area, although none are especially abundant.

Helen (S) and Hiawassee (N) are the nearest towns.

getting there: From the jct of GA-75 and GA-75A at the N end of Helen, drive N on GA-75 0.9 mi to FS-283 on the R (the turn, which is nearly a hairpin onto a gravel road, is marked only by a very small sign for High Shoals Scenic Area). Turn R on FS-283 and drive 1.3 mi to an easily recognizable parking area on the L. The road is rough, fording the creek and climbing the mountain, but passable in a passenger vehicle, except under high-water conditions, when the ford can become problematically deep.

topography: High Shoals Creek rises high on Tray Mtn and runs most of its course along the NW slope of the mtn before joining forces with Corbin Creek to form the Hiawassee River. Through the High Shoals SA, the creek tumbles over a series of waterfalls, and the surrounding terrain is steep. White pine/hemlock forests and rhododendron communities dominate along the creek. Hardwoods become predominant farther up the slope. Elevations range from 2,400 to 3,045 ft. **maps:** USGS Tray Mtn.

starting out: High Shoals Falls has just enough slope and dry-looking rock to be tempting to climb, but giving in to that temptation has resulted in more than one fatal fall. This area is dangerous and warrants respect. The parking area, which may or may not be marked with a sign, is outside the SA, but the trail soon penetrates it. The SA has no facilities.

Dogs must be kept on a leash or otherwise confined, except when used for hunting.

activities: Hiking, Camping, Fishing.

hiking: While the falls of High Shoals Creek are main attraction of the *High Shoals Trail*, they aren't its only rewards. This 1.2-mi (1-way), blue-blazed trail, an ideal short day-hike, begins well up a slope, winds down to the creek and crosses it, follows a gentle stretch of the stream and then descends to the area around the falls. Spurs lead to viewing platforms beneath the two largest falls. The hike is easy going in, but moderate on the way out with a couple difficult climbs. Major turns along the well-maintained trail and spurs are signed, well traveled and easy to recognize. Less-traveled paths are all switch-back cut-offs (pig paths, as forest rangers call them) that should be avoided.

camping: Backcountry camping is permitted within the SA, and there are nice sites for camping on a creek-side flat shaded by big white pines and hemlocks. The flat is between the trail and the creek, on the L, just past where the route crosses High Shoals Creek on a footbridge. Camping is also possible close to the parking area, just a few steps down an unmaintained trail to the L of the blue-blazed hiking trail.

fishing: High Shoals Creek is a small stream, and most of it is quite shallow, but its cold waters hold native brook trout. From the falls upstream to where the stream gets too small to fish is probably less than 2 mi, but that depends on how low an angler is willing to crawl. The best stretches are those that dip away from the trail, but caution is strongly advised in the area around the falls.

lodging: The Mountain Memories Inn (706/896-VIEW or 800/335-VIEW) overlooks Lake Chatuge and the mountains of both GA and NC. The guest rooms at this romantic inn all have private entrances, private baths, Jacuzzi tubs and sitting areas. A full breakfast buffet and evening desert buffet are served daily. Rates range from $100 to $125/night. The inn is approximately 10 mi from the SA.

Swallow Creek Area

The Swallow Creek Area is somewhat difficult to define because it takes in much more than the watershed of its namesake creek. The entire northwestern slope of Tray Mountain is broadly associated with the name Swallow Creek because most of it lies within the borders of the Swallow Creek Wildlife Management Area. However, the Tray Mountain Wilderness and the High Shoals Scenic Area (see separate entries), both part of the wildlife management area, are generally distinguished from the rest of the area. The crest of Blue Ridge, which the *Appalachian Trail* follows, forms part of the area's eastern border. Though not a designated wilderness, Swallow Creek is a rugged backcountry with no facilities and only scattered access from the west and the north. The area is lightly traveled but has some wonderful rock formations, unnamed waterfalls and botanically rich northern coves, including Ramp Cove, best known for its massive buckeyes and abundant ramps. The streams that drain this area, although small, offer decent prospects for trout fishermen. Opportunities for hiking and camping are limited to wilderness-type exploration, with no maintained trails or designated campgrounds. Along with turkeys, deer and bear, wild boar are sometimes seen in the Swallow Creek area.

Hiawassee (NW) is the nearest town.

getting there: Swallow Creek Rd provides the best access to Swallow Creek itself and the N end of this backcountry. From the jct of US-76 and GA-17/75, just E of Hiawassee, drive E on US-76 6.4 mi to Swallow Creek Rd on the R. Swallow Creek Rd turns to gravel and enters the NF at a sign for the Swallow Creek WMA. • Access to the area S of Kelly Ridge is possible off FS-26-2. From the jct of US-76 and GA-17/75, drive S on GA-17/75 3.6 mi to Mill Creek Rd on the L. Turn L and drive 1.2 mi before forking L onto FS-26-2, which is gravel.

topography: The Blue Ridge runs NE to SW and then N to S from Dicks Creek Gap to the Summit of Tray Mtn, and the N half of the ridge forms the E border of the Swallow Creek area. The area is defined by Kelly Ridge, a major E-W spur that divides the Swallow and Mill Creek watersheds, and by a series of creeks that generally flow E to W from high on the Blue Ridge toward the Hiwassee River. Forest types vary notably, but include oak/hickory, white pine/hemlock, mixed deciduous and northern cove hardwood forests, plus laurel/rhododendron thickets along creeks. The terrain is steep and rugged, with elevations ranging from 2,100 to 4,276 ft. **maps:** USGS Tray Mountain, Macodania; ATC Springer Mountain to Bly Gap.

starting out: There are no facilities in the Swallow Creek area. A $2 daily or $30 annual parking fee is required for parking at Dicks Creek Gap, which is a good access point for exploration beginning on the *Appalachian Trail*. Dogs must be on a leash, except while hunting, which is popular in this area, especially in the areas of the FS roads.

activities: Fishing, Hiking, Camping.

fishing: Swallow, Dismal, Mill and Corbin creeks all offer some opportunity to trout fisherman although no single stream offers much more than 1 mi of fishable water. Swallow Creek gets some hatchery trout near the FS boundary waters, but most of these waters support wild trout populations that are dominated by small but colorful rainbows. A few brook trout can be found in headwaters branches, but casting conditions are tight to impossible. The creeks are generally small, but steep enough to create some good pool habitat. Most stretches go through tunnels of rhododendron, making for difficult casting. Swallow Creek and Mill Creek are the most accessible, as Swallow Creek Rd and Mill Creek Rd parallel fishable sections. Dismal Creek is accessible by a very rough, unnamed road that splits off Swallow Creek Rd near the WMA entrance. Corbin Creek can be accessed near its headwaters by FS-698.

hiking: Excepting the *AT*, which borders the area for 5.3 mi from Dicks Creek Gap to Addis Gap, no hiking trails are maintained. Nevertheless, good opportunities exist for hikers who enjoy backcountry exploration with a compass and topo map. Kelly Ridge, accessible off the *AT* or by several creeks that drain it, is a popular area to explore, and unofficial trails do follow the ridge and split some of its coves. The *AT*, accessible from Dicks Creek Gap, 8 mi E of Hiawassee, is blazed with white rectangles and well maintained. With elevations ranging from 2,675 ft to 4,276 ft, this stretch contains a lot of ups and downs and is quite demanding. Addis Gap is not directly accessible by car, but the old roadbed that connects FS-26 and FS-26-2, both of which are now gated about a mi shy of the gap, provides access from either side of the ridge.

camping; Backcountry camping is permitted throughout the NF, except where posted as prohibited. Primitive car camping is possible from scattered points along Swallow Creek Rd and FS-26-2, but in most places both roads skirt mountainsides, with no level ground on either side. There are no developed campgrounds.

lodging: Creekside Retreat (706/896-1857) is a 4-room, fully-furnished cabin that shares 7 wooded acres only with the property owners' private dwelling. The cabin is 40 feet from Hightower Creek, a trout stream, and only 3 mi from Dicks Creek Gap. Myrlon Carmean, who along with his wife, Francis, owns the retreat, runs a shuttle service for hikers who are taking an AT hike that will end at Dicks Creek Gap. The cabin costs $475/week and is available year round.

Southern Nantahala Wilderness

North Georgia's final frontier, the Southern Nantahala Wilderness is the least developed backcountry in the Chattahoochee National Forest and the most difficult to access. The total wilderness is actually split between North Carolina and Georgia, and 16 developed trails provide foot access to North Carolina's 10,900-acre portion. Through the 13,600 acre Georgia portion, however, the *Appalachian Trail* is the only maintained footpath. Only unofficial routes that follow old fire roads, ridgetops and creekbeds provide access through most of this wilderness, which is as rugged as any spot in Georgia, with high peaks, cliff faces, waterfalls, boulderfields and impenetrable thickets of laurel and rhododendron. Adding to the difficulties, the Georgia portion of the Southern Nantahala Wilderness is bounded by private land and by tracts of undeveloped Forest Service land, so gaining access even to the edge of the wilderness presents a challenge.

That said, this wilderness is as spectacular as it is remote, with steep southern slopes characterized by virtually undiscovered cliffs and waterfalls, heath balds atop high peaks, and rich northern coves of hardwood species normally found much farther north. Wildlife species include bears and ruffed grouse. For the backcountry hiker/camper who takes precautions and is accustomed to using topo maps and a compass, the Southern Nantahala Wilderness is as good as it gets.

Hiawassee (W) and Dillard (E) are the nearest towns.

getting there: Although scattered points provide other access possibilities, most exploration begins with the *AT*, at Blue Ridge Gap or Dicks Creek Gap. Blue Ridge Gap is at the edge of the wilderness, but the final stretch of road leading to it is a borderline jeep road. Much improvement has been done to this road, but clearance is still an issue for many passenger vehicles. From Hiawassee, drive 8 mi E on US-76 to Upper Hightower Rd on the L. Turn L and drive 3.7 mi to a fork in the road where the L fork is marked as a private drive. Take the R fork onto FS-72 and drive 1.2 mi to the gap. Though 5.6 mi from the edge of the wilderness, Dicks Creek Gap is easy to access. On US-76, continue 2.8 mi past Upper Hightower Rd. The gap is well marked as an *AT* crossing, and parking is on the L.

topography: The Blue Ridge and Tennessee Valley Divide split the Georgia portion of the Southern Nantahala Wilderness, with creeks W and E of the divide tumbling toward the Hiwassee and Tallulah rivers, respectively. Hightower Bald, the highest peak in GA's portion of the wilderness at 4,568 ft, is on a spur off the Blue Ridge. NC peaks in the wilderness reach higher, with some over 5,000 ft. Forest types vary enormously by elevation and orientation, but spruce/fir, oak/hickory/northern cove hardwood and white pine/hemlock forests can all be found, along with extensive laurel/rhododendron thickets. The terrain is almost invariably steep. **maps:** USGS Macedonia, Dillard, Hightower Bald; ATC Bly Gap to Springer Mtn; USFS Southern Nantahala Wilderness and Standing Indian Basin.

starting out: There are no facilities in the Southern Nantahala Wilderness. Nearest supplies are in Hiawassee. A $2 daily or $30 annul parking fee is required for access at Dicks Creek Gap.

activities: Hiking, Camping.

hiking: The *AT* runs 34 mi through the Southern Nantahala Wilderness, but only 3 mi of the trail are in GA. The premier hiking opportunities in this part of the wilderness are off the main trail, however, across ridge tops, down remnant fire roads and up coves and creek bottoms. USGS quads and the USFS *Southern Nantahala Wilderness and Standing Indian Basin* map are strongly recommended. Although no trails other than the *AT* are named and maintained, a network of routes used by backcountry explorers can be followed through much of the wilderness.

camping: Backcountry camping is permitted throughout the wilderness. No-trace camping is strongly encouraged. Good campsites and water are available at Bly Gap, just N of the NC border on the *AT*.

lodging: The Hiawassee Inn (800/711-6961) caters to the outdoors crowd, even offering a free shuttle service to hikers, and it draws a lot of business from hikers, hunters and fishermen in the area. The inn, which has been completely refurbished over the past couple years, has 15 rooms, plus a cottage with a hot tub. Rooms cost $45–60/night, depending on the season.

Vogel State Park

Although small, covering only 280 acres, Vogel State Park is centered around a 22-acre mountain lake, and its trails provide a great link with extensive backcountry areas. Set at the base of Blood Mountain, the park itself is for the most part flat and largely developed with campsites, cabins, a lake and picnic facilities, but high peaks rise all around it, and most of the land beyond its borders is part of the Chattahoochee National Forest. Established in the 1930s, with the lake and original cabins built by the Civilian Conservation Corps, Vogel is Georgia's second oldest state park.

Fishing is possible both in the lake and in the small stream that feeds it, and campers have several options. Hiking is popular in and around the park. Vogel is also very popular with picnickers and vacationers who enjoy the mountain lake scenery. Because the park is quite developed for its size and surrounded by backcountry, wildlife is not abundant. During years of low mast production, bears occasionally roam down into the park in search of food, but generally they stay farther up the mountain.

Blairsville (N) and Cleveland (SE) are the nearest towns.

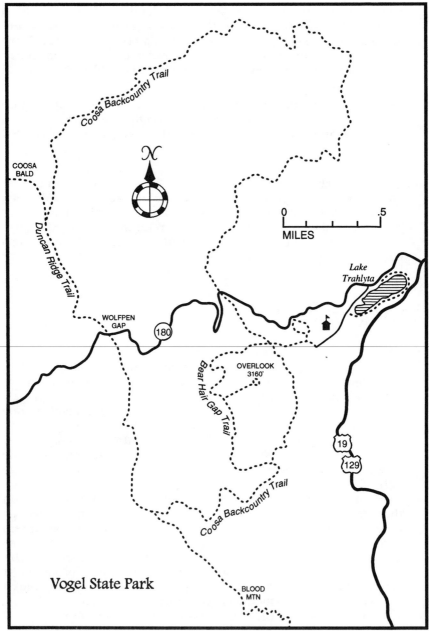

COOSA
BALD

Coosa Backcountry Trail

N

Duncan Ridge Trail

0 .5
MILES

Lake
Trahlyta

WOLFPEN
GAP

180

Bear Hair Gap Trail

OVERLOOK
3160'

19

129

Coosa Backcountry Trail

Vogel State Park

BLOOD
MTN

contact: Superintendent, Vogel State Park, 7485 Vogel State Park Rd, Blairsville, GA 30512; 706/745-2628; www.gastateparks.org.

getting there: From the traffic circle in Cleveland, Drive N on US-129 11.4 mi to Turners Corner at the jct of US-19 and US-129. Continue N on US-19/129 11.1 mi to the park entrance on the L.

topography: Vogel sets in a high cove and centers around a small lake that impounds Wolf Creek, which splits the park through the middle, flowing SW to NE off Blood Mtn, toward the Nottley River. The park is surprisingly flat, considering its mountainous location, except right along its edges where the land begins sloping upward toward surrounding peaks. Forest types are very diverse in and around the park and include evergreen, deciduous and mixed forests of several kinds. Elevations range from 2,200 to 2,600. **maps:** USGS Coosa Bald.

starting out: The park visitor center, open 8 AM to 5 PM daily, has maps and brochures. The visitor center also has a gift shop and handles registration for cabins and the campground and permits for hiking the Coosa Backcountry Trail. The park is open from 7 AM to 10 PM daily.

Alcoholic beverages are prohibited in public areas. All pets must be on a leash of 6 ft or less. Neither campers nor cabin users are permitted to gather firewood within the park.

activities: Camping, Hiking, Fishing.

camping: Backcountry camping is permitted on the *Coosa Backcountry Trail*, which is administered by the SP, although most of its route runs through NF land. Campsites are not designated, but all campsites must be at least 100 ft from the trail and campers are asked to "leave no trace." A free permit is required for day-hiking or backpacking along the 12.7-mi loop.

Two pioneer camps have 3-sided shelters but no other facilities. Water is available at the trailhead, 0.3 mi from the camps. The pioneer camps are wooded, with Wolf Creek cutting through them. Camps cost $20/night for up to 15 campers, plus $1 for each additional person. Maximum group size is 25. Pioneer camp reservations should be made through the park office.

The park's developed campground has 110 sites spread across an open forest dominated by pines. Wolf Creek cuts through the campground. The campground includes 17 walk-in sites, which require a hike of up to 0.3 mi from parking areas and which have no electric hook-ups or water. Walk-in sites have picnic tables and tent pads. Some have fire rings and/or grills and lantern posts. The walk-in sites offer more privacy than the car-camping sites, many of which are quite close together. The campground is large enough to offer sites of all sizes and levels of privacy, if the good ones are available. The campground stays full on weekends through summer and fall. Car-camping sites offer tent pad, fire ring/grill, lantern posts and picnic table, plus water and electricity. Restrooms have flush toilets and hot showers. The campground is open year round. Sites cost $9–17/night.

hiking: Only the 1-mi *Trahlyta Lake Trail* and the 0.7-mi *Byron Herbert Reece Nature Trail* stay within park boundaries, but Vogel SP administers more than 18 mi of hiking trails, and its routes offer something for everyone. The 2 short trails are both easy to hike, but quite different in character, with one circling the lake and staying near its edge and the other winding through the forest, with interpretive plaques along the way.

The *Bear Hair Gap Trail* and the *Coosa Backcountry Trail* are and 4 mi and 12.7 mi, respectively, providing great options for day-hiking and/or backpacking. The *Bear Hair Gap Trail*, which is moderate in difficulty, leads to a nice overlook of the park and surrounding peaks. The *Coosa Backcountry Trail* is a difficult loop that includes an ascent of Coosa Bald, a 4,160-ft peak. This trail can be covered in a day by fit and determined hikers, but park rangers strongly recommend using it as a backpacking trail. Free permits, which are required for day-hiking or for camping on the *Coosa Backcountry Trail*, are available at the park visitor center.

The *Lake Trahlyta Trail* begins near the visitor center. The 3 other trails share a single trailhead, near the entrance to the campground. The trailhead is marked by a large sign that maps out the routes and shows how they are color-coded. The trails are blazed.

fishing: 22-acre Lake Trahlyta is stocked once or twice per year with trout, but bass, bream and channel catfish generally offer the best action for fishermen. Private boats are not allowed on the lake and only pedal boats are rented, so fishing is almost exclusively from the banks. The *Trahlyta Lake Trail* and park roads together provide access all the way around the lake, and most of the banks are either cleared or lightly forested, making for easy bank-fishing.

Wolf Creek and its tributaries also offer limited stream fishing for trout. The creeks, which total less than 1 mi of fishable waters are stocked occasionally, but are small and bushy, making for tight casting. In summer water levels can get very low. A trout stamp is required for the streams, which are seasonal, but not for the lake, which is open year round.

lodging: Vogel SP's 36 cottages range from single-room structures to large 3-bedroom cottages that sleep up to 10 people. 6 of the cottages are historic log cabins that were built by the CCC in the park's early days. The others are more contemporary, but wood siding gives them a natural appearance. All cottages are fully furnished and have fireplaces and charcoal grills. None have telephones or televisions. Cottages cost $50–100/night. The minimum stay is 2 nights, 3 nights over holidays, or 7 nights from Jun to Aug. Cottages may be reserved up to 11 months in advance by calling 800/864-7275.

Smithgall Woods/Dukes Creek Conservation Area

Acquired in 1994 as a gift-purchase from Charles A. Smithgall for half its assessed value, Smithgall Woods/Dukes Creek Conservation Area is one of the showcases of Georgia's state parks system. The 5,562-acre foothills tract was pieced together through numerous purchases over many years by Mr. Smithgall and lovingly cared for under his ownership. The area is designated as a Heritage Preserve, which perpetually protects it from significant development or uses that would alter its character. Though logged and even mined for gold earlier this century, the landscape has recovered nicely and the forest is gradually maturing.

4 miles of blue ribbon trout waters, 5 short hiking trails, a network of limited-access dirt and gravel roads for mountain bikers and a group camping area provide excellent recreational opportunities, but facilities are limited and access is controlled to protect the integrity of the area and the experience of users. Smithgall Woods also has nice picnic areas in various areas along Dukes Creek.

Helen (N) is the closest town.

contact: Smithgall Woods/Dukes Creek Conservation Area, Tsalaki Trail, Helen, GA 30545; 706/878-3087; www.gastateparks.org.

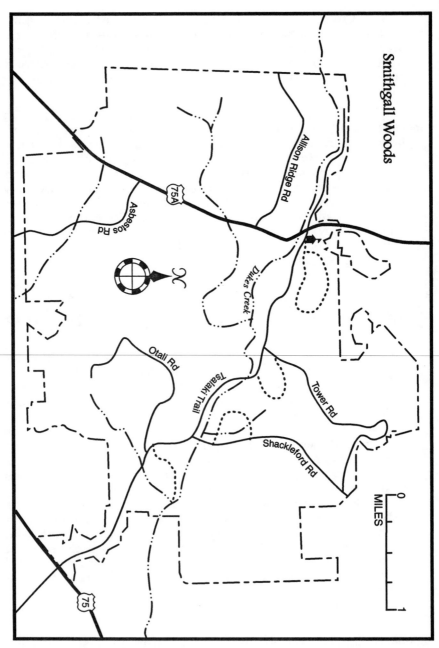

getting there: From the jct of GA-75 and GA-75-A at the N end of Helen, turn S on GA-75-A and drive 2.5 mi to the entrance on the L, which is well marked, with a sign, rock wall and gate.

topography: A foothills tract, Smithgall Woods' main peaks of Hamby and Little Hamby mountains are significantly lower than mountaintops immediately N and W on adjacent tracts of FS land. Dukes Creek, oriented NW to SE as it tumbles toward the Chattahoochee, is the area's defining feature. The forest of mixed pines and hardwoods is fairly young through most of this tract and lacks many mature white pines or oaks. Elevations range from 1,350 to 2,000 ft. **maps:** USGS, Helen, Cowrock.

starting out: All private vehicles must park at the visitor center, on the L just inside the gates, and all visitors must register. The visitor center has maps, brochures and an information counter, plus restrooms, a drink machine and a water fountain. As primary management is carried out by the Parks Division, a Georgia ParkPass is required. The visitor center is open 8 AM to 4 PM on weekdays. Hours are longer on W and Sa–Su, but vary according to season. Guided tours and shuttle rides into the area are available on W and weekends only.

activities: Fishing, Hiking, Mountain Biking, Camping.

fishing: Limited fishing is allowed on 4 mi of Dukes Creek, which offer Georgia's best prospects for trophy-class trout on public waters. Huge browns and rainbows abound in this small stream, which drops gently as it crosses the area. The stream cuts through a tunnel of rhododendron, but is sufficiently open for careful fly-casting. The trout are tough customers, having been caught before and having seen every imaginable fly or lure. Nymphs generally offer the best prospects.

Only artificial lures with barbless hooks are allowed in any angler's possession, and all fish caught must be immediately released. Fishing is allowed on W, Sa and Su only and is restricted to 15 anglers at a time, with reservations taken and strongly recommended. Two shifts of anglers each fish half a day from Mar through Oct. That's reduced to a single, full-day shift from Nov through Feb.

hiking: Smithgall Woods offers little for serious hikers who seek a challenge or a full-day commitment, but 5 trails totaling 6 mi are well designed for educating visitors and allowing them to get a deeper look into the area. Two are interpretive; others lead to features like an old gold mine or a waterfall. All are short, ranging from 0.25 to 2 mi, easy to follow, and easy or moderate to walk. 2 begin at the visitor center. Others require either a hike to the trailhead or a shuttle ride.

mountain biking: Mountain bikers have more than 12 mi of road to ride on the Smithgall Woods, including the entire limited-access road system and scattered, gated fire roads. The main roads, mostly gravel or dirt, are well maintained, but they include several creek crossings and significant climbs up Big Hamby and Little Hamby mountains. The fire roads, rough and unmaintained, are short, one-way spurs. All roads are interconnected, so a variety of routes is possible.

camping: Only group camping is permitted. One group per night may use the group camping area, which consists of 10 tent pads, a fire ring and pit toilets. Only organized groups with adult leaders may use the area, and reservations are required. Camping costs $5/camper nightly, with a $50 minimum.

lodging: Grampa's Room, a 135-year-old farmhouse in scenic Nacoochee Valley, has two antique-furnished guest rooms. If the big white home and its rocking chair porch don't make someone feel like they are visiting grandparents, the full country breakfast will. Rates for two people are $65/night. Grampa's room is located on GA-17, E of Helen. Call 706/878-2364 for reservations and info.

Chattooga Ranger District

Chattahoochee National Forest

Deceptive in its name, the Chattooga Ranger District takes in no part of the Chattooga River watershed. Instead it's the Chattahoochee, Georgia's best-known river, that rises high along the slopes of this district. Encompassing more than 118,000 acres in White, Habersham, Stephens, Lumpkin, Union, Towns and

Banks counties, this district lies along the southeastern edge of Georgia's mountain region, with landscapes that range from relatively high Blue Ridge peaks to moderate Piedmont ridges.

Most of the best opportunities for backcountry adventure in the Chattooga RD lie along the SE slope of the Blue Ridge, where a vast area of largely unbroken woodlands contains 2 scenic areas, 4 recreation areas and major portions of the Raven Cliffs, Mark Trail and Tray Mountain wilderness areas. Several Chattahoochee feeders rise near the RD border, as do headwaters streams in the Chestatee River watershed.

Farther E, where the hills are more modest in height and pitch, the district is divided into scattered smaller tracts, with access only at Panther Creek, via a small rec area and a trail. To the SE, Lake Russell Recreation Area and WMA offer additional opportunities. Hiking, trout fishing, camping, and mountain biking are all major activities within the district.

Cleveland (S), Helen (S), Clarkesville (S), Cornelia (W) and Toccoa (E) are the nearest towns.

contact: Chattooga Ranger District, US Forest Service, Burton Road, Clarkesville, GA; (706) 754-6221; www.fs.fed.us/conf/

getting there: GA-17, -348 and -356 are the major roadways that provide access to the Chattooga RD. The district RS is 0.4 mi N of Clarkesville on GA-197 on the R.

topography: Escarpment topography creates numerous dramatic falls and cliffs as the Blue Ridge Mountains drop off to the Piedmont. The rugged terrain includes forests of oaks/hickories, and mixed hardwoods/pines and pines/hemlocks, plus laurel/rhododendron communities along numerous streams. Scattered tracts, including Yonah Mountain and Lake Russell, surround monadnocks or isolated mountains that rise apart from major ranges. Elevations range from 700 to 4,430 ft. **maps:** See below under individual areas.

starting out: The district RS, open weekdays 8 AM to 4:30 PM, offers free maps and brochures and sells FS topo maps of wilderness areas and annual parking permits for fee areas.

activities: Hiking, Fishing, Camping, Mountain Biking.

hiking: The *Appalachian Trail* follows the Blue Ridge for 27 mi along the NW border of the Chattooga RD, and like most of the Georgia portion of the trail, this section consists of almost no flat ridges, instead ever alternating between ascents to peaks and descents to gaps. For day-hikers, the district contains 20 different trails ranging from less than 1 mi to more than 6 mi, creating opportunities for hikes of almost any level of difficulty. Numerous trails within the district lead to or past major waterfalls.

fishing: The headwaters of the Chattahoochee River highlight the offerings of the Chattooga RD, but tributary trout streams tumble off all the mountains along the Blue Ridge. This is tiny-stream fishing, mostly for wild fish, including brook trout in a few branches. On tracts farther E, portions of the Soquee River, Big Panther Creek and the Middle Fork of the Broad River all offer opportunities to fish for stocked trout.

camping: Backcountry camping is permitted throughout the district, except where otherwise noted, which is mostly around designated recreation areas. Containing 3 wilderness areas and a significant stretch of the *Appalachian Trail*, the Chattooga RD offers terrific opportunities for backpacking outings. 4 different recreation areas within the district have developed campgrounds.

mountain biking: Mountain biking is not permitted on most trails on the district, but riders make good use of both gated and ungated FS roads, especially around the upper Chattahoochee watershed and near the edges of the Tray Mountain Wilderness Area. Mountain biking is growing quickly in popularity in this part of Georgia so riders are continuing to discover and develop routes.

Raven Cliffs/ Dukes Creek Falls Area

Best known for its namesake cliffs and the unusual waterfall on Dodd Creek whose lower drop actually falls through a crack in the cliffs, the 9,115-acre Raven Cliffs Wilderness also takes in the spine of the Blue Ridge from Hogpen Gap to Neels Gap. It is a playland for backcountry adventurers who cherish the tops of mountains and their extreme upper slopes, where branches rise, gather to form speckle streams, tumble over falls and dig steep gorges. Adjacent to the wilderness, Davis and Dukes creeks fall dramatically to form the centerpiece of the Dukes Creek Falls Scenic Area. The main falls, which plunges an estimated 250 feet, is actually on Davis Creek, a Dukes Creek feeder stream, but the main stream comes in beside it over a lesser falls, the final drop in a long series of Dukes Creek cataracts.

Hikers can pick from 5 different routes in this area, and fishermen find wild trout exclusively, including native brook trout. Backcountry camping is permitted throughout most of the Raven Cliffs/Dukes Creek Falls area, and there are some very nice places to camp. A few picnic table are also located near the parking lot at the Dukes Creek Falls Trail, and an overview, just 0.1 mi down the trial, offers a nice look at the falls from across the gorge. A trail that is being developed will eventually provide foot access from the Raven Cliffs Wilderness to the Dukes Creek Falls Scenic Area. Wildlife includes white-tailed deer, wild turkeys and black bears.

Helen (E) is the closest town.

getting there: From the jct of GA-75 and GA-75A at the N end of Helen, turn S on GA-75A and drive 2.2 mi to GA-348 (Richard B. Russell Scenic Parkway) on the R. GA-348 leads to the entrance to the Dukes Creek Falls area at 1.7 mi on the L and follows the E border of the wilderness for 7.7 mi to the parking area for Tesnatee Gap. Access to the wilderness, all on the L, is via FS-245 (2.7 mi); *Raven Cliffs Trail* (3.0 mi); *Appalachian Trail* at Hogpen Gap (7.0 mi); and Tesnatee Gap (7.7 mi).

topography: Most of the Raven Cliffs Wilderness lies along the steep southern slope of the Blue Ridge, and the rugged terrain is defined by high ridges, waterfalls, cliffs and the narrow upper gorges of Cowrock Creek, Towns Creek and the Dukes Creek watershed. N and S facing slopes, along with a wide range of elevations, make for forest types that range from dry rim/cliff habitats to lush fern communities. Deciduous forests and white pine/hemlock forests make up much of the canopy. Elevations range from 3,846 ft atop Levelland Mtn to 1,625 ft where Dukes Creek flows off NF land. **maps:** USGS Cowrock, Neels Gap; ATC Springer Mtn to Bly Gap.

starting out: Dukes Creek Falls is a fee area ($3). Restrooms with pit toilets and an information board are available at the parking lot, which is paved. The wilderness has no facilities. Repelling is not permitted at Raven Cliffs.

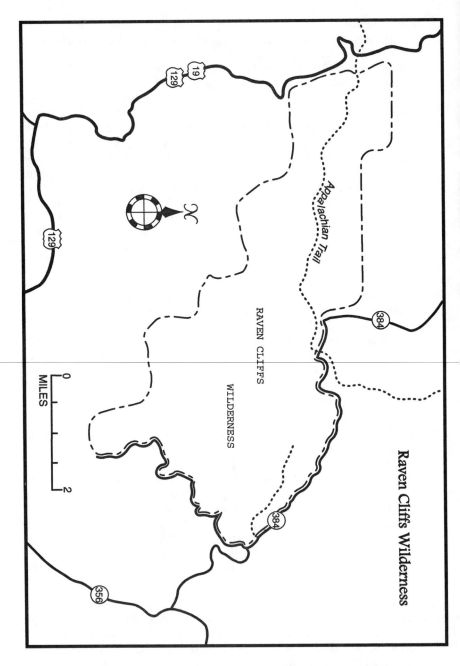

Raven Cliffs Wilderness

activities: Hiking, Camping, Fishing.

hiking: Highlights along area hiking trails are the namesake Raven Cliffs, numerous falls along Dodd, Davis and Dukes creeks, spectacular overviews of ridgelines and creek gorges from the *Appalachian Trail* and from the top of Wildcat Mountain, and the lush evergreens that the *Whitly Gap Trail* cuts through. Hiking opportunities abound, with 5 separate routes that total 13.9 mi and range from the 1-mi trek to the base of Dukes Creek Falls to a 6.4-mi section of the *AT.* Most trails are moderate, although some sections of the *AT* are difficult, as is the 2-mi *Logan Turnpike Trail,* an old wagon road through Tesnatee Gap into the steep upper gorge of Town Creek. The *Dukes Creek Falls* and *Raven Cliffs Falls* trails, both blue blazed, are heavily used, and their parking areas and trailheads off GA-345 are easy to find. The *AT* enters the wilderness at Hogpen Gap, and is also accessible at Tesnatee Gap, where the *Logan Turnpike Trail* begins. The *Whitly Gap Shelter Trail* begins 0.2 mi from Hogpen Gap, as a spur to the L off the *AT.*

camping: Backcountry camping is permitted, except as otherwise noted, but the USFS is considering establishing designated sites along the *Raven Cliffs Trail,* which is easily accessible and borders on over-use for a designated wilderness. For the same reason, no camping is permitted within 0.25 mi of FS-245 on the wilderness side (R, if driving from GA-348). The 6.4-mi section of the *AT* that cuts through W half of the wilderness has several campsites along it and good access at both ends, making it ideal for an overnight backpacking trip and a good taste of both trail and wilderness.

fishing: The headwaters streams that drain the Raven Cliffs Wilderness offer limited opportunity for extreme small-stream fishermen. The appeal of these waters is that they contain only wild fish, mostly native brook trout, but all except Dodd Creek are quite inaccessible, and all, Dodd included, are tiny, steep and sometimes treacherous. Dodd Creek is accessible at scattered points from the *Raven Cliffs Trail,* but most access is by wading. Dukes Creek, downstream of the falls, offers about a mi of good water for wild rainbows. Although the creek remains small, its bed is sufficiently steep and boulder-strewn to form nice pools and provide decent casting room. The *Dukes Creek Falls Trail* leads to the stream immediately downstream of the falls. Access downstream of there is by wading.

lodging: The Edelweiss German Country Inn (706/865-7371), which sets on 3 wooded acres that overlook Yonah Mtn, is operated by the Beyer family, who moved to America from Germany in 1962. Then inn has outstanding German food, extensive gardens and a nice nature trail that loops through the property. Rooms in the main inn, some with Jacuzzi tubs, and fully-furnished one-bedroom cabins, are available. Inn stays include a full German-style breakfast. Rates range from $55–124/night. The inn is located 3 mi S of Helen.

Mark Trail Wilderness

Established in 1991, the Mark Trail Wilderness covers 16,400 acres in Towns, Union and White counties and is divided between the Brasstown and Chattooga ranger districts. This mountaintop wilderness straddles the Blue Ridge, from Unicoi Gap to Hogpen Gap, plus Hickorynut Lead, a major spur ridge. The *Appalachian Trail* follows the Blue Ridge from Unicoi Gap to Hogpen Gap through the wilderness, following the ridge through an unusual southeast to northwest turn around the headwaters of the Chattahoochee River in the northern part of the wilderness. At Chattahoochee Gap, where both ridge and trail return to their normal northeast to southwest orientation, is Chattahoochee Spring, a good water source and the official source of the river that eventually runs through Atlanta on its way to the Gulf of Mexico.

Beyond the *Appalachian Trail*, the only designated trail is the *Jacks Knob Trail*, which begins near the summit of Brasstown Bald and ends at Chattahoochee Gap. Only the trail's final 2 miles are within the wilderness. Much of the Mark Trail Wilderness is bounded by National Forest land, including the Raven Cliffs Wilderness along its southwestern edge, so access is possible from various points. However, the terrain is steep and the forest often dense, so any exploration off the 2 main trails is via ridgetops, creek bottoms and old fire roads and requires first-rate backcountry skills and regular attention to a compass and topo map. The southeastern quadrant of the wilderness, which surrounds Hickorynut Lead, has no trails coursing it. This wilderness support deer, bear, grouse and wild turkey.

Helen (SE) is the nearest town.

getting there: To reach Hogpen Gap, from the jct of GA-75 and GA-75A at the N end of Helen, turn S on GA-75A and drive 2.2 mi to GA-348 (Richard B. Russell Scenic Parkway). Turn R and drive 7 mi to the Gap, the parking area for which is on the R. To reach Unicoi Gap from the same starting point, drive N on GA-75 8.0 mi to the gap, which is well marked and has parking on the R.

topography: Straddling the Blue Ridge and Hickorynut Lead, the Mark Trail Wilderness contains mostly high elevations. The terrain is very steep, except along the ridges, and is covered by forests that are dominated by hardwoods, especially along moist northern slopes. Laurel/rhododendron communities are common along mountaintops and headwaters branches. Elevations range from 2,400 to 4,045 ft. **maps:** USGS Jacks Gap, Cowrock, Tray Mtn; ATC Springer Mtn to Bly Gap.

starting out: The Mark Trail Wilderness has no facilities. Nearest supplies are in Helen.

activities: Hiking, Camping.

hiking: The 13.6-mi section of the *AT* that runs from Unicoi Gap to Hogpen Gap is among the least difficult stretches in Georgia, slipping off the crest of the ridge through a couple stretches and following old roads that are for the most part level. The trail cuts through nice hardwood forests as it wraps around the headwaters of the Chattahoochee River. The initial climb from Unicoi Gap to Blue Mtn, if you're hiking the trail from N to S, is challenging as it gains more than 1,000 ft in 1.4 mi. Beyond that there are no major ascents for hikers traveling in either direction. The trail, of course, is blazed with white rectangles and well maintained. The 4.5-mi, blue-blazed *Jacks Knob Trail*, a National Recreation Trail, connects the *AT* and the Mark Trail Wilderness with the Brasstown Wilderness. The trail skirts the top of Jacks Knob and then descends Hiwassee Ridge to Jacks Gap before turning upward to climb Brasstown Bald. The trail is well marked and well maintained. Access from the Mark Trail Wilderness side is only by the *AT*, 4.4 mi from the nearest road access at Unicoi Gap.

camping: Camping is allowed throughout the wilderness, but access is difficult, except by the 2 trails. There are two shelters, the Blue Mountain Shelter and Low Gap Shelter, along the *AT*, and plenty of campsites and water sources.

lodging: Nacoochee Valley Guest House (706/878-3830) overlooks one of the most scenic valleys in Georgia, just outside Helen. An English cottage-style home built in 1920, the guest house is surrounded by extensive gardens and sets among huge old trees, including a 150-year-old pin oak with a 2,000-square-ft deck built all around it. 3 guest rooms all have private baths. The home's original master bedroom, now one of the guest rooms, has the original fireplace and wood floors. The inn also has a fine dining restaurant, which is continental, but with a French flair. Guest rooms cost $85–110/night and include a full breakfast.

Upper Chattahoochee River Area

The Upper Chattahoochee River area takes in high mountain slopes around the river's headwaters, but the actual Blue Ridge, the top of the mountain and the extreme headwaters of the Chattahoochee all lie within the adjacent Mark Trail Wilderness. Although neither pristine nor dramatic in character, this large backcountry tract of mountain land includes an outstanding and often-overlooked waterfall, Horse Trough Falls, along with encompassing many miles of the upper 'Hooch and its steep tributaries. The entire area is coursed by a long, winding Forest Service road, which provides good access for campers and trout fishermen. Gated and ungated Forest Service roads in the Upper Chattahoochee area are also favored by local mountain bikers. There is a picnic area along the upper river and a developed campground.

Helen (SE) is the closest town.

getting there: From the jct of GA-75 and GA-75A at the N end of Helen, Drive S on GA-75A 0.1 mi to Poplar Stump Rd and turn R. Poplar Stump turns gravel and becomes FS-44, which is marked as FS-52 on old maps, and winds 14.8 mi through the Upper Chattahoochee River area, coming out on GA-75, near Unicoi Gap. Drive 10 mi to the Upper Chattahoochee River Campground, which is very well marked on the L. 4.5 mi from GA-75A, FS-44 turns right across a bridge over Low Gap Creek, while a dead-end spur goes straight; the turn is not marked.

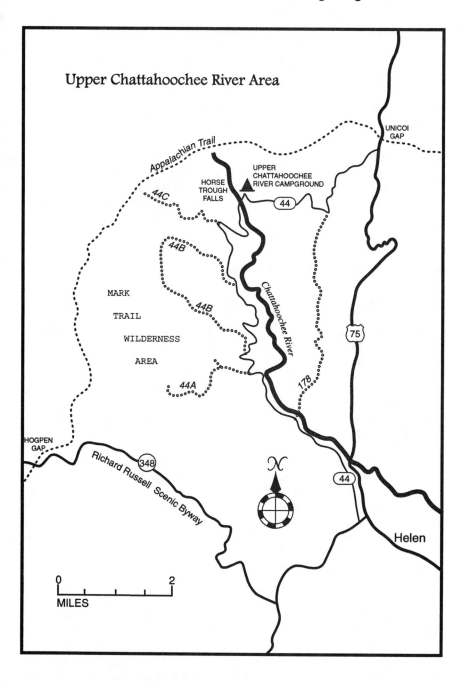

Upper Chattahoochee River Area

topography: The Upper Chattahoochee River, which generally runs N to S through the center of this tract, gathering feeder flows as it goes, is the area's defining feature. Ridges rise on both sides of the river, but SE slopes are dominant, falling off the Blue Ridge to the NW. The terrain is steep and land heavily forested, mostly with mixed pine/hardwood stands. Elevations range from 1,550 to 3,000 ft. **maps:** USGS Helen, Cowrock, Jacks Gap, Tray Mountain.

starting out: An information board is posted at the edge of the NF, which is also the border of the Chattahoochee WMA, but this area has no facilities outside of the campground. Pets must be on a leash or otherwise confined at all times. Hunting is popular here, so blaze orange is advised for backcountry exploration during spring turkey season and fall deer season.

activities: Mountain Biking, Fishing, Camping.

mountain biking: Although no trails are designated specifically for mountain biking, riders make use of all the FS roads, both gated and ungated, through the Upper Chattahoochee area, which together encompass 31.9 mi. FS-44 is twisty and scenic enough to make for a nice ride; the entire 14.8-mi trip, ridden top to bottom, is suitable for beginners. FS-178, gated at both ends, leaves FS-44 2.3 mi N of GA-75A on the R and rejoins it 10.6 mi farther up the mountain. The roads together make a good, 15.7 mi loop route, although the ride is difficult in either direction because what goes down must come up, at least if you're returning to the starting point.

Other gated roads, all off FS-44 on the L, include FS-44A, a 3.4-mi, one-way moderate to difficult spur; FS-44B, a 7-mi moderate to difficult loop; and FS-44-6, a very difficult 1.6-mi spur that climbs almost to the crest of the Blue Ridge along the border of the Mark Trail Wilderness. All routes are double-track, but some sections of gated roads are quite rugged and would be suitable only for 4WD, if vehicles were permitted on them. Horseback riding is also permitted.

fishing: The first couple miles of Poplar Stump Rd follow the Chattahoochee, but through heavily posted private land. Once on the NF, the road soon strays out of sight of the river and is sometimes well above it or even separated from it by a ridge. The first public waters, which are easily accessible from the road, are very heavily fished. The river is of moderate gradient, dropping just enough to form some very large pools. For the more adventurous, the Upper Chattahoochee remains fairly decent-sized water for several miles and contains both stocked trout and stream-bred rainbows and browns, including some large browns. All access, after the road turns away from the river, is by wading or climbing around pools along banks that are steep and wooded. Upstream of the Upper Chattahoochee River Campground, the river contains wild brook trout. Several Chattahoochee feeders also have interesting offerings for wild trout, including brookies in their headwaters, but all of these are quite small by most trout fishermen's standards.

camping: backcountry camping is permitted throughout the area, except where otherwise noted, but only gated FS roads used mostly by mountain bikers lead away from the main road, so backcountry access is limited. Camping is popular in a flat area near Low Gap Creek and at scattered other spots along FS-44, but the only official campground, with facilities, is the Upper Chattahoochee Campground.

The developed campground, situated on a fairly open, linear flat at the confluence of Henson Creek and the Chattahoochee River, offers 34 campsites, some of which front the river or creek. The gravel sites, fairly well spaced but without a lot of privacy because of the open landscape, are medium-sized, and each offers a picnic table, fire ring/grill and 2 lantern posts. Some sites near the back of the campground are large and nicely secluded. 3 restrooms have pit toilets. Camping costs $8/night. The campground is open from late Mar through mid-Dec. Horse Trough Falls, a significant falls on a small Chattahoochee feeder, is just a few steps from the back of the campground.

lodging: The Stovall House (706/878-3355), an 1837 farmhouse in Sautee Valley, has 5 guest rooms, each with a private bath and furnished with family antiques. The house sets on a hill amidst 26 acres, and views of the mountains that rise around the valley are outstanding from a swing on the large wrap-around porch. Rooms cost $80/night, double occupancy, which includes a continental breakfast.

Anna Ruby Falls Scenic Area

Curtis and York creeks, tumbling 153 and 50 feet, respectively, join forces at the bottom of the drop, together forming the centerpiece of the 1,600-acre Anna Ruby Falls Scenic Area. Although most visitors come only to see the dramatic twin falls and walk the 0.4-mile trail to their base, hikers do have a couple other options, and the opportunity to fish for trout exists along a portion of Smith Creek, which forms at the bottom of Anna Ruby Falls, where the two smaller streams come together. Eleven picnic tables, each with its own grill, are also popular with area visitors.

Helen (SW) is the closest town.

getting there: From the jct of GA-75 and GA-75-A at the N end of Helen, drive N on GA-75 for 0.4 mi and turn R on GA-365. The road into the rec area is 2.3 mi ahead on the L and well marked. After turning L, drive 2.6 mi to the pay station.

topography: Anna Ruby Falls SA surrounds Smith Mountain, but the creeks flow off Tray Mountain. While the area's ridges aren't especially high, the terrain is steep, as evidenced by the falls that define it. White pine and poplar dominate much of the forest, with oaks and hickories prevalent up the slopes and hemlocks abundant along Smith Creek. Elevations range from 1,900 to 3,468 ft. **maps:** USGS Helen, Tray Mountain.

starting out: A $3 parking fee or $30 forest service annual parking pass is required. A Georgia ParkPass, required for visiting Unicoi State Park, which the entry road cuts through, does not cover entry to the SA and often causes confusion. A visitors center/gift shop is open daily 10 AM to 6 PM. There are also flush toilets, a water fountain, drink machine and pay telephone outside the visitor center. The SA is open 9 AM to dusk, year-round.

activities: Hiking, Fishing.

hiking: 3 trails in this area total slightly more than 5 miles, with most of that mileage contained in the 4.5-mi *Smith Creek Trail*, which actually begins in the scenic area, near the base of the falls, but ends in Unicoi SP. Blue-blazed and moderate in difficulty, the *Smith Creek Trail* defies its own name by quickly leaving the creek and then staying away. The short trails include the *Falls Trail*, a

0.4-mi moderate path beside Smith Creek that leads to the base of Anna Ruby Falls, and the *Lion's Eye Trail*, 0.2-mile paved, interpretive path deigned for visually impaired users, with rails of steel cable for guidance and 27 interpretive signs written in large print and Braille.

fishing: No fishing is allowed from the falls to the footbridge at the lower end of the picnic area, but Smith Creek is open to fishing during trout season from the picnic area downstream about 2 mi into Unicoi SP. Limited natural reproduction takes place in Smith Creek, but most fish caught are stocked rainbows. The stream is small to medium-sized, open enough for careful casting and fairly easy to wade in most places. Wading upstream is more popular than bank-fishing through the SA.

lodging: Tanglewood Cabins, just 2 mi from the entry road to Anna Ruby Falls SA on GA-356, offer 52 cabins tucked away in the woods, each on an acre of land. The cabins, through rustic in design, are fully furnished, including fireplaces, decks with a grills and air conditioning. Rates begin at $75/night. Call (706) 878-3286.

Tray Mountain Wilderness

High-elevation slopes and ridges comprise most of 9,702 acre Tray Mountain Wilderness. Known for extraordinary views, not only from its summit but from various spots along its ridge, Tray Mountain reaches 4,430 ft. Long and narrow and running north to south, the wilderness surrounds the crest of the Blue Ridge, taking in upper slopes on both sides. The southeastern quadrant of the wilderness does stretch farther from the ridge, with elevations that drop sharply through the dramatic and isolated region surrounding the headwaters of the Soquee River.

Tray Mtn's upper slopes are difficult to access or penetrate, except by the *Appalachian Trail*, which runs north to south through most of the wilderness, ever following the ridge as it alternates between peaks and gaps. The Soquee watershed is bounded by private lands at the southern border of the wilderness, so any access is by bushwhacking along slopes that are sometimes broken by cliffs. The *AT* provides good access for hiking and camping, however, and backcountry explorers who are willing to go at it with only quads and compass to guide them find marvelous mountainsides and no company. Mtn bikers, meanwhile, enjoy the FS roads that lead to wilderness access points and run along its borders. Explorers are as likely to see a bear or jump up a grouse on Tray Mtn as they are anywhere in north Georgia.

Helen (SW) is the nearest town.

getting there: From GA-75 and GA-75A at the N end of Helen, drive N on GA-75 0.7 mi to FS-79. Turn R and drive 8.0 mi to Tray Gap. FS-79 is gravel and a bit rough, and it climbs the mountain through steep switchbacks, but it is suitable for passenger vehicles under most conditions.

topography: One of GA's highest peaks, Tray Mtn is part of the Blue Ridge, which runs central through much of the wilderness. Tray Mtn also lies along the Tennessee Valley Divide, and raindrops that fall on its slopes might flow toward the Savannah, Chattahoochee or Tennessee rivers, depending on which side they hit. The terrain is steep; cliffs, boulders and unnamed waterfalls are all common. Deciduous forests are dominant through the wilderness. Elevations range from 1,692 to 4,430 ft. **maps:** USGS Tray Mtn, Lake Burton, Clarkesville, Helen; ATC Springer Mountain to Bly Gap.

starting out: There are no facilities in the Tray Mountain Wilderness. Nearest supplies are in Helen.

activities: Hiking, Camping, Mountain Biking.

hiking: From Addis Gap to Tray Gap, the *AT* extends 6.4 mi across the backbone of the Tray Mountain Wilderness, with the highpoint of the hike literally at the highest point, atop Tray Mtn, from which views of mountains to the N and S are outstanding. Like anywhere along the *AT*, the path is well-beaten, marked with frequent white, rectangular blazes and easy to follow. The ascent of Tray Mtn is strenuous from either direction, but most of this stretch is fairly flat, at least by *AT* standards. Access to Addis Gap is by FS-26 or W Wildcat Rd off GA-197. It's 8.1 mi from the highway to a gate that blocks further vehicular travel. From there it's about a mi to the *AT*.

Backcountry hikes along unmarked and unmaintained routes using former fire roads and creekbeds are also possible from various entry points along the wilderness. Descending from the main ridge is difficult in most places, however, because of the pitch of the landscape and the density of the undergrowth.

camping: Backcountry camping is permitted throughout the wilderness. Sites are not designated, but flat ground and reasonable access to much of the wilderness are rare. Good sites are scattered along the *AT*, including some at Addis Gap, a former shelter site. There is also a shelter at Montray Gap, just N of Tray Mtn.

mountain biking: Bikes are prohibited within the wilderness, but all of the FS roads that converge at Tray Gap offer great rides. 3 gravel roads cover just shy of 30 mi and offer 4 possible downhill rides. Although down the mountain, these routes include steep descents on loose track and demand some mtn biking experience. FS-79 in particular has some screaming downhills, going either direction from Tray Gap, and the 7-mi stretch from the gap to Chimney Mountain Rd, off GA-356, is a rutted, rocky jeep road that demands advanced to expert riding skills. FS-698, 10.3 mi long, is the easiest route. All rides begin at Tray Gap. For bikers who have the legs and lungs to take on any of these roads uphill, loops are possible, using stretches of paved highway as connectors.

lodging: Set on 22 wooded acres just a few miles from the S border of the Tray Mountain Wilderness, the Royal Windsor Bed & Breakfast (706/878-1322) offers a touch of Old England in the N Georgia mountains, from food to furnishings to innkeeper Don Dixon, who moved to the states from London. The inn, which sets on a hilltop, has 4 guest rooms, all with private baths. Rooms cost $95–145 /night and include a candlelit "Royal English Breakfast."

Panther Creek Recreation Area

Spreading over a series of steep shoals and dropping more than 100 feet, Panther Creek forms one of North Georgia's most scenic waterfalls. While the recreation area named for the creek is quite small and open for day-use only, it provides the jumping-off point for the *Panther Creek Trail*, which follows the creek past numerous smaller shoals and to the falls and provides the only access to a substantial backcountry tract. Hiking, backcountry camping and trout fishing are all popular activities. The recreation area itself consists of little more than a parking lot and picnic area, but picnic facilities are nice, including large group shelters with fireplaces.

Clarkesville (S) is the nearest town.

getting there: From Clarkesville, drive N on Historic US-441 9.6 mi to the rec area entrance on the L.

topography: Despite lying SE of the Blue Ridge, where most Georgia lands level off quickly, Big Panther Creek creates steep-sided gorges and crashes repeatedly over shoals and falls as it descends toward the Tugaloo River. The terrain is somewhat demanding in places as the creek and trail wind between rocky outcrops and a forest dominated by white pine and hemlock. Rhododendron and laurel shroud much of the creek corridor, but some moist open slopes support diverse wildflower communities. Elevations range from 700 to 1,600 ft. **maps:** USGS Tallulah Falls, Tugaloo Lake.

starting out: Panther Creek sometimes gets crowded on weekends. Limited overflow parking is available across the highway, near the trailhead. A $2 parking fee or $30 annual pass is required at the rec area. An information board, water fountain and restrooms with pit toilets are near the parking lot.

activities: Hiking, Fishing, Camping.

hiking: The *Panther Creek Trail* , one of North Georgia's most popular day-hiking routes, begins across Historic US-441 from the recreation area. The blue-blazed and easily followed trail runs 6 mi to the confluence of Panther and Davidson creeks, but most users take on only the 3.5-mi section from the rec area to Panther Creek Falls. Hiking the trail is easy to moderate, with only a couple tough areas to negotiate and footbridges for some tributary crossings and one spanning the main creek.

fishing: Big Panther Creek and its tributaries are all designated trout waters that are open year-round. The creek is stocked regularly through summer within the rec area. Trout can be fished for throughout the watershed, which is more than 5 mi of stream, but siltation and marginal elevations cause habitat quality to diminish quickly downstream of the rec area. Within the rec area, the short stretch of small stream is fished mostly from the banks with bait. Some wild brown trout can be found downstream, especially in less-accessible gorge sections, where wading anglers use spinners and large weighted flies.

camping: Camping is not permitted within the rec area, but backcountry camping is popular along the *Panther Creek Trail.* Much of the trail is within the creek's gorge and therefore steep on both sides, but flat areas suitable for setting up camp are scattered along the route.

lodging: Just a few miles from the rec area, Glen-Ella Springs (706/754-7295) sets on 17 acres between a dirt road and Little Panther Creek. An 1890 hotel, Glen-Ella has 16 guest rooms, rustic in appearance but complete with amenities. Rocking chairs line the 2-tiered front porch. Extensive gardens and a swimming pool are behind the inn. Rates begin at $100/night and include a full breakfast.

Lake Russell Recreation Area

Despite being more than 20 miles removed from any actual mountain range, Lake Russell fits in nicely with the mountainous Chattahoochee NF and offers fairly good opportunities for backcountry exploration. Along with the developed rec area, popular for its lakeside picnic areas and beach, the area includes the 17,300-acre Lake Russell WMA, which is also on NF land. The namesake lake, which covers 100 acres, sets between modest ridges along the southwestern edge of this isolated tract of NF land. The rec area surrounds the lake and 3-acre Nancytown Lake, which lies just upstream of Lake Russell. The WMA, to the N and E, includes the ridges on both sides of the Middle Fork of the Broad River. Hikers, fishermen, and campers all have multiple options in the Lake Russell area, and one trail offers a challenging ride for mountain bikers.

Cornelia (S) is the closest town.

getting there: From Historic US-441 in downtown Cornelia, make a hard L on US-123. Drive 2.0 mi to Lake Russell Road on the R, which leads into the rec area.

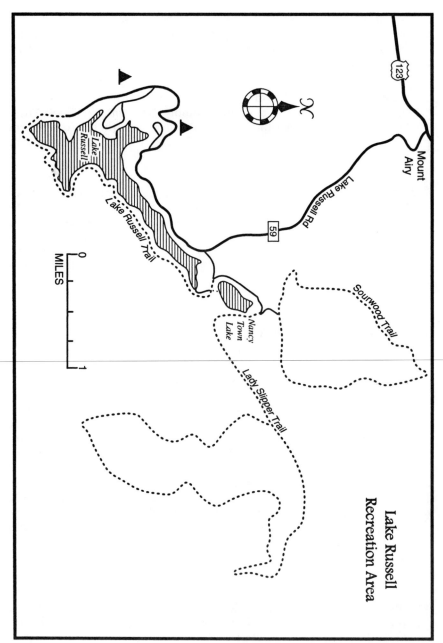

Lake Russell
Recreation Area

topography: Lake Russell WMA and rec area lie in the Piedmont but include Currahee Mountain, a 1,740-ft monadnock, and the hills around it, which creates a mix of mountain-like and Piedmont terrain. Pines dominate young forests through much of the area, with a shrub layer that is often nearly impenetrable. Rhododendron/laurel communities are dense at higher elevations and along river drainages. Elevations range from 992 to 1740 ft. **maps:** USGS Ayersville, Lake Russell, Toccoa, Baldwin.

starting out: The swimming area has restrooms with flush toilets and showers, plus a water fountain and drink machine. Alcoholic beverages are not allowed in the day-use area. A $2 parking fee or $30 USFS annual pass is required. Information boards at various locations within the rec area offer limited direction. The day-use area is open daily 6 AM to 10 PM. The rec area is open Memorial Day through the end of Oct. The lake is open year-round.

activities: Hiking, Fishing, Camping, Mountain Biking.

hiking: 5 trails at Lake Russell offer 5 different experiences, cover 19 mi, and range from 1.5 mi to 6.2 mi. *Broad River Trail* follows a tumbling stream; *Lake Russell Trail* circles the namesake lake; *Sourwood Trail* leads past a pretty waterfall; *Rhododendron Trail* descends Chenocetah Mountain; and *Lady Slipper Trail* leads to great overviews. All but the *Lady Slipper Trail* are open to foot-traffic only and offer fairly easy hiking. *Lady Slipper Trail* is also open to equestrians and mountain bikers.

Trails are all blazed blue, but blazes are sometimes infrequent and faded. Lake Russell, Sourwood and Lady Slipper, all loop routes, begin and end near Nancytown Lake, within the rec area. For the Rhododendron Trail, from Lake Russell Rd, turn L on US-123 and drive 1.3 mi to Chenocetah Dr and turn L. Trailhead is at 1.0 mi, near the top of the mountain, across from a marble sign and well marked. Broad River Trail begins on the WMA, off FS 87.

fishing: 100-acre Lake Russell, which holds bass, bream, crappie and catfish, is the main attraction to fishermen, and numbers of boating, and bank-fishing anglers are roughly even. Much of the shoreline is wooded, but the *Lake Russell Trail* and numerous "fishermen's trails" combine to offer good shoreline access. Countless downed trees, dragged out into the water, and Christmas trees bound together and sunk as fish attractors, provide the best cover for bass and bream and crappie. Nancytown Lake is stocked with trout through spring and early summer and also holds bream and bass. Bank-access is pretty good all the way around the lake. No boating facilities exist.

All the streams Lake Russell WMA are classified as trout waters, but most are small, overgrown and very marginal trout habitat. Only areas near FS road crossings on the Middle Fork of the Broad River, where stocking sometimes takes place, offer viable fishing opportunities, and fishing is almost all from the banks, with bait. All streams on Lake Russell are seasonal.

camping: The Lake Russell Campground consists of two loops through fairly open woods just a short walk from the lake. 42 sites, 7 of which are doubles, are generally fairly large and well spaced, and each has a gravel tent pad, fire ring/grill, picnic table and lantern post. Bathrooms have cold shower and flush toilets, and water is available near them. Campground is open Memorial Day through October. Single sites cost $8/night. Double sites cost $10/night. Sites are available on a first-come first-served basis, but capacity is reached only on occasional summer weekends.

A group camp is located near Nancytown Lake and available by reservation only for groups of up to 100. Most campers will set up in a large open field, but a few sites are tucked away in the surrounding woods, and facilities include drinking water, a fire ring, pit toilets and a picnic pavilion with a fireplace. The group camp costs $25/night for groups of 1 to 50 or $40/night for groups of 51 to 100. Reservations and arrangements should be made through the district office (706/754-6221).

mountain biking: The 6.2-mi *Lady Slipper Trail* is not for the faint of heart. It begins with a long climb and includes some screaming down-hills, tight single-track and highly technical turns. It is a good ride for experienced bikers that leads to some great views. The trail is poorly marked in places but fairly well worn from bikes and horses.

Unicoi State Park

Though not quite in the mountains, Unicoi State Park has a definite mountain flair, with high peaks nearby, ridges rising on both sides, a trout stream tumbling through it, and one of the region's most impressive waterfalls just a few miles upstream. The park has a privately operated lodge and conference center on the property and a scenic 53-acre lake tucked between its ridges.

The park is popular with travelers and picnickers, many of whom are visiting nearby Helen for the day or the weekend. Most park visitors don't stray more than 100 feet from any paved road, but Unicoi offers some intriguing opportunities for backcountry exploration. The most celebrated offering is an outstanding mountain biking trail that has been used for several major races. Fishermen enjoy lake and stream fishing possibilities, and opportunities exist for hiking and camping. While the park is fairly small, covering just 1,081 acres, adjacent Forest Service holdings expand opportunities for hiking and trout fishing beyond the park border. Wildlife includes deer, wild turkeys and occasional bears.

Helen (SW) is the closest town.

contact: Superintendent, Unicoi State Park, P.O. Box 997, Helen, GA 30545; 706/878-3983, 706/878-3982; www.gastateparks.org

getting there: From the jct of GA-75 and GA-75A at the N end of Helen, drive N on GA-75 for 0.4 mi and turn R on GA-365. The main road into the park, which is also the road to Anna Ruby Falls, is 2.3 mi ahead on the L.

topography: Lying on the lower E slope of the Blue Ridge, Unicoi SP is more hilly than mountainous. Its roads and trails sometimes wind and climb, but over modest grades; and Smith Creek, which dissects the park, tumbles gently along most of its course. Dominant forests are made up of white pines, Virginia pines and a good mix of hardwoods. Elevations range from 1,580 ft to 1.850 ft. **maps:** USGS Helen.

starting out: Unicoi SP has no visitor center, but maps and brochures are available at the park office, which is to the R along the main park road, or at the front desk of Unicoi Lodge. Restrooms, pay phones and water fountains can be found at various points, including at the lodge and campground trading post. Because Unicoi SP and Anna Ruby Falls lie adjacent and parking passes are required for each, confusion is common. The two passes are not interchangeable.

Pets must be on a hand-held leash of no longer than 6 ft, and alcoholic beverages are not permitted in common areas.

activities: Mountain Biking, Fishing, Camping, Hiking.

mountain biking: The 7.5-mi mountain-biking loop has played host to several national racing events and is a favored destination of serious north Georgia riders. The one-way, counter-clockwise route is difficult, with numerous technical turns, creek crossings, long ascents and steep descents. A couple stretches are linked by fire road, but most of the route is single-track. Turns are well-marked and the trail is heavily used, though mountain biking is the only permitted use. Access is possible from two points: behind the lodge, and off Chattahoochee St in Helen. While the parking lot near the Helen trailhead is not on park property, a Georgia ParkPass is still required. ParkPasses can be purchased at the Helen Welcome Center, also on Chattahoochee St.

fishing: A 53-acre lake in the middle of the park is fed by Smith Creek. The lake was recently re-opened after having been drained and restocked with bass, bream and catfish. Bank-fishing and boat-fishing are popular, but no private boats are allowed. Canoes and jonboats are available for rent. 7 Fishing platforms create very good access for non-boating anglers.

Roughly 2 mi of Smith Creek run through the park, 1 mi upstream of the lake and 1 mi downstream. The upstream portion is designated as seasonal trout waters and is stocked heavily from Memorial Day to Labor Day. It also supports some wild rainbows and browns. A small to medium-sized stream of moderate grade, Smith Creek is tight for casting in places but easy to wade. Where the state park ends, the national forest begins, giving anglers another 2 mi of public, fishable waters before they reach waters closed to fishing near Anna Ruby Falls. Around the picnic area, anglers can get in and out of the creek at several points or move along the banks; upstream of there all access is by wading.

Downstream of the lake, 1 mi of the creek falls under a new delayed-harvest regulation. Only artificial lures with single hook may be used, and all fish must be released from Nov 1 to May 14. From May 15 to Oct 31, the stream reverts to general regulations. During the delay period, a free permit is required to fish the creek. Permits are available from the front desk. The stream character is very similar to the upstream portion, but a trail has been developed along the creek to provide good access.

camping: A developed campground E of the lake includes 52 car-camping sites, 22 walk-in sites, and a village of 16 primitive, three-sided structures used mostly for group camping. Car-camping sites are medium-sized to large and offer varying degrees of privacy. The campground is hilly and wooded, and some sites back up to a small stream. All sites have picnic tables, tent pads, lantern posts, fire ring/grills, water and electricity. 13 also have sewage hook-ups. Sites cost $18/night for RVs, $16/night for tents.

Walk-in sites, all on the Hickory Hollow spur, are generally smaller but more isolated and much nicer than car-camping sites, and each has a picnic table, tent pad, lantern post, and grill/fire ring. Water is available for every three or four sites. The Squirrels Nest, as the village of primitive shelters in known, has no other facilities, except for a community fire ring. The three-sided structures set on a hillside and are somewhat isolated from the rest of the campground. Sites cost $10/night at either area.

Restrooms with flush toilets and hot showers are convenient to all camping areas. The campground also has a trading post, where pay phones are found, and laundry facilities. For reservations, call 800/864-7275. All sites can be reserved, and the campground is typically full on weekends from spring through fall.

hiking: Hiking trails in Unicoi SP are all easy to moderate and lend themselves to short day-hikes or interpretive walks. 5 trails, including a small portion of the *Smith Creek Trail*, most of which is on FS land, wind across wooded ridges, along sections of Smith Creek and around the park's lake. The trails, all of which are well marked at trailheads and blazed along the way, total 7 mi. The 0.5-mi *Frog Pond Nature Trail*, which has interpretive signs along the way, is the shortest route. The 3-mi (one-way) *Unicoi/Helen Trail*, which as the name suggests, leads to the town of Helen, is the longest. *Smith Creek Trail* begins across from the Little Brook camping loop. The others begin beside the lodge's upper level parking area.

lodging: Unicoi Lodge, though operated by a private concessionaire, is on park property and managed in close conjunction with Unicoi SP. Choices of accommodations include 100 lodge rooms and 30 different 1-, 2- and 3-bedroom cottages. The large wood-sided lodge has a restaurant, full conference facilities, and 4 common areas, all with fireplaces. The cottages, located in 4 different areas, vary in style, but all are complete with either fireplaces or wood-burning stoves and are fully furnished. Some cottages offer views of the lake; others are close to Smith Creek. Cottages range from $55–135/night. Lodge rooms range from $59-$99/night. For reservations, call 800/864-7275.

Tallulah Ranger District

Chattahoochee National Forest

Streams of every size drain the Tallulah Ranger District, among them the Chattooga National Wild and Scenic River and the namesake Tallulah River. Waterfalls abound, including dozens of significant drops that, due to their remoteness or the size of the streams they fall along, are not even named on maps. The Blue Ridge runs close to the western border of this district, so much of the landscape is characterized by its steep southeastern slope. The district, which includes high peaks and narrow river gorges, encompasses nearly 154,000 acres, almost entirely in Rabun County. Approximate borders are formed by the Blue Ridge to the west, by the Habersham County line to the south and by the North Carolina and South Carolina lines to the north and east, respectively.

Hikers, campers, fishermen, paddlers and mountain bikers all find fabulous places to play on the Tallulah RD. Beyond the Southeast's only National Wild and Scenic River, the district also takes in Georgia's second-highest peak, nearly 20 mi of the *Appalachian Trail*, 37 mi of the *Bartram Trail*, and a string of scenic mountain lakes. There are a few developed recreation area, which range from a small picnic area to a lakeside area with a campground and swimming beach. While no single wilderness lies totally within the boundaries of the Tallulah RD, the district contains portions of the Ellicott Rock, Southern Nantahala and Tray Mountain wildernesses. Additionally, a large portion of the Chattooga River watershed is contained in a vast, undeveloped backcountry. Black bear, wild boar and timber rattlesnake are among the wildlife species sometimes seen in this rugged region.

Clayton and Dillard, which surround the Tallulah RD, are the nearest towns.

contact: Tallulah Ranger District, US Forest Service, P.O. Box 438, Clayton, GA 30524; 706/782-3320; www.fs.fed.us/conf/.

getting there: US-76 provides the main access to Tallulah RD lands that lie W of US-441, while Warwoman Rd splits the vast tract between US-441 and the South Carolina border. The RS is located in Clayton, toward the S end of town, on US-441.

topography: The Blue Ridge and its escarpment, the Eastern Continental Divide and the Chattooga and Tallulah river watersheds are all defining features of the rugged Tallulah RD. Waterfalls and cliffs abound, especially along the eastern slope of the mountains, where the land falls off dramatically toward the Piedmont. Forest types range from northern hardwoods, high in the mountains to white pine/hemlock forests and rhododendron communities along river banks. Elevations range from 4,696 ft atop Rabun Bald to 891 ft. **maps:** See below under individual areas.

starting out: The district RS, open weekdays 8 AM to 4:30 PM, has nice interpretive displays detailing both human and natural history in the area. They also offer free maps and brochures and sell FS topo maps of the Chattooga River and some wilderness areas, plus annual parking permits for fee areas.

activities: Hiking, Camping, Fishing, Canoeing/Kayaking, Mountain Biking.

hiking: A dozen maintained trails cover 75 mi on the Tallulah RD and lead to many of its most dramatic features, including the top of Rabun Bald, the banks of the Chattooga River and several waterfalls. Routes range from the 0.4-mi nature trail at Warwoman Dell Picnic Area to a 37-mi section of the *Bartram Trail* and cover the entire range of difficulty levels. Several miles of unmeasured, unmaintained and unnamed trail also wend through this district, especially within the Southern Nantahala Wilderness and in the upper watershed of the West Fork of the Chattooga River. Nearly 20 mi of the *AT* follow the Blue Ridge from the NC line S to the summit of Tray Mtn along the border between the Tallulah and Brasstown ranger districts.

camping: Backcountry camping is allowed anywhere on the district, except where otherwise noted, which primarily includes day-use recreation areas and a few other popular spots that are threatened by over-use. No camping is allowed within 50 feet of the Chattooga River. 9 campgrounds in the district, 1 of which is primarily for equestrians, range from very rustic, with established sites but no facilities, to fully developed.

fishing: Fishing opportunities are both abundant and varied on the Tallulah RD. Most trout fishing is within the watersheds of the Tallulah and Chattooga rivers, but that includes more than a dozen fairly substantial flows and countless tiny feeders. Some waters are heavily stocked. Others contain wild fish exclusively, including native brook trout in headwaters sections. The Chattooga also offers good fishing for redeye bass through much of its flow, and a series of small lakes breaks the flow of the Tallulah, each offering good prospects to fishermen.

canoeing/kayaking: The Chattooga River is one of the nation's premier paddling destinations. 4 separate sections of river (including its West Fork) offer 4 very different paddling experiences. Sections I and II are beginner/intermediate. Section III calls for advanced paddling skills. Section IV is an experts-only run, with 10 rapids in 7 mi rated Class IV or higher. The Tallulah RD also has some outstanding but treacherous flood-level creek runs, including Overflow Creek with its numerous waterfalls. Flatwater paddlers enjoy the Tallulah River lakes.

mountain biking: The Stonewall Falls Loop Area, developed specifically for mountain bikers, is the main attraction on the Tallulah RD, but countless mi of FS roads, both gated and ungated, also provide opportunities for every skill and fitness level throughout the district.

lodging: Housed in a working gristmill at the edge of a valley just NW of Clayton, Sylvan Falls Mill (706/746-7138) sets at the base of an impressive set of falls and is surrounded by herb gardens. The mill, built of wormy chestnut in 1840, has changed little over the years, except that the original wood wheel was replaced by a 27-foot steel wheel. The inn has 3 guest rooms, each with a private bath. Breakfast is served on the screen porch which is built over the stream, beside the turning wheel. Rooms cost $95/night.

Tallulah Lakes Area

Four steep-sided narrow lakes along the Tallulah River, Lake Burton (2,775 acres), Seed Lake (240 acres), Lake Rabun (834 acres) and Tallulah Falls Lake (65 acres), wind through the mountains of Northeast Georgia. Although the lakes themselves are bounded primarily by private holdings, each has some public access, and the mountainsides that enclose the lakes contain significant tracts of national forest land.

Fishing is good on all the lakes, and each has appeal for paddlers. Around them are opportunities for hiking and camping. The best backcountry areas are W of Lake Burton, where a vast tract of the Chattahoochee NF rises all the way to the crest of the Blue Ridge, and a couple major creeks provide good fishing and cut through scenic gorges. Along the E bank of Lake Rabun, a developed recreation area offers a large, campground, a nice hiking trail and a popular swimming beach and picnic area.

Clayton (E) and Clarkesville (S) are the nearest towns.

getting there: From US-441 in Tallulah Falls, drive N 1.7 mi to Old US-441 (marked by a brown Rabun Beach sign). Turn L and drive 2.6 mi to Lake Rabun Rd and turn L. The first entrance to Rabun Beach Campground is 4.9 mi up this very twisty but paved road on the R. Lake Rabun Rd also parallels Seed Lake. Lake Burton is best accessed from GA-197, between Clarkesville and US-76.

topography: Modest foothills bound the Tallulah Lakes directly, with spur ridges to the W of Lake Burton rising to the Blue Ridge. The lakes are narrow and riverine, oriented N to S initially and then turning toward the SE. The final lake in the chain, tiny Tallulah Falls, dams the extreme upper end of Tallulah Gorge, and its N shore is part of the state park that surrounds the gorge. Major Tallulah River feeders, all of which flow into Lake Burton, are Dicks, Moccasin and Wildcat creeks. Elevations range from 1,550 to 4,276 ft. **maps:** USGS Lake Burton, Tiger, Tray Mountain, Hightower Bald; ATC Springer Mtn to Bly Gap.

starting out: A $2 daily or $30 annual parking fee is required for day-use at Rabun Beach (including the trailhead at the back of the campground), Wildcat Creek, and Moccasin Creek. A bathroom with flush toilets, water fountain and pay phone are available at the Rabun Beach Campground, near the hiking trail. Otherwise there are no facilities in this area. Pets must be on a leash.

activities: Fishing, Hiking, Camping, Canoeing/Kayaking, Mountain Biking.

fishing: Each lake in the Tallulah chain has its own mix, but together the lakes offer good opportunities for spotted bass, largemouth bass, catfish, crappie, bream and yellow perch. Most fishing is done from boats, except on Tallulah Falls, which has no formal launching facilities. Bream and perch fishing are good from the banks, with the best access at Moccasin Creek SP on Lake Burton, Nacoochee Park and Rabun Beach on Lake Rabun, and Tallulah Gorge SP on Tallulah Falls Lake.

Trout fishermen find the best opportunities on Wildcat and Moccasin creeks, both of which are small and shrouded in laurel and rhododendron. Wildcat, which FS-26 (West Wildcat Rd), parallels, is heavily stocked and heavily fished, mostly from the banks. The lower end cuts through posted private lands but there are 4 mi or so of fishable waters on public land. Access is by the road or by wading upstream. Moccasin Creek has two distinct personalities. Its lower reaches run flat through Moccasin Creek SP. This stretch is easily accessed, with grassy banks, and heavily stocked, but open for fishing only to children 12 and under, senior citizens and handicapped anglers. Upstream of the special section and limited private holdings, Moccasin is a small, steep stream that is tough to wade because of its size and gradient and numerous fallen trees, but it has good offerings of wild browns and rainbows. Both streams are seasonal. Moccasin Creek remains large enough to fish for about 2 mi.

hiking: Waterfalls are the reward at the end of 3 short trails along Tallulah River tributaries that feed the lakes. Up the mtn, 5.3 mi of the *AT* follow the crest of the Blue Ridge from Dicks Creek Gap S to Addis Gap, at the N end of the Tray Mtn Wilderness. Dicks Creek Gap is easily accessible by car, as the trail crosses US-76 here. Addis Gap is accessible from a 1-mi spur road from the end of FS-26, 8.1 mi from GA-197. Although this is a short stretch of the AT, elevations range from 2,675 ft to 4,276 ft.

The falls trails offer easy hikes along well-trodden paths. The 1.6 mi *Angel Falls Trail* begins at the back of the Rabun Beach Campground and leads to two waterfalls. The *Hemlock Falls Trail*, which has silver metal blazes, is 1 mi long and follows Moccasin

Creek. The parking area is 0.7 mi up a gravel road that is directly across GA-197 from the Lake Burton Fish Hatchery. The 0.4 mi *Minnehaha Falls Trail* is off Bear Gap Rd. From Rabun Beach Campground (directions above) continue 2.2 mi to an unnamed paved road on the L, which dips down and crosses a 1-lane bridge just downstream of Nacoochee Dam (Seed Lake). Across the bridge, fork L on Bear Gap Rd (gravel) and drive 1.5 mi. The trail, which may not be marked, begins with steps that cut into the mtn right beside the road.

camping: Backcountry camping is limited in this part of the NF, because it is not permitted below Hemlock Falls (where there is an attractive but illegal site), along Wildcat Creek (except in two designated areas), or in the Rabun Beach Recreation Area. The best backcountry camping opportunities are along the *AT*.

The 2 campgrounds along Wildcat Creek, 2.8 mi and 4.4 mi from GA-197 up FS-26, offer 30 sites combined. Both campgrounds are in flat areas of sparse woods and close to but not on the creek. Sites are small, close together, and basic, but each does have a picnic table, tent pad, lantern post and fire ring/grill. Pit toilets and water are available. Sites cost $5/night. Both areas are open year round. There is also a group of established campsites, some with lantern posts and grills, beginning at mi 5.4 on both sides of the road. This is not an official campground, and there is no charge for camping.

The Rabun Beach Campground offers 100 sites, 20 of which have electric hook-ups. The roads through the 2 interconnected loops are winding and hilly and both areas are densely wooded. Medium-sized to large sites offer decent privacy, and each has a tent pad, fire ring/grill, lantern post and picnic table. Restrooms have flush toilets and cold showers. Sites cost $10–16/night. the campground is open from late Apr through Oct.

canoeing/kayaking: All four lakes are extremely scenic, with steep banks and clear water. Unfortunately, Burton, Seed and Rabun all get heavy pleasure boating traffic—for their respective sizes—from Memorial Day to Labor Day. Summer paddling trips, therefore, are best restricted to weekdays and taken early in the morning. Tallulah Falls, with no power boats and little development along its sometimes-cliff-lined banks, offers the most intimate paddling experience, although its 63 acres are quickly covered.

mountain biking: Although there are no actual mountain biking trails, riders do make use of FS roads, the most popular being FS-26, an 8.1-mi route from near Addis Gap to GA-197 along Wildcat Creek. The route, though double-track and not terribly rough by mountain bikers' standards, has some good downhills and offers great scenery, with the creek tumbling beside and often well below it. For more adventurous riders, various old fire roads, in no way maintained and long closed to vehicular traffic, spur off FS-26 and FS-164.

lodging: Established as a camp for workers during the building of Lake Burton in 1916, LaPrade's (706/947-3312) opened as a fish camp in 1925, after the lake was completed, and has been a popular base camp for traveling adventurers ever since. 20 rustic cabins, set high up a wooded hillside above the lake, have porches with rockers, gas heat and basic furnishings. Cottages vary in size but some sleep as many as 8. There is a full-service marina, with boat rentals, bait and tackle and guide service available. Cabin stays cost $40/person/night and include 3 full meals of Southern cooking, served family-style and all-you-can eat. Kids 3–9 are half-price; under 3, free.

Tallulah River

Flowing out of North Carolina, where it rises high on the slopes of Standing Indian Mountain, the Tallulah River enters public land just S of tiny Tate City and tumbles through the Chattahoochee National Forest for the next 5 miles. A fairly large stream through much of this stretch, the Tallulah crashes through massive boulders and over small falls in some places and in others spreads lazily across shallow gravel bars. A Forest Service road that parallels this stretch, along with three developed camp-grounds and plenty of trout in the river, make it a very popular area.

The *Appalachian Trail* follows the crest of the Blue Ridge Mtns, W of the river, running NE to SW as it alternates between peaks and gaps. Much of the land between the river and the trail is public, but access is limited. The Coleman River, the Tallulah's major headwaters feeder, comes in from the NE, flowing off the Blue Ridge and out of the Southern Nantahala Wilderness; it's surrounded by the Coleman River Scenic Area.

Trout fishing is extremely popular both in the Tallulah River and in its largest feeder, the Coleman River. Hikers pick from a short trail or a section of the *AT*. Most camping occurs in one of three developed campgrounds, although backcountry camping is permitted throughout much of the area. Mountain bikers, meanwhile enjoy an easy ride up the Tallulah. Deer and bears make use of the area.

Clayton (E) is the closest town.

getting there: From the jct of US-441 and US-76 W in Clayton, drive W on US-76 8.3 mi to Persimmon Rd. Turn R and drive 2.3 mi to Tallulah River Rd (FS-70) on the L. FS-70 comes alongside the river at 3.0 mi and stays close to it for the next 5 mi, passing the Tallulah River, Tate Branch and Sandy Bottom campgrounds.

topography: The Tallulah River rises right in the center of an unusual turn in the Blue Ridge, where, like the top half of a diamond, the main ridge runs SW to NE and then turns to a NW to SE orientation. The Tallulah and all its major feeders flow directly off the Blue Ridge, but the Georgia portion of the main river flows through a valley of only moderate grade. Backcountry explorers can find cliffs, boulders and countless waterfalls never named on any map well up the slopes, but access to the steepest areas is very limited. Deciduous and white pine/hemlock forests predominate. The river's elevation is 2,000 ft where it leaves the NF. Mountains immediately beside the river rise to 3,000 ft. **maps:** USGS Hightower Bald; ATC Springer Mtn to Bly Gap.

starting out: An information board is located on the L side of FS-70 where it first meets the river. Parking along the river is restricted to designated areas, which are scattered all along its length and clearly marked. A $2 parking pass or $30 annual pass is required for day-use of the area. The river gets crowded on weekends between Memorial Day and Labor Day. Pets must be on a leash.

activities: Fishing, Hiking, Camping, Mountain Biking.

fishing: The 5-mi stretch of the Tallulah River that FS-70 parallels supports some wild rainbow and brown trout, but it is also regularly stocked in support of heavy fishing pressure, and hatchery fish make up most of the catch. The river is only of medium size at the upper end of this run, but gains volume quickly as it picks up feeders. Many stretches tumble through boulder-strewn mini-gorges, creating long, deep pools. Bait-fishing from the bank is popular, but the river can also be waded, especially through the upper half. Rhododendron and other vegetation crowd the banks in many places, but the river is plenty wide to permit casting. The Tallulah is open year-round.

The Coleman River, on which fishing is restricted to the use of artificial lures, is wild trout water. Although small, the Coleman is sufficiently open in its final couple miles for comfortable fishing. It is steep in places, making for fairly tough wading, and numerous fallen trees further complicate matters. The *Coleman River Trail* follows the stream for about a mile. Beyond that all access is by wading. Fly fishing with attractor pattern dry flies is the most popular approach. The Coleman's headwaters support good populations of native brook trout. Rainbows and browns inhabit the rest of the river. The Coleman, like all other Tallulah River feeders, is a seasonal stream.

hiking: The *Coleman River Trail*, a 1-mi footpath that begins along FS-70 just past the Tallulah River Campground on the R, is a nice hike along a small but energetic mtn stream, through a mature evergreen forest that includes some huge white pines. It's an easy route that's well trodden. Small footbridges across seasonal branches are falling apart, but they aren't really needed for the crossings.

The *AT* follows the Blue Ridge SW for 8.8 mi from Bly Gap to Dicks Creek Gap and flanks the valley of the free-flowing portion if the Tallulah River, beginning 0.2 mi north of the NC line. The first 3.2 mi are through the Southern Nantahala Wilderness. The entire section stays on or near the top of the ridge. Bly Gap is 1,165 ft higher in elevation than Dicks Creek Gap. Access to the *AT* is good at Dicks Creek Gap, where the trail intersects US-76, 19 mi W of Clayton. The nearest access at the NC end is 6.8 mi N of Bly Gap.

camping: Backcountry camping is permitted throughout most of the NF, but is prohibited outside campgrounds along much of the Tallulah River. The *Coleman River Trail* has a couple nice sites for backcountry camping along the end of it, and the *AT* through this stretch has several good camping areas, with a shelter at Plumorchard Gap.

The Tallulah River, Tate Branch and Sandy Bottom camp-grounds, all riverside, together offer 48 campsites, each with a tend pad, fire ring/grill, picnic table and lantern post. All 3 campgrounds have pit toilets and water available, but no water at individual sites. Tallulah River also has a pay phone.

The Tallulah River Campground is heavily wooded, and the loop through it is hilly and winding. 17 medium-sized sites are attractive and provide good privacy. Tate Branch and Sandy Bottom are both set on riverside flats in more open woods, providing less privacy. Sandy Bottom is farthest up the FS road, however, and is the least likely to be crowded of the 3 campgrounds. Tallulah River and Sandy Bottom are open from late Mar through the end of Oct. Tate Branch is open year 'round. At Tallulah River, sites cost $10/night. At the other 2 campgrounds, sites cost $8/night.

mountain biking: The 9-mi (one-way) trip from Persimmon Rd to Tate City on FS-70 makes a nice, easy riverside ride. The well-packed double-track road, with its modest grades, is suitable for beginners, but even experienced bikers enjoy the ride for its scenery.

lodging: Tucked away in a creek-side cove outside the town of Tiger, Mountain Oaks Bed & Breakfast (706/782-4625) is housed in a half-century-old, hand-hewn log cabin. Three guest rooms, all with private baths, are situated in the main house and an adjacent cabin. Each stay includes a full breakfast, by the fireplace or on the deck. Rooms cost $74 for one night or $70/night for 2 or more nights.

Stonewall Falls Loop Area

A dedicated mountain-biking area, the Stonewall Falls Loop Area was developed cooperatively by the USFS and the local biking community. The namesake Stonewall Falls is not a single waterfall but a series of shoals and drops, some 30 or 40 feet high, along Stonewall Creek, as it tumbles off Glassy Mountain. Beyond riding the loop trail bikers can also camp beside the creek, near the base of the last set of falls.

Tiger (N) is the closest town.

getting there: From Clayton, drive S on US-441 2 mi to Tiger Connector on the R, just past the Stecoa Creek bridge. Turn R and drive 1.2 mi to Old US-441 at the 4-way stop in Tiger. Turn L and

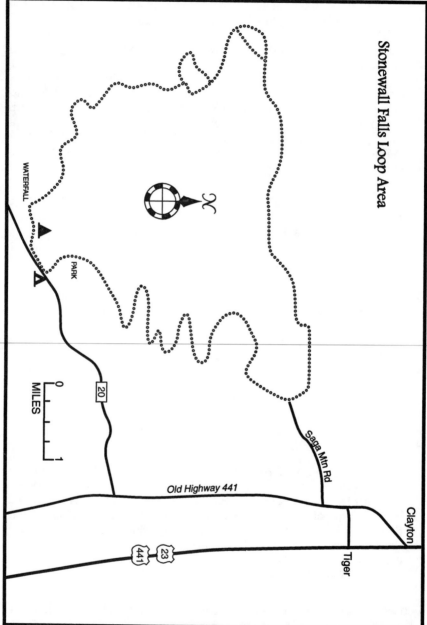

drive 2.3 mi to FS-20 on the R, which is marked by a brown FS sign, but is tricky to recognize because the sign faces traffic on FS-20, instead of Old US-441. Drive 1.4 mi on FS-20 into the Stonewall Falls area and turn R at the T-intersection to the gravel parking area.

topography: This foothills area features ridges that are modest in both height and pitch, especially for the Tallulah RD. Forests are deciduous, up the ridges, but dominated by pines and hemlocks along Stonewall Creek. Worley and Crumpleton ridges, Stonewall Creek and the series of falls that break the Creek's flow are the area's defining features. Trail elevations range from 1,875 to 2,380 ft. **maps:** USGS Tiger.

starting out: A $2 daily or $30 annual parking fee is required. A self-pay station and information board, with a basic trail description, are located off FS-20 on the way in.

activities: Mountain Biking, Camping.

mountain biking: The 8.3-mi *Stonewall Falls Loop* includes a mix of old FS roads, fire roads and single track and is rated moderately difficult. Trail elevations vary approximately 500 ft, and the route includes a couple long climbs, a narrow, single-track descent and four stream crossings. Highlights include a great mountain view of surrounding peaks from the top of Saga Mountain and the Stonewall Creek Waterfalls. The trail is designed to be ridden counter-clockwise.

camping: primitive camping is available around the falls. A few flat openings within sight of the lowest set of falls lend themselves nicely to camping. Although open to anyone, this area is intended for and used almost exclusively by mountain bikers. Maximum stay is 7 nights.

Warwoman Creek Watershed

While most of Warwoman Creek runs through private land, the creeks that provide this Chattooga feeder with most of its flow drain the steep slopes north of Warwoman Valley and together with the mountainsides they drain form an extensive backcountry.

Several streams, plus a fairly extensive network of Forest Service roads, provide access to these mountains, the loftiest of which is Rabun Bald, Georgia's second-highest peak. Facilities are nonexistent throughout the backcountry, where the terrain is rugged. The slopes are steep, creating dramatic cliffs and falls, including several spectacular unnamed waterfalls that are found only by "bushwhacking" or by working up or down the small streams the falls interrupt. Fishing is excellent for anglers who like small streams, and hikers can pick from the longest and shortest trails in the Tallulah Ranger District. Campers also have a couple options in the watershed. Picnickers enjoy the Warwoman Dell Picnic Area. The area supports a good bear population.

Clayton (W) is the nearest town.

getting there: From the intersection in Clayton where US-76 W leaves US-441, drive E on Rickman St. Drive 0.5 mi to the stop sign and veer R onto Warwoman Rd. The road, which extends 13.9 mi to GA-28 and skirts the N side of Warwoman Valley, connects with all the FS roads that provide access to Warwoman Creek, its tributaries and the ridges that divide them. Warwoman Dell Picnic Area is at 2.4 mi on the R. Earls Ford Rd is at 7.8 mi on the R. Sarahs Creek Rd (FS-156) is at 8.9 mi on the L.

topography: Warwoman Creek forms a broad valley from which the Blue Ridge rises abruptly to the NW, with the summit of Rabun Bald (4,696 ft), the high-point along the ridge. Several small, steep creeks, which parallel one another as they tumble down the SE slope of the mtns, help define the landscape. Hardwood forests cover most of the mountainsides, but white pine/hemlock forests and rhododendron thickets are common along the creeks. **maps:** USGS Rabun Bald, Satolah.

starting out: The Warwoman area has no facilities beyond parking pull-offs and scattered information boards, which generally contain only information about the NF as a whole or possibly the Tallulah RD. Nearest supplies are in Clayton. Pets must be on a leash or otherwise confined, except for hunting.

activities: Fishing, Camping, Hiking.

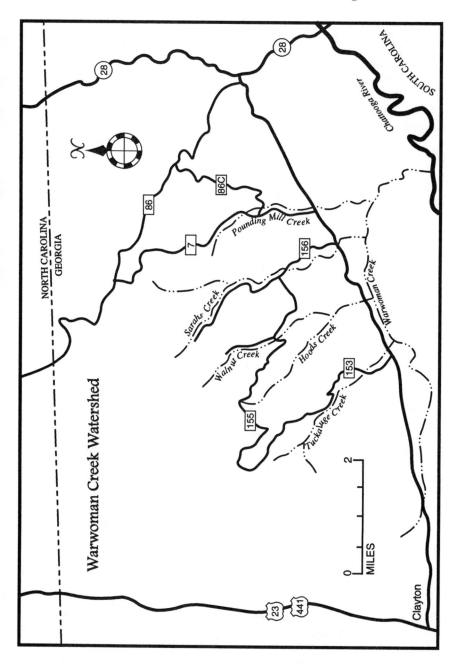

fishing: Wild trout abound in all the small streams of the Warwoman Creek watershed, and most creeks have browns toward their lower ends, rainbows through middle reaches and brookies in the headwaters. Small and clear, these waters demand finesse. Steep and overgrown, they are tough to wade and fish. However, fishing pressure is light and both the terrain and the colors of the trout are spectacular. Only Sarahs Creek, near the ford on Sarahs Creek Road, and lower Warwoman Creek are stocked. Warwoman Creek is of medium size through its lower reaches, and as it runs through a valley it is much easier to fish than its feeders. Dicks Creek Rd parallels lower Warwoman Creek, and bait fishing from the banks is popular through this section. The final 0.5 mi of the stream, before it flows into the Chattooga, is accessible only by wading downstream.

Tuckaluge Creek, Hoods Creek, Walnut Fork and Sarahs Creek are the main mountain streams. No trails stay close to any of them, so access is from scattered FS road crossings and then by wading in the streams themselves. Hoods Creek and Walnut Fork fall under special regulations, and only artificial lures may be used. All streams in this watershed are seasonal.

camping: Backcountry camping is permitted throughout most of this area, but within the Chattooga Wild and Scenic River corridor, which Warwoman Creek enters for its final run, camping is prohibited within 50 ft of any stream or trail and within 0.25 mi of any road.

Two easily accessible areas within the Warwoman watershed are popular for car-camping, although no sites are designated or formally established. One is at Sarahs Creek, 2.1 mi from Warwoman Rd on FS-156, near where the road fords the creek. The other is along Earls Ford Rd, a mile or so from Warwoman Rd, where the road cuts close to Warwoman Creek. Sarahs Creek will soon be developed into a regular campground, however, with a fee structure, pit toilets and sites that are designated and developed, each with lantern post, grill, tent pad and picnic table.

hiking: 37.4 mi of trail course this part of the forest, but 37 mi of that fall under a single route, the Georgia portion of the *Bartram Trail*. The *Warwoman Dell Nature Trail*, a loop from the picnic area of the same name, makes up the other 0.4 mi. The *Bartram Trail* actually begins high up a mountain within the West Fork watershed, and ends near the confluence of the West Fork with the main stem of the Chattooga. It enters the Warwoman Creek watershed upon crossing the top of Rabun Bald at mi 2.9, however, and remains there through most of its horseshoe-shaped route. This long trail, which begins near the NC border on Hale Ridge Rd and ends beside Russell Bridge (GA/SC-28), is accessible at 6 different points, so various day hikes are possible. From the northernmost trailhead to Warwoman Dell, the trail is moderate to strenuous, but the mtn views, mature forests and waterfalls are spectacular. The second half is easy to moderate. The entire trail is well maintained and blazed with white, metal diamonds. The route, which shares its final 9.8 mi with the *Chattooga River Trail*, includes 2 wet fords toward the end, the second of which, across the West Fork, can be difficult on high water. The Tallulah RD office has a *Bartram Trail* brochure that lays out the route and shows all access points. The Russell Bridge trailhead is on the S side of GA-28, right beside the bridge, which spans the Chattooga River. The parking area, a pull-off with an information sign, is on the N side of the highway.

lodging: The Beechwood Inn, (706/782-5094) a restored 1922 inn, sets on a hillside among terrace flower gardens, and its wrap-around porch affords great mountain views. The building is rustic, and the 6 spacious guest rooms are furnished in antiques. All have private baths, most have fireplaces and some have private decks. A full breakfast is served to guests on the sun porch. Rates range from $85–125/night. The inn is open from May to Oct.

West Fork Watershed

Georgia's largest tributary of the Chattooga River, the West Fork and much of its watershed fall within the Chattooga National Wild and Scenic River corridor. Most of the waters that join to form the West Fork actually rise high on North Carolina mountainsides, but they soon enter Georgia, which contains the bulk of the water-shed's stream miles.

The West Fork itself officially forms at 3 Forks, where Holcomb, Overflow and Big creeks join forces, all over waterfalls and nearly at a single confluence. These creeks, among Georgia's most remote, all flow through spectacular gorges and crash over numerous falls, most of which have no names because they are too tough to get to for most folks to ever visit them. The West Fork itself runs a violent course though a deep, rugged gorge for its first

3 mi and then calms substantially for its final remaining 4 mi run to the Chattooga River.

For fishermen, hikers, campers and paddlers, the West Fork watershed is as impressive a backcountry area as any in N Georgia, and it runs almost exclusively through NF land. However, access is quite limited, facilities are nonexistent and the terrain is demanding.

Clayton (SW) is the closest town.

getting there: From the intersection in Clayton where US-76 W leaves US-441, drive E on Rickman St. Drive 0.5 mi to the stop sign and veer R onto Warwoman Rd, which is the main road that crosses at an unusual 5-way intersection. Drive 13.7 mi on Warwoman to Overflow Rd (FS-86) on the L, just past the bridge that spans the West Fork. FS-86 runs 7.4 mi up the West Fork watershed to the headwaters of Holcomb Creek, where it dead-ends into Hale Ridge Rd (FS-7). The West Fork Campground is on FS-86, 1 mi from Warwoman Rd on the L. FS-86B, which branches off FS-86 5.0 mi from Warwoman Rd, runs 3.8 mi to the headwaters of Overflow Creek, near the NC line.

topography: Holcomb Creek rises well up the E slope of Rabun Bald, Georgia's second-highest peak. Other West Fork feeders rise even higher along the Blue Ridge, just across the NC border. The creeks front countless cliffs and pour over dozens of waterfalls as they tumble off the steep SE slope of the Blue Ridge and collect to form the West Fork. The terrain is rugged and the undergrowth thick. Deciduous forests dominate upper slopes while white pine/hemlock forests are prominent along creeks and rivers. Impenetrable laurel and rhododendron thickets are also common along creeks. Elevations range from 4,450 to 4696 ft. **maps:** USGS Satolah, Rabun Bald.

starting out: A $2 daily or $30 annual parking fee is required for camping or for launching a canoe or kayak at the West Fork Campground. There are no facilities, beyond pull-offs for parking, in the West Fork watershed. Pets must be on a leash.

activities: Fishing, Hiking, Camping, Kayaking/Canoeing.

fishing: The West Fork is best known by anglers for a put-and-take rainbow trout fishery in its lower 3 mi, especially around the FS-

86 and Warwoman Rd bridges and the West Fork Campground. Farther upstream, however, the river offers outstanding backcountry trout fishing for a mix of wild fish and helicopter-stocked fish all the way to 3 Forks. From 3 Forks upstream, 4 mi of Overflow Creek, and 5 mi of Big Creek are pure wild trout waters, while Holcomb Creek offers everything from freshly stocked rainbows to native brook trout, depending on which stretch you visit. Upstream of the FS-86 bridge, the only access is at 3 Forks, 1 mi down a trail. From there all access up the creeks is by wading or along steep-sided , heavily overgrown banks. Cliffs and waterfalls are frequent.

All the wild trout waters in the West Fork watershed, including the upper West Fork and various tiny tributaries, offer very tough going with repeated steep drops, bluff-bounded pools and countless downed trees. Stream sizes cover the entire range. Fly fishing and ultralight spinner fishing are most common for these waters, except through the lower West Fork, which attracts more bait-fishermen. The West Fork and the Overflow Creek watershed are year-round waters. All other waters are seasonal.

hiking: From the summit of Rabun Bald, which two trails in this area ascend, to several impressive waterfalls, hiking trails in the West Fork watershed offer great reward. The trails actually lend themselves best to day-hikes, although the first 3 mi of the 37-mi *Bartram Trail* are within the West Fork watershed. 4 trails in this area total 8.4 mi, with the shortest route being the 1.2-mi hike to the 3 Forks and the longest being nearly a tie between the 2 routes that climb Rabun Bald—the *Rabun Bald Trail* and the first leg of the *Bartram Trail*, each measuring close to 3 mi.

The *Holcomb Creek Falls Trail*, a loop route that leads past 2 major waterfalls, and the *3 Forks Trail* are both moderate. However, 3 Forks officially ends short of the streams, and the final approach to the forks is tough, any way you tackle it. The best way is probably to bear L at the end of the trial, ford Holcomb Creek just above a small waterfall and long ravine, and then pick your route over a short but steep ridge to the confluence of Overflow and Big creeks. The first stretch of the *Bartram Trail* and the *Rabun Bald Trail* are both difficult; Rabun Bald is the toothiest, beginning nearly 800 ft lower in elevation but climbing to the same mountaintop in 0.1 mi less distance.

All trails in the area are easy to follow. None are open to any uses other than hiking. 3 Forks begins at John Teague Gap, 4.1 mi from Warwoman Rd on FS-86. The *Bartram Trail* and *Rabun Bald Trail* both begin on FS-7. The *Bartram Trail* trailhead is just

1.1 mi from the NC border and is well-marked with a large wooden sign. The *Rabun Bald Trail* begins 2.7 mi S of the FS-7/ FS-86 jct and is marked by a sign but is more readily recognized by a parking area that is big enough for 2 or 3 cars on the L, just before the trailhead on the R. The *Holcomb Creek Falls Trail* begins right at the jct of FS-86 and FS-7, and the trailhead is well marked with an engraved rock.

camping: Backcountry camping is permitted throughout the area except where marked as prohibited by signs. Within the Chattooga Wild and Scenic River corridor, which extends up the entire West Fork and includes roughly 1.3 mi of Overflow creek and 0.5 mi each of Holcomb and Big creeks, no camping is allowed within 50 ft of any stream or trail or within 0.25 mi of any road.

The West Fork Campground is very primitive, with only pit toilets and a community gravel parking area for facilities. A sign notes that camping is restricted to designated sites, but the sites, simply clearings along the forested riverbank that are interconnected by unofficial trails, are neither numbered nor marked. Sites offer average privacy. Some offer excellent views of the river. Camping cost is only the $2 daily or $30 annual parking fee.

kayaking/canoeing: The lower West Fork, from the FS-86 bridge downstream to the Chattooga, is an easy 4-mi trip that is suitable for beginners and runnable year round. The scenery is outstanding, and only 2 rapids earn a Class II rating. The best access is at the West Fork Campground, where there is parking and where launching is easy. The take-out is on the main Chattooga, 1.7 mi downstream of the confluence at the Highway 28 Access, which is on the SC side of the river directly off SC-28. Some land between the campground and the main branch of the Chattooga is privately owned and posted, and boaters are warned to stay in their boats as matters of river ownership and access rights remain unsettled.

Upstream of the FS-86 bridge, a flood-level, experts-only run begins at the FS-86B crossing of Overflow Creek, 7 mi upstream of the bridge. This route begins tight and drops several hundred feet through numerous Class III to VI rapids with major strainers common. Banks are often vertical, so scouting rapids and portaging are impossible in some areas. Even expert boaters taking all safety precautions should only consider taking on Overflow and the upper West Fork with someone who has run this stretch before.

Chattooga National Wild & Scenic River

The Chattooga National Wild and Scenic River is best known for fabulous whitewater and for big brown trout in deep pools,. Rising high on the slopes of North Carolina's Whiteside Mountain, the Chattooga leaves the Tar Heel state at Ellicott Rock and for the next 40 miles forms the dividing line between Georgia and South Carolina. From Whiteside to Lake Tugaloo, where the free-flowing Chattooga ends, the river alternates between violent sections of rapids and placid runs.

Lands surrounding the Chattooga are divided among the Chattahoochee, Sumter and Nantahala national forests, in Georgia, South Carolina and North Carolina, respectively. All three forests claim a portion of the Ellicott Rock Wilderness, named for the rock that marks the tri-state border. No trails pierce the wilderness in Georgia, however, and no roads lead to its edges. Opportunities for boating, fishing, hiking and camping are all outstanding and diverse within the river corridor. The Chattooga is famous for 5 Falls, where the river crashes 75 ft through 5 Class IV and V rapids in less than 0.25 mi, but 20 mi up the same river, there is an outstanding run for beginning and intermediate paddlers. Fishermen, likewise, can pick from rugged sections with big, wild brown trout that are several mi from the nearest road crossing, or they can fish for freshly stocked rainbows within sight of Burrells Ford Bridge.

Clayton (W) is the nearest town.

getting there: From US-441 and US-76 E in Clayton, drive E on US-76 8.5 mi to the river. The US-76 access area is 0.2 mi ahead on the L. 2.4 mi from the river on the L is Chattooga Ridge Rd, which leads to several boating access points and connects US-76 with GA/SC-28. • The best access to the headwaters is at Burrells Ford. From the intersection in Clayton where US-76 W leaves US-441, drive E on Rickman St 0.5 mi to the stop sign and veer R onto Warwoman Road. Drive 13.9 mi to the end of the road at GA-28. Turn R and drive 1.8 mi to FS-646. Turn L and drive 5.5 mi to the FS parking lot on the R, just before the Burrells Ford bridge. FS-646 is a rough gravel road, but it is suitable for passenger vehicles. Along with deer and wild turkeys, the Chattooga corridor supports a decent black bear population.

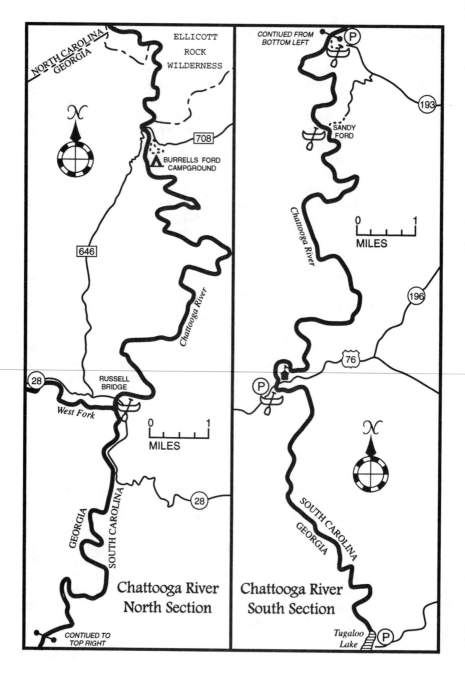

Chattooga River
North Section

Chattooga River
South Section

topography: The steepest portion of the Chattooga is through its first 20 miles or so, as it plunges over the Blue Ridge escarpment. Throughout the Chattooga's course, however, its valley remains steep and narrow, and rock walls, which sometimes rise straight from the boulder-strewn river bed, alternate with steep laurel banks and hemlock slopes. Deciduous forests dominate farther up the slopes. A classic drop-and-pool river, the Chattooga rages through strings of steep, powerful rapids, but whitewater portions are always divided by calm waters. Elevations range from 891 to 3,676 ft. **maps:** USGS Rainy Mountain, Satolah, Tugaloo Lake, Tamassee (SC), Whetstone (SC), Highlands (NC), Cashiers (NC).

starting out: For regulatory purposes, the Chattooga is divided into sections 0-IV (Section I is the West Fork, covered in a separate chapter). Russell Bridge or GA/SC-28 divides sections 0 and II, Earls Ford divides sections II and III, and US-76 divides sections III and IV. The US-76 access, on the SC side, has a huge parking lot, pit toilets/changing rooms, and a large pavilion with several informational displays detailing the river's offerings, along with its history, hazards and regulations. Well-maintained information boards are likewise found at most of the popular access areas.

The Wild and Scenic River designation protects the river from any development, and commercial activities are severely limited. Special regulations also affect individual backcountry explorers. No motorized vehicles are allowed within a 0.25-mi corridor of the river. Other special regulations are covered under individual activities.

activities: Kayaking/Canoeing, Fishing, Hiking, Camping.

kayaking/canoeing: Paddlers of every skill level find waters to suit their preferences on the Chattooga, which offers 26.5 mi open to boating on 3 distinct sections. Section II, 7 mi long, is suitable for beginning boaters. Section III, 12.5 mi, requires intermediate to advanced paddling skills. Section IV is an experts-only run, with 10 rapids rated Class IV or higher in 7 mi. The Chattooga's rapids are steep and technical, and the scenery is often spectacular, with house-sized boulders, sheer rock faces and waterfalls dropping directly into the river.

Because of the dangers in the Chattooga's rapids, extra rules are in place, beginning with a prohibition against paddling any waters upstream of Russell Bridge. Registration is required for all river runs (self-registration forms are available at put-ins), and every party must include at least 2 paddlers. On section IV, 2 or more paddlers and 2 or more boats per party are required. Helmets are required for any decked craft downstream of Earls Ford, and for all paddlers from Woodall Shoals downstream. Life jackets must be worn by all paddlers downstream of Earls Ford.

Section II begins at Russell Bridge, but much better river access is at the SC-28 access, 1.4 mi from the bridge on SC-28. Section III access points, Earls Ford, Sandy Ford and *Fall Creek Trail*, are all off Chattooga Ridge Rd and easy to get to. The main access for Section IV is the US-76 access, but a shortened trip is possible from just upstream of 7-Foot Falls. The take-out is on Lake Tugaloo. All popular boating access points are on the SC side of the Chattooga.

fishing: Big brown trout can be caught anywhere in the Chattooga, but the best trout fishing generally occurs from the NC border to Rock Gorge, 10 mi downstream. Catchable-sized rainbows are stocked through the summer at Burrells Ford Bridge and Russell Bridge, and sub-adult browns are helicopter stocked from Burrells Ford to Rock Gorge each fall. Wild browns are the Chattooga's mainstay, however, and there are fish in the river that reach double-digit weights. Bait fishing is popular near the bridges, but wading with a fly rod or spinning rod and artificials is much more popular through remote areas. The lower river is dominated by Coosa redeye bass, which look and act much like smallmouth bass.

Burrells Ford is the main access point for trout fishermen, and preferences of working upstream or downstream from that point are about evenly divided. The Chattooga is a large flow from the NC line. Portions are easy to wade or work from the edges. Others demand extreme care or are impassable, forcing anglers up the mountain to get around them.

hiking: The *Chattooga River Trail* parallels the river for 20.5 mi in GA, including 9.8 mi that are shared with the *Bartram Trail*. However, much of the route runs high up the ridge, instead of riverside. Beyond spurs of roughly 0.25 mi, which simply take explorers from the edge of the corridor to various places along the river, the only other hiking trail on the GA side is the 0.8-mi *Raven Rock Tail*, which leads to the Chattooga beside a Class IV rapid in the shadows of a 200-foot cliff. Hiking trails stay closer to the river in SC, paralleling Section 0 all the way to Ellicott Rock.

The GA portion of the white-blazed *Chattooga River Trail*, begins beside the US-76 bridge, in a small parking area with an information board; the trailhead is marked with an engraved rock. The trail ends beside Russell Bridge, where there is also a small parking area and information board. This trail is well maintained, easy to follow and moderate in difficulty. It does include 2 wet fords, at Warwoman Creek and the West Fork of the Chattooga. The West Fork ford, over a gravel bar beneath a small rapid, is usually easy, but it can be too deep for safe crossing on high water.

The *Raven Rock Trail*, blazed with white metal diamonds, begins at the end of FS-511B, which requires a high-clearance vehicle to negotiate. Walking the road from FS-511 only adds about a mile to the hike, however.

camping: Backcountry camping is permitted within the Chattooga corridor, but restrictions are in place to protect both the river and the integrity of backcountry experiences. No camping is permitted within 50 ft of the Chattooga River or any trail or within 0.25 mi of any road. The *Chattooga River Trail* has several nice sites along it for backpackers

The only developed campground is at Burrells Ford, on the SC side, 0.4 mi from the bridge. It offers minimal facilities and still requires a 350-yard walk from the parking area. Several clearings are scattered along this fairly flat, forested area. Most have lantern posts, some have picnic tables and fire rings constructed of rocks. The area has a hand pump for water and pit toilets. The campground is open year round at no charge.

lodging: The York House (706/746-1068 or 800/231-YORK), the state's oldest inn to have remained in continuous operation, has been accommodating visitors to N Georgia's mountains since 1896. The elegant inn sets on the edge of a valley, facing the Blue Ridge to the NW, and has massive hemlocks around it. 13 guest rooms, all decorated with turn-of-the-century antiques, have private baths, and stays include a full breakfast with gourmet coffee. Every room connects directly with a two-tiered porch. Rates range from $69–119/night.

Black Rock Mountain State Park

Named for the dark color of its biotite gneiss cliffs and boulders, Black Rock Mountain State Park straddles the crest of the southern Blue Ridge Mountains and contains the highest elevations in Georgia's state parks system. Receiving 80 inches of rainfall in a typical year, the park's forested slopes are botanically rich—almost jungle-like in appearance—and support a fabulous array of spring and summer wildflowers.

Though best known for roadside overlooks, mountaintop vacation cottages and pretty picnic areas, most of Black Rock Mountain's 1,803 acres fall within the park's backcountry. Hiking is the primary means for getting away from developed parts of the park, whether on a day-hike or an overnight excursion on the backcountry loop. Campers, too, find several kinds of opportunities within the park's boundaries, while fishermen enjoy the offerings of Black Rock Mountain Lake. Wildlife includes bear, grouse, deer, and turkey.

Clayton (S) is the closest town.

contact: Superintendent, Black Rock Mountain State Park, Mountain City, GA 30562; 706/746-2141; www.gastateparks.org.

getting there: From the jct of US-441 and US-76 W in Clayton, drive N on US-441 for 3 mi into Mountain City and turn L on Black Rock Mountain Parkway, which enters the park at 1.5 mi.

topography: Sheer cliffs and 100-year-old deciduous forests characterize the rugged landscapes of Black Rock Mountain SP, which sets astride the Eastern Continental Divide. Hardwood forests are only occasionally broken by younger pine stands or laurel/rhododendron communities along rocky north slopes. Elevations range from 3,640 ft atop Black Rock Mountain to 2,175 ft along Taylor Creek at the park entrance. **maps:** USGS Dillard.

starting out: The best starting point for exploring the park is the visitor center, located 1.8 mi past park entrance on the L and open 8 AM to 5 PM daily. Inside are displays depicting the natural and cultural history of the area. Maps and other information are available, along with restroom facilities, a drinking fountain and a pay phone.

Alcohol is prohibited in public areas. All pets must be kept on a leash.

activities: Hiking, Camping, Fishing.

hiking: The park's 3 trails, moderate to strenuous, total 9.4 mi and are well-marked and easy to follow. Winding through ferns and wildflowers beneath canopies of oaks and hickories, 2 of the 3 trails follow high ridges. A third trail, the 0.2-mi *Ada-Hi Falls Trail*, leads to the modest but pretty cascade it is named for. The 2 longer trails begin behind a well-marked pull-off along Black Rock Mountain Rd. The Ada-Hi Falls trailhead, recently moved, is at the Cowee Overlook.

camping: Backcountry camping is allowed at 2 designated sites along the *James E Edmonds Backcountry Trail*. The sites have no facilities, but are fairly large, in scenic spots along the route and easy to recognize. One site is approximately 2.5 mi from the trailhead; the other is near the loop route's midpoint. Reservations are required, and the sites cost $3/person.

Through not quite in the backcountry, 11 tent-only walk-in campsites are also in the park, each a short walk from a collective parking area and restrooms with flush toilets and hot showers. The sites are medium-sized and nicely concealed by forest, space between them, and hilly terrain; each offers a tent pad, lantern post, fire-ring/grill and picnic table. Sites cost $14/night.

The park also has 48 campsites for tent or RV use with the same amenities, plus water, electricity and cable television hook-ups. Many of these sites, though only medium-sized and fairly close together, are concealed by dense vegetation and by the steep landscape. Along with flush toilets and hot showers, campers in this area have a pay phone, laundry facilities, drink machine and a small trading post at their disposal. Sites cost $14/night for tents; $16/night for RVs. The campground is open year round.

Camp Tsatu Gi, available for group camping only, includes 4 Adirondack-style structures with bunk frames, a rustic log cabin with a loft, wood stove and grill, and a big fire ring in the center of camp. Camp rental is $75/ night.

For camping reservations, except for Camp Tsatu Gi, call 1-800-864-7275. For Tsatu Gi reservations, call the park office.

fishing: Bass, bream, catfish and trout can all be caught from 17-acre Black Rock Mountain Lake. Only bank-fishing is allowed, but much of the lake is surrounded by grassy banks, providing plentiful access. No trout stamp is required.

lodging: The park has 10 rental cottages, including 2- and 3-bedroom designs. The cottages, fairly modern but with natural-looking wood siding, set high on the mountain, and some offer views of nearby mountains and valleys. All cottages are fully furnished Some have fireplaces; others have wood-burning stoves. Cottages cost $65 to $90/night, with a 2-night minimum, Sep to May and a 7-night minimum, Jun to Aug. For cottage reservations, call 1-800-864-7375.

Tallulah Gorge State Park

Quartzite cliffs rise straight from the pools of the Tallulah River, which loses almost 600 feet of elevation in less than two miles between the walls of Tallulah Gorge. Made famous by Karl Wallenda's tightrope act in 1970, the gorge is half a mile wide, two miles long and nearly 1,000 feet deep in places. Although much of the river's flow bypasses the gorge for power-generation purposes, it is still impressive as it meanders through house-sized boulders and tumbles over five separate waterfalls that range in height from 17 to 96 feet, plus countless smaller cascades.

The park, which covers 3,000 acres both inside and outside of the gorge, has been open only since 1993 and is still in development. Overnight exploration is not allowed inside the gorge, but day-hikers can discover a fascinating place to explore, and experienced climbers can enjoy some of Georgia's finest cliffs. Limited numbers of expert boaters get their chance to run the lower gorge five weekends per year, when special water releases from an upstream dam return the Tallulah River to its past splendor. Outside the gorge, trails that range from easy footpaths to fairly rugged routes through rolling woodlands appeal to both hikers and mountain bikers. Fishermen find bass in a 63-acre lake and a 600-acre lake and trout in the moving waters upstream of the smaller lake. Camping opportunities include a developed car campground and a backcountry area along the edge of a mountain lake. Deer and wild turkeys are the most prevalent wildlife species in the park, but bears occasionally use wooded areas outside the gorge.

Clayton (N) is the closest town.

contact: Superintendent, Tallulah Gorge State Park, P.O. Box 248, Tallulah Falls, GA 30573; 706/754-7970; www.gastateparks.org

getting there: From the jct of US-76 E and US-23/US 441 in Clayton, drive S 10.2 mi to the main park entrance on the L.

topography: The gorge alone supports 8 separate ecosystems, ranging from hemlock/white pine forests along its lower slopes to dry rim and cliff habitats, where only hardy oaks and pines, usually small and gnarled, survive. Park elevations range from 2,200 ft atop hillsides outside the gorge to 890 ft at the lower end of the gorge. The terrain, often vertical, is demanding and potentially dangerous. **maps:** USGS Tallulah Falls, Tugaloo Lake, Tiger.

starting out: The Jane Hurt Yarn Interpretive Center is the place to begin all park exploration. Along with interactive displays and a fabulous film about the gorge and the park, there are maps, brochures, restrooms, water fountains and pay phones. The interpretive center also distributes permits, which are necessary for all access into the gorge and for use of the multi-use trail. The interpretive center is open 8 AM to 5 PM daily.

Gorge access is not permitted during rainy periods or on days of water releases for whitewater boating, and only ranger-led hikes are permitted in the gorge during aesthetic water releases, which take place periodically during spring and fall.

Alcohol is prohibited in public areas, and pets must be on a leash of 6 ft or less.

activities: Hiking, Mountain Biking, Fishing, Kayaking/Canoeing, Camping.

hiking: Hiking opportunities are outstanding and varied, although the trail system is still being developed. 2 trails into the gorge are currently open to hikers. Once between the walls, adventurers can pick their own path, keeping in mind that no travel is permitted upstream of Hurricane Falls. The hike in by either route is moderate, but travel within the gorge and the hike out are strenuous. The *Hurricane Falls Trail* follows a long series of steps into the gorge. A second set of stairs is being built across the gorge, and eventually the two paths will be linked by a suspension bridge over Hurricane Falls. Outside the gorge, hikers have 4 routes to pick from that range from 0.5 to 15 mi in length. 2 short, easy routes along the rims, a moderate hiking trail, a moderate to difficult network of multi-use trails, and the trails into the gorge total well over 20 mi. Some trails are blazed; all have some form of markers at jcts and trailheads. A trail map, available at the interpretive center, shows locations of trailheads, which are scattered across the park but easy to find. The park requires permits for entry into the gorge and for the *Stoneplace Trail*, which is open to hiking and mountain biking. Quotas of 100 hikers per day apply to gorge entry only. A 3-mi route along an old railroad grade beside the upper Tallulah River is being developed. The flat, paved path will be open to hiking, biking, jogging and skating.

mountain biking: Mountain bikers enjoy use of the *Stoneplace Trail* and a series of unmarked and unblazed spurs off of it. The marked trail is 5 mi, one-way, and leads to the banks of Lake Tugaloo, but the total mileage of the trail system is roughly 15 mi. Multi-use trails follow old logging and powerline-access roads through fairly steep terrain and are moderate in difficulty. More trail miles, including sections of single-track that will create loops with existing spurs, are being developed. A free permit is required for riding on the *Stoneplace Trail*.

kayaking/canoeing: When water is released through Tallulah Gorge, on 5 weekends each year in Apr and Nov, expert boaters take on one of the South's greatest runs. The put-in, just below Hurricane Falls, is at the end of a 1-mi gorge-access trail that consists of a series of steps and decks. The take-out is on Lake Tugaloo, which the river backs into at the lower end of the gorge. The run, which is less than 2 mi long but takes most of the day—with permitting procedures, carrying boats, scouting, playing, paddling the lake and shuttling—includes amazing scenery, 3 named waterfalls, and numerous Class IV and V rapids. Water releases are 500 cfs on Sa and 700 cfs on Su. 100 boaters per day, pre-selected by a drawing, plus 20 walk-ons, receive permits to run the gorge during water releases. Call or write the park office for details on permit application procedures.

camping: A backcountry camping area on the banks of Lake Tugaloo is near the end of the 5-mi *Stoneplace Trail*. The camping area is completely primitive, with just a single, 3-sided shelter. Backcountry camping costs $3/person and is available to 10 campers/night in the area around the shelter, on a first-come, first-served basis.

Most camping in the park is at a developed car campground. 50 medium to large sites are located in a flat, fairly open forest of mostly pines. Each site has a picnic table, fire ring/grill, lantern post, water and electricity. 6 additional tent sites lack water or electricity and are somewhat removed from the others. Restrooms, hot showers, pay phones and a laundry room are available at the campground, which is open year round and typically stays full on weekends from Apr through late Nov. Sites cost $10/night for tents and $12 for trailers. Reservations (706/754-7979) are recommended.

fishing: Tallulah Falls Lake, which covers 63 acres between the cliffs at the head of Tallulah Gorge, offers good fishing for bass, bream, and channel catfish. Some bank access is available around the park's picnic area, and small boats, like canoes or float tubes, which can be hand-launched, can be used to explore the deep, clear lake, which receives very little fishing pressure. The park also offers limited access to 600-acre Lake Tugaloo, which the gorge backs into. The lake is accessible by foot or bike on the *Stoneplace Trail* or by car. Boats can be hand-launched. Some bank-fishing is possible, but the banks are very steep and wooded. The lake doesn't hold large numbers of fish, but its bass and bream are typically quite large. Walleyes and catfish are also present. Limited trout fishing is available in the moving waters at the head of the lake, but wading is difficult and access is spotty.

The Piedmont

The Piedmont Region Key Map

1. Red Top Mountain SP
2. Kennesaw Mountain NBP
3. Chattahoochee River NRA
4. Sweetwater Creek SP
5. F.D. Roosevelt SP
6. Sprewell Bluff SP
7. Panola Mountain SP
8. Indian Spring SP
9. High Falls SP
10. Fort Yargo SP
11. Hard Labor Creek SP
12. Oconee River Area
13. Ocmulgee River Area
14. Lake Sinclair Area
15. Piedmont NWR
16. Watson Mill Bridge SP
17. A.H. Stephens SHP
18. Richard B. Russell SP
19. Bobby Brown SP
20. Mistletoe SP

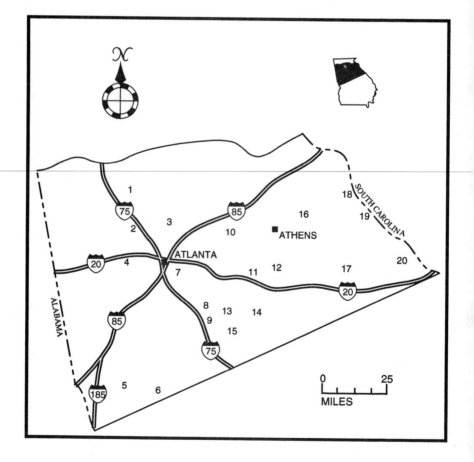

Weather & Climate Readings in Atlanta

Month	Avg High F°	Avg Low F°	Precipitation (Inches)	Snowfall (Inches)
Jan	50	32	4.8	1.0
Feb	55	35	4.8	0.6
Mar	64	42	5.8	0.4
Apr	73	50	4.3	0
May	80	59	4.3	0
Jun	86	66	3.6	0
Jul	88	70	5.0	0
Aug	87	69	3.7	0
Sep	82	64	3.4	0
Oct	73	52	3.0	0
Nov	63	43	3.9	0.1
Dec	54	35	4.3	0.2

Introduction

The transition zone between the mountains and the Coastal Plain, Georgia's Piedmont region is large, making up more than one-third of the state's total land mass. From the foot of the Blue Ridge Mountains and ridges of northwest Georgia, the Piedmont extends south to a line that runs east-southeast roughly from Columbus to Augusta. Known as the Fall Line, this is where the Piedmont falls off, sometimes dramatically, to the upper coastal plain.

The word Piedmont means foothills, and the region is indeed made up of hills. The hills are gentle in slope and modest in size, however, rarely resembling small mountains, as a term meaning foothills would seem to suggest. Elevations decrease gradually as you move south through the region, with the average elevation dropping from more than 1,500 feet to around 300 feet. The rolling landscapes of the Piedmont are very consistent, with the only noteworthy features being large granite outcrops or monadnocks, like Stone Mountain or Panola Mountain. The scenery becomes much more dramatic around the fall line, where the abrupt drop in the landscape creates features like High Falls, a string of steep shoals that drops more than 100 feet and looks like it belongs in the mountains. Columbus, Macon and Augusta are right at the Fall Line, all on major rivers, following a pattern that's consistent throughout the south Atlantic Region. The rapids at the Fall Line marked the end of the line for boating traffic, so cities where established at those sites.

The Piedmont, much more so than the rest of state, has been radically altered by human presence. Farming, timber cutting, and development have left little remnant of the mixed forests that once covered the region. Some large tracts have returned, but most woodlands are made up of planted pines on huge tree farms. Rivers, once free-flowing through strings of shoals, have been harnessed for energy behind hydroelectric dams. Most of the region's largest rivers, including the Etowah, Chattahoochee, Ocmulgee, Oconee and Savannah, have major impoundments, and dams are traditionally built on the most lively sections of rivers. In the heart of the region is Atlanta, the South's largest city. Atlanta's metropolitan area has a population pushing the 3 million mark, and it extends a good 30 miles in every direction.

Natural areas suitable for backcountry travel and adventure are widely scattered throughout the Piedmont and most cover less than 2,000 acres. The most significant exception is the area encompassed by the Oconee National Forest and the Piedmont National Wildlife Refuge, which together cover more than 150,000 acres. Even that is scattered across dozens of tracts, however, with towns, timberlands and some industrial lands between them. The other exception worth noting is F.D. Roosevelt State Park, Georgia's largest state park, which covers 10,000 and has a 40-mile trail system atop an unusual and beautiful Appalachian outcrop near the southern limits of the Piedmont region.

Of the backcountry areas covered in this section, two-thirds are state parks. Many are centered around a unique natural feature or an area of historical significance, and often the two go hand in hand. For example, mill ruins at Sweetwater Creek, Watson Mill Bridge and High Falls state parks are all linked with major strings of rapids on the rivers. Two of the most unique sites covered are administered by the National Park Service, and both are within the Atlanta metropolitan area. Kennesaw Mountain National Battlefield Park offers more than 16 miles of hiking trail on the edge of Marietta. The Chattahoochee River National Recreation Area, meanwhile, is spread along 48 miles of river in 14 separate units. Natural areas not covered include several wildlife management areas, most of which have no developed trail systems and are not managed for the activities covered in this guidebook.

Although backcountry areas are widespread and typically small, there are terrific opportunities for exploration hidden among them. For example, behind a sign that simply says "Nature Trail" in Indian Springs State Park, an unassuming little path soon winds into a fabulous old-growth forest beside trees that have escaped the saw for hundreds of years because Indians considered the area around the springs sacred. Some form of hiking, fishing, and camping is available at almost all the sites listed. Although less abundant, there are places to ride mountain bikes and a handful of fine rivers for paddling.

Deer and wild turkey are by far the most abundant large wildlife species in this region, and both exist in amazingly high numbers given the amount of development. Deer, in fact, are overpopulated in many Piedmont parks, where they find pockets of woodland habitat and where hunting is not permitted. Beavers, squirrels, ducks, geese, and an array of woodland birds are among other wildlife species frequently seen in Piedmont backcountry areas.

Red Top Mountain State Park

Situated on an Allatoona Lake peninsula, Red Top Mountain State Park covers 1,950 acres. The lake, which covers 11,860 acres, is deep, pretty and green, except after heavy rains, which turn it Georgia-clay red. It is popular with fishermen and pleasure boaters, and can get crowded on summer weekends. While the park has some of the development that might be expected so close to Atlanta—lodge and conference center, miniature golf, tennis courts, etc—it also has a fine trail system and offers good opportunities for camping and fishing. Picnic tables and grills, including nine large group shelters, are scattered around the park.

The park also ranks among the best places in Georgia for seeing white-tailed deer. Several food plots have parking areas beside them and are designated as wildlife viewing areas, but observant park visitors will spot deer along the roads and trails, in the campground, behind the lodge and really just about everywhere else. Deer are so common, in fact, that signs are needed throughout the park to remind visitors not feed them and to stop only in designated parking areas along roads.

Cartersville (N) is the closest town.

contact: superintendent, Red Top Mountain State Park, 653 Red Top Mountain Rd SE, Cartersville, GA 30120; 770/975-0055; www.gastateparks.org/.

getting there: From I-75 at Cartersville, drive S 2 mi to Exit 123, which is Red Top Mountain Rd. Turn L at the end of the ramp, and drive 1.5 mi, across the lake and into the park.

topography: Despite the name, there are no mtns here, just Piedmont ridges. The red in the name refers to the reddish appearance of the soil, which comes from a high iron ore content. The park covers one major peninsula, but the shoreline wraps around numerous points and coves, with the most significant cuts formed by small creeks that drain the park's ridges. Few spots are flat, but none of the hills are terribly high or steep. The park is mostly wooded with a mixed pine/hardwood forest. **maps:** USGS Allatoona Dam.

starting out: A good starting point is the park visitor center, 0.6 mi past the park entrance on the L. Inside are maps, brochures, interpretive displays, gifts and information. Restrooms and a drink machine are also available. The visitor center is open daily, with hours that vary seasonally. Park hours are 7 AM to 10 PM. All pets in the park must be on a leash of no more than 6 ft. Maps and information are also available at the front desk of the lodge.

activities: Hiking, Camping, Fishing.

hiking: 5 trails, which range from 0.75 mi to 5.5 mi, total 11.5 mi and offer a good mix of opportunities for day-hikes. Most routes lead to or follow the lakeshore at least part of the way, and all wind through wooded areas. Deer and squirrels are abundant along all the routes. The *Lakeside Trail* is paved, mostly flat and handicapped-accessible. A 0.5-mi section of the 3.5-mi *Sweetgum Trail* has several interpretive stops, keyed to a brochure. The 5.5-mi *Homestead Loop*, which includes both lakeside and ridgetop sections, plus dips into a couple small hollows, makes the best day-hike. Trails are mostly easy, with occasional moderate slopes, and are well marked at trailheads and blazed by color. Footbridges are provided for occasional crossings of small creeks. All trails are accessible either from the visitor center parking lot or the lodge area.

camping: Camping facilities include a large developed campground and pioneer camp or group camp. The campground has 12 large, linear sites with water, electricity and cable hook-ups for RVs only, 74 sites for tents or small RVs, and 6 walk-in, tent-only sites. The tent and trailer sites, which vary quite a bit in size, are fairly close together, but the woods and underbrush offer decent privacy. Some offer views of and access to the lake. Each site includes a picnic table, tent pad, fire-ring/grill, lantern post, electric hook-up and water. The lakeside walk-in sites are the most secluded and nicest, but they do not have electricity or water. 5 restrooms, scattered through the campground, have flush toilets and hot showers. RV sites cost $16/night; other sites cost $12/night. Reservations can be made up to 11 months in advance (800/864-7275), but individual sites are selected on a first-come, first served basis. The campground is open year round.

The pioneer camp, available by reservation to groups of up to 100, has only pit toilets and a foul-weather shelter. Isolated from the rest of the park, the area is cleared, but surrounded by woods and lakefront. The pioneer camp costs $25/night.

fishing: The best fishing in 11,860-acre Allatoona Lake is for striped bass, hybrid bass, spotted bass, channel catfish and crappie, but a mix of other species are found in the lake. Most fishing is done by boat, and the park has two boat ramps and a marina, but fishermen wanting to work the banks also find plenty of shoreline to work in the park. The best bank-fishing prospects are for spotted bass or crappie around fallen trees that stretch out into the lake or for channel catfish off the ends of points.

lodging: The park has 33 lodge rooms and 18 cottages. The lodge, which has a swimming pool and a restaurant, overlooks a nice cove, and the 1-mi *Lakeside Trail* begins right behind the lodge. Numerous bird feeders, food plots and other habitat work make the area around the lodge excellent for spotting wildlife. The cottages, natural in appearance, but not really rustic, are situated atop the ridge of a narrow peninsula. None are quite lakefront, but most have views of the water through the trees. All are fully equipped, including central heating/air, fireplaces, decks and grills. Lodging rates begin at $79/night. Cottages have a 2-night minimum stay. For rates and reservations, call 800/864-7275.

Kennesaw Mountain National Battlefield Park

A historic park, established to commemorate the 1864 Atlanta campaign and to protect earthworks that still remain from the battle, Kennesaw Mountain's 2,284 acres nonetheless create a nice backcountry pocket in the heart of the Atlanta metropolitan region. The Battle of Kennesaw Mountain was the last stand of Confederate troops before General William T. Sherman took Atlanta in the summer of 1864. Led by Gen Joseph E. Johnston, Confederate forces held off Union troops for two weeks, using still-visible trenches atop the ridges of Big and Little Kennesaw Mountains. Casualties, mostly to Union troops, exceeded 3,000. The park, administered by the US National Park Service, is not open for overnight use, but its network of trails lends itself a host of day-hiking options. Most visitors never get past the 1-mile stretch of trail that leads to the top of Kennesaw Mountain, and many visit the mountaintop only by shuttle or simply use picnic

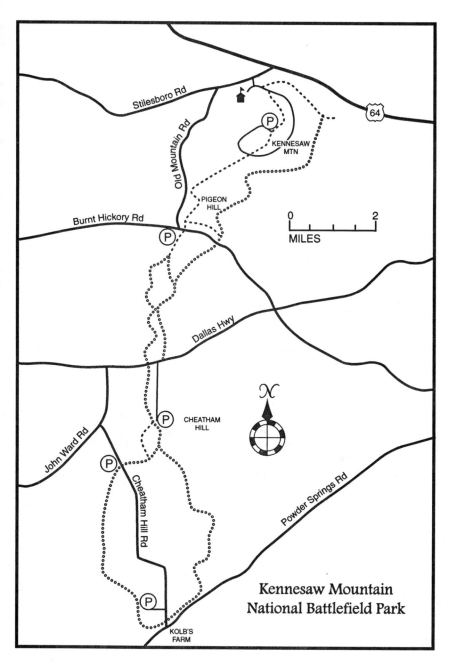

Kennesaw Mountain
National Battlefield Park

areas that are scattered around the park. Deer and squirrels are the most common wildlife species.

Marietta (E) and Kennesaw (E) are the closest cities.

contact: Superintendent, Kennesaw Mountain National Historic Park, 900 Kennesaw Mountain Dr, Kennesaw, GA 30144; 770/427-4686; www.nps.gov.

getting there: From the jct of US-41 and Bells Ferry Rd, at the N end of Marietta, turn L on Bells Ferry Rd and drive 0.2 mi to Old US-41. Turn R on Old US-41 and drive 1.4 mi to Stilesboro Rd. Veer L on Stilesboro to the visitor center parking lot entrance on the L. All turns are clearly marked with brown signs.

topography: A monadnock, Kennesaw Mtn looms over Marietta and can be seen from many places in town. Although the peak reaches only 1,808 ft, that's 700 ft higher than the elevation at the visitor center, just 1 mi down the trail. The mountain actually has two major peaks, with Little Kennesaw Mtn topping out at 1,600 ft. The terrain is steep in places, although S of Pigeon Hill, ridge elevations drop off and pitches are generally more modest. The park is mostly wooded with mixed pines and hardwoods typical of the Piedmont. **maps:** USGS Marietta.

starting out: A new visitor center, to be completed by summer 1999, will have a new film detailing battle history, museum exhibits and interpretive displays, along with maps, information, and restrooms. A temporary building, beside where the new structure is being constructed, currently serves as the visitor center, and maps and information are available inside. Pit toilet and a pay phone are also currently available. Visitor center hours are 8 AM to 5 PM daily. Park hours vary, according to season and location, but all areas are closed by dark.

Possession of metal detectors is prohibited at Kennesaw Mountain, and picnics are not allowed in fields along trails, unless marked as "activity areas." All pets must be on a leash, and pet owners are required to pick up after their animals. "Pet mitt" dispensers can even be found at various locations around the park.

activities: Hiking.

hiking: The park has 16.2 mi of interconnected trails that ascend all major mountains and hills and lead past various earthworks, cannons and monuments, including the Illinois Memorial at Cheatham Hill, site of 3,000 Union casualties. The trails are amazingly empty, most of the time, considering that downtown Marietta is just a couple mi away.

The trails, well maintained and signed but not blazed, are neither named nor designated as parts of specific loops, but most of the trail miles are contained in two parallel paths, which run N to S through the park and occasionally reconnect. The W trail, which goes over Big and Little Kennesaw mtns and Pigeon Hill, takes on most of the park's steepest terrain. Horseback riding is also permitted on much of the trial system. Footbridges cross scattered small creeks. All trails are accessible from the visitor center, but access is also possible from 4 other points.

Chattahoochee River National Recreation Area

The Chattahoochee River National Recreation Area is unique not only for its location within the Atlanta metropolitan area but for its make-up of 14 separate units along 48 miles of river. A series of pocket wildernesses amid densely populated Atlanta suburbs, the NRA includes a total of 4,100 acres. The units, all riverside, are wooded and provide surprisingly good insulation from the hustle and bustle of the densely populated areas that surround them. The NRA, managed primarily for outdoor recreation, provides some very good places to play along the Chattahoochee. The river, which is quite large by this point in its journey, can be lazy, clean and green, or swift and muddy. The entire 48-mi stretch alternates between long, deep pools and rocky, shoal areas. Since this is the tailwater section below Lake Sidney Lanier, power generation schedules dictate the character of the river.

Trout fishing is very good from Buford Dam, which impounds Lake Lanier, almost to the Atlanta city limits, and the entire stretch of river lends itself well to canoeing and kayaking. Hikers and mountain bikers, meanwhile, find good networks of trails on various units of the NRA, which is owned and operated by the US National Park Service. A few units have no access at present, serving only to protect the river from further suburban encroachment. 11 units at least have a parking lot and picnic tables, and most of those also have restrooms, canoe launches, boat ramps or trail systems. The NRA is a work in progress, with more land along

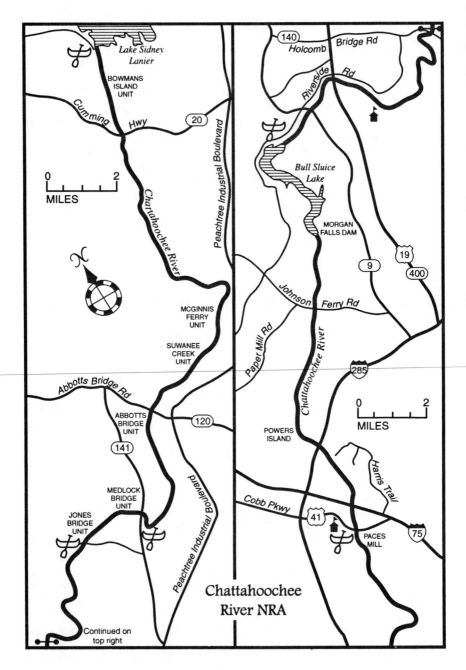

Chattahoochee
River NRA

Continued on top right

the river continually being added and access to various units being improved as funds allow. Deer and squirrels are the most common woodland wildlife species. Wood ducks and wading birds often can be seen on the river.

Buford (E), Roswell (W), Marietta (W) and Atlanta (S) are the nearest cities.

contact: Superintendent, Chattahoochee River National Recreation Area, 1978 Island Ford Parkway, Atlanta, GA 30350-3400; 770/399-8070 or 770/952-4419; www.nps.gov.

getting there: GA-141, GA-140 and GA-9 serve as major corridors between different parts of the park, but a host of individual roads that spread from near Buford to Marietta lead to individual units.

Park headquarters is at the Island Ford Unit. From GA-400/US-19, take Exit 7 (Holcomb Bridge Rd) and drive W 0.3 mi to Dogwood Rd on the L. Drive S on Dogwood, which will become Riverside Dr, 3.0 mi to GA-9 (Roswell Rd). Turn L on GA-9 and drive 0.2 mi to Roberts Dr on the L. Turn L and drive 1.7 mi to the entrance on the L, which is well-marked with a large brown sign, as are all Chattahoochee NRA units.

topography: Modest shoals separate long pools throughout the tailwater portion of the river. Park units are generally hilly and wooded with forests dominated by oaks and hickories. Feeder streams of various sizes course most units, but the Chattahoochee River is clearly the defining feature of the NRA. **maps:** USGS Buford Dam, Suwanee, Duluth, Norcross, Chamblee, Roswell, Mountain Park, Sandy Springs, Northwest Atlanta.

starting out: Park headquarters, at the Island Ford Unit, has maps for many individual units, plus a good brochure/map that details facilities at each unit. There are also restrooms, drinking fountains, pay phones, and an information counter, from which annual passes are available. Headquarters is open year-round 8 AM to 4 PM on weekdays; 10 AM to 4 PM on weekends. Park units are open sun-up to sun-down. All units that have public access also have information boards, with maps and any pertinent information for that particular area.

A $2/day or $20/year parking fee is required for most units. Pets must be on a hand-held leash at all times. Camping and hunting are prohibited in the park. Glass containers are prohibited on the river. A Coast Guard-approved personal floatation device must be aboard every craft (float tubes included) for each person aboard, and must be worn by all river users (waders included) between Buford Dam and GA-20.

activities: Fishing, Hiking/Mountain Biking, Canoeing/Kayaking.

fishing: From Buford Dam downstream to the Atlanta city limits, the Chattahoochee River offers fine trout fishing, with the coldest, cleanest water up close to the dam but the best insect hatches through the lower half of the run. Beyond yielding fast action when river conditions are good, the 'Hooch also has a reputation for producing double-digit-weight brown trout. Depending on the area and on water levels, the river can be fished from the banks, waded, floated in a canoe or float tube, or fished from a motorized boat; all are popular methods. The best shoals for low-water wading are found at the Bowmans Island, Jones Bridge, Island Ford, Cochran Shoals and Palisades units. The best access points for fishing by motorized boat are at Abbotts, Medlock and Jones bridges.

Water releases through Buford Dam and Morgan Falls Dam, 35 miles downstream, can cause water levels to rise several feet and the river to become both dangerous and difficult to fish. Projected water releases through Buford Dam are available by calling 770/945-1466 or listening to AM 1610 on the radio. Expected water flow below Morgan Falls Dam (given as low, moderate or high) is available by calling 404/329-1455.

The entire stretch of the river through the NRA units is considered trout water, so a trout stamp is required. Rainbow, brown and brook trout are stocked in the river. Only artificial lures may be used from the GA-20 to GA-141 crossings. The river is open year-round.

hiking/mountain   biking: At times following the river, at times ascending ridges, 43 mi of trail provide a great mix of hiking opportunities on the Chattahoochee NRA. Highlights of the trails include historic ruins of mills and homes, great views of the river and its tributaries and surprisingly good opportunities to see wildlife, including beavers, mink, muskrats, various wading birds, and woodpeckers. Trails are mostly easy to moderate but contain occasional difficult climbs, Individual units have trail networks that range from 1 mi at Johnson Ferry South to 7 mi at Gold Branch. Trail systems all begin at parking areas, and trailheads are easy to locate. Trails are well-marked on maps and generally easy to follow; some trails are blazed. Footbridges are provided as needed to cross creeks. Scattered unofficial trails, especially along river-front sections, can be confusing. Poison ivy abounds throughout the river corridor, so it's important to stay on the trails.

Mountain biking is only allowed on 6 miles of interconnected trail on the adjacent Cochran Shoals and Sope Creek units. The unnamed, yellow-blazed trails, which include both single-track and double-track, are moderate in difficulty.

canoeing/kayaking: Paddling the Chattahoochee offers an interesting mix of scenery. Most of the river corridor is actually quite secluded, with steep, wooded banks enclosing the river and occasional rock bluffs rising straight from the water's edge. 10 bridges do cross the tailwater run, however, and in places golf fairways or executive homes replace woodlands. The river, lazy on low water but swift when the water is up, is always suitable for paddling. Some rocky shoals become Class II white water at high water levels.

With boat ramps or canoe launches at 9 locations from Bowmans Island to Paces Mill, paddlers can plan trips of just about any length. The shortest stretch between access points is 2 mi; the longest is 12 mi. No portage route is available around Morgan Falls Dam, so possible paddling routes are divided into the 32 mi from Buford Dam to Chattahoochee River Park and the 8.5 mi from below Morgan Falls Dam to Paces Mill. Chattahoochee River Park and the Morgan Falls Dam access are not part of the NRA, but both are public, easily accessible out of Roswell, and included on the NRA brochure/map.

A private concessionaire located on the property of the Johnson Ferry North Unit offers shuttle service and canoe/raft rentals on the river's lower 6.5 mi from Memorial Day through mid-Sep.

Sweetwater Creek State Conservation Park

Located just west of Atlanta, Sweetwater Creek State Conservation Park offers a nice pocket of backcountry in the midst of the capital city's suburbs. Most of the park's 1,986 acres are divided among various access points around a 215-acre lake and a large day-use backcountry area along Sweetwater Creek. Along the tumbling creek are ruins from a factory built in 1859 but occupied and burned by Union troops during the Civil War and never rebuilt. Remnants of the old millrace, road, and community store also exist. Though quite prone to turning muddy, the large creek is very scenic as it tumbles over numerous shoals, including one steep rapid that is somewhat generously called Sweetwater Falls. The area around the lake is popular with picnickers and fishermen. The area around the creek is primarily a hiking destination, although it also offers fairly good fishing prospects. The park has no campground and is open for daytime use only. Deer and squirrels, plus various ducks on the pond, are the most commonly seen wildlife.

Lithia Spring (N) is the nearest town.

contact: Superintendent, Sweetwater Creek State Conservation Park, P.O. Box 818, Lithia Springs, GA 30122; 770/732-6871; www.gastateparks.org.

getting there: From I-20 W of Atlanta, take Exit 12. Turn S on Thornton Road (GA-6) and drive 0.5 mi to Blairs Bridge Rd, which has no street sign but is marked by a brown sign for Sweetwater Creek SP. Turn R and drive 2.2 mi to Mt Vernon Rd. Turn L and drive 0.5 mi to the park, most of which lies L of the road. The second entrance on the L leads to the park office and visitor center. The third entrance on the L, Factory Shoals Rd, leads to the hiking trails.

topography: Sweetwater Creek and George H. Sparks Reservoir, which floods a small tributary of the creek, are the main features of a Piedmont landscape that is forested with mixed pines and hardwoods. The creek tumbles through a significant set of shoals. The park's terrain is steeper than most surrounding areas because it sets directly atop the Brevard Fault. **maps:** USGS Austell, Mableton, Ben Hill Cambellton.

starting out: The park office, open 8 AM to 5 PM daily, has maps and information, including good trail maps. The bait shop, housed in the same building, also has information, but it is closed on Mondays. There are restrooms, drink machines, pay phones and a water fountain in the area of the office. The park is open from 7 AM to 10 PM, but the area around the trails closes at sunset.

Swimming and wading are prohibited in Sweetwater Creek. Alcoholic beverages are prohibited in the park. Pets must be on a leash of 6 ft or less.

activities: Hiking, Fishing.

hiking: 4 trails that wind through the backcountry around Sweetwater Creek provide a good mix of day-hike opportunities, with individual trails ranging in length from 1 to 4 mi. Highlights include the ruins of the old factory and mill village, overviews of the creek's numerous shoals, rich tributary coves, ridges and very good wildflower displays. The trails, which total 9 mi, are interconnected, so a variety of loops is possible. The red-blazed *History Trail* and the blue and white-blazed *Non-Game Wildlife Trails* are on the W side of the creek. While the newly established, yellow-blazed *Sweetwater Creek Trail* crosses the creek on an old trestle and forms a loop along the opposite shoreline and ridge. Trails are generally moderate to hike, although the second half of the *History Trail*, from the factory ruins to Sweetwater Falls, includes some difficult footing along narrow, rocky sections and a couple short but steep climbs. All trails are well marked with rectangular blazes. Some past trails that are no longer maintained are sufficiently well trodden to cause confusion, but false routes have no blazes. There are footbridge and steps where needed. The first half of the *History Trail*, which is the most frequently hiked section in the park, has an accompanying interpretive brochure. The trails begin at a parking lot off Factory Shoals road, and the main trailhead is signed.

fishing: Crappie are the most sought-after species in 215-acre George H. Sparks Reservoir, but the lake also offers good prospects for bass, bream and catfish. Fishing is popular from the banks and from boats. A fishing pier is located in a small picnic area across Mt Vernon Rd from the office entrance. Private boats are permitted on the lake, but only electric motors may be operated, and a $2 launch fee is required. Canoes and jonboats may be rented for $3/hour, $8 for 4 hours or $12 for 8 hours.

Sweetwater Creek also offers decent prospects for bass, bream and catfish. Only bank-fishing is permitted, however, and the steep, wooded banks make access difficult in many places.

F.D. Roosevelt State Park

Georgia's largest state park at 10,000 acres, F.D. Roosevelt State Park is quite appropriately named. President Roosevelt was drawn to the Pine Mountain area after being stricken with polio in 1921 because of the reported therapeutic value of some nearby warm springs, and he soon built his "home away from home," the Little White House, just down the mountain from where the park now exists. FDR's favorite picnic spot, Dowdell Knob, is near the center of the state park named for him and looks off the south side of Pine Mountain. Also, much of the park, including its cottages, swimming pool and visitor center, were built by Roosevelt's Civilian Conservation Corps. The park covers much of Pine Mountain, a long, plateau-like outcrop of the Appalachian Mountains. Modest waterfalls and mountaintop overviews are outstanding and seem out of place so far south in Georgia.

The park has an outstanding trail system, with more than 40 miles of well-maintained hiking trails, plus a separate network of equestrian routes and a stable run by a private concessionaire. Camping opportunities range from backpacking along the *Pine Mountain Trail* to car camping in the developed campground. Fishing is available in 15-acre Lake Delano. The park has several nice picnic areas, including some with great overviews off the south side of Pine Mountain. White-tailed deer and wild turkey are common wildlife species.

Pine Mountain (W) and Warm Springs (NE) are the nearest towns

contact: Superintendent, F.D. Roosevelt State Park, 2970 GA-190, Pine Mountain, GA 31822; 706/663-4858; www.gastateparks.org.

getting there: From Pine Mtn, drive S on US 27 3.2 mi to GA-190. The park entrance is on the L.

topography: Most of the park sets atop Pine Mtn, a long plateau that runs W to E and is a distant outcrop of the Appalachian Mountains. Though most slopes are modest atop the mtn, along its edges the terrain drops sharply to flat valleys to the N and S. Forests contain typical Piedmont mixes of pine and hardwoods. The elevation at Dowdell is 1,400 ft, which is 800 ft higher than Pine Mountain Valley. **maps:** USGS Pine Mountain, Shiloh.

starting out: The park visitor center is housed in the old Roosevelt Inn, a 2 story stone structure that overlooks Pine Valley and was constructed by CCC workers. The visitor center is open 8 AM to 5 PM M– Th and Sa–Su, 8 AM to 10 PM F. Maps and information are available, along with restrooms, a water fountain and pay phones. The park is open from 7 AM to 10 PM daily.

Alcoholic beverages are prohibited in public areas. Pets must be on a leash of 6 ft or less.

activities: Hiking, Camping, Fishing.

hiking: 40 mi of trail, with routes ranging from the 3.2-mi *Mountain Creek Nature Trail* to the 23-mi *Pine Mtn Trail*, provide opportunities for a tremendous variety of hikes within F.D. Roosevelt SP. Rock formations, waterfalls, mtn overviews and a good mix of forest types are among the sights along the way. Most of the trail system stems off the main *Pine Mtn Trail*, and several loops are possible for day-hikes or backpacking trips. The 6.7-mi *Wolfden Loop*, popular for its namesake wolf den, plus several pretty cascades along a small but lively stream, is the most popular day-hike in the park. The entire trail system was developed by and is maintained by the Pine Mtn Trail Association. The *Pine Mtn Trail* is blazed blue, and its approach trails are blazed white. The *Mtn Creek Nature Trail*, which begins and ends at the campground Trading Post and is not linked to the rest of the trail system, is blazed red. Trails are very well marked, with signs at all junctures telling distances and directions. Most trails are moderately difficult. The *Mtn Creek Nature Trail* is easy, with only a few modest slopes. Numerous trailheads are scattered along GA-190. The *Pine Mtn Trail*'s W terminus is near the park's main entrance on GA-190, across from the Callaway Country Store. The E terminus is beside the WJSP TV tower off GA-85. Trail maps are sold for $2.15 at the park office.

camping: Backcountry camping is permitted at 11 designated campsites along the *Pine Mtn Trail*. Sites, which are marked with signs, are undeveloped, except for having fire rings, and minimum-impact camping is expected. Campfires are permitted in fire rings only. Some sites are as close as 0.5 mi to a car access point, but several can be reached only by hikes of 3 mi or more. Reservations guarantee a site, but are not site-specific, so with 23 mi of trail and the sites well distributed, it is important to know how many sites are reserved and if possible which direction other backpackers have gone. A backcountry permit is required from the visitor center, and permits will not be issued less than 2 hours before sunset. Camping costs $3/person per night, with a maximum of $15/campsite. Maximum capacity for campsites is 15 people.

Car camping is also possible at a large developed campground near Lake Delano. The campground has 140 sites in a series of loops. Campsite sizes and levels of privacy vary markedly in different areas, as much of the campground is flat and very open but with some portions that are hilly and more densely forested. Sites closest to the lake generally offer the least space and privacy. All sites have a picnic table, tent pad and fire ring/grill, plus water and electricity. Many have lantern posts. 5 separate restrooms have flush toilets and hot showers. Pay phones, a Trading Post and laundry facilities are also available. Sites cost $12/night for tents and $14/night for RVs. The campground is open year round.

4 pioneer camping areas are isolated from the rest of the park and from each other, although all are down the same road. Each consists of a small clearing in a dense forest, with picnic tables, space for several tents, a 2-sided wooden shelter, water, pit toilets and a fire ring. Pioneer camping costs $1/person, per night, with a minimum of $15/night.

fishing: Lake Delano, which covers 15 acres near the campground and picnic areas, has bass, bream and catfish. Bank-fishing is more popular than boating, and access is good. Campers may fish at night, but other park visitors may not fish past 10 PM. Fishing boats may be rented from 8 AM to 5 PM. Private boats are not permitted.

lodging: The park has 21 1- and 2-bedroom cottages, all fully furnished, with fireplaces, picnic tables and grills. Some are traditional log cabins with stone foundations; others are more contemporary designs, with brown wood siding. 4 stone cottages built by CCC workers in the 1930s set on the edge of a mtn spur, behind the visitor center, and overlook a pretty valley. Cottages cost $50–80/night. There is a 2-night minimum stay year-round and a 7-night minimum through summer. For reservations call 800/864-7275.

Sprewell Bluff State Park

Despite its lower Piedmont locale, Sprewell Bluff looks like it belongs in North Georgia, with high bluffs rising on both sides of the rock-strewn Flint River. The mountains that the river cuts through to form the bluffs are part of the Pine Mountain range, an extreme southern outcrop of the Appalachian Mountains. The park is long and narrow, with 1,400 acres stretched along the river bank. Most activity centers around the park's picnic area, a broad flat area of gravel and open woods between the bluff and the river. A hiking trail begins there, although it quickly climbs off the flat and then follows the bluff-line upstream. The park offers good fishing, both by wading and from its banks, along with being a good access point for canoeing an kayaking on the Flint River. Squirrels, wading birds and wood ducks are the most wildlife apt to be seen near the river. Deer use the woods atop the bluff.

Thomaston (E) is the nearest town.

contact: Superintendent, Sprewell Bluff State Park, 740 Sprewell Bluff Rd, Thomaston, GA 30286; 706/646-6026; www.gastateparks.org.

getting there: From Thomaston, Drive N on GA-74 5.7 mi to Old Alabama Rd and turn L. Drive 5.5 mi on Old Alabama Rd to the park entrance.

topography: High bluffs rise on both sides of the Flint River as it flows over gentle shoals. Much of the park's acreage is atop the bluff along the E bank, but the main access area is a riverside flat in the shadow of the bluff. The flat is sparsely wooded, while the top of the bluff is mostly forested with a mix of pines and hardwoods. Elevations atop the ridge are approximately 1,000 ft.
maps: USGS Roland, Sunset Village.

starting out: Sprewell Bluff has no visitors center, and facilities are limited to a parking area, boat ramp, picnic tables and grills and pit toilets. The park is open from 7 AM until sunset.

Alcoholic beverages are prohibited. Pets must be on a leash of no longer than 6 ft.

activities: Fishing, Hiking, Canoeing/Kayaking.

fishing: The Flint River offers excellent fishing for shoal bass, a black bass species similar to a variety of smallmouth that is found in only a few river systems which drain into the Gulf of Mexico. The park offers good fishing access. Wading is the best way to access the most water, as the river is quite wide, but the park's long stretch of flat, open bank allows fishermen to cast to a fair amount of water without getting wet. Float-fishing from a canoe and using the boat to access other wadable shoals downstream is probably the best overall way to fish the river. Catfishing is also popular in a couple deep holes within casting range of the park's banks.

hiking: The park has one trail, simply labeled as "hiking trail," that can be accessed from a marked parking area at the top of the bluff, just past the park entrance, or from the back of the picnic area. The 3-mi route loops along the river bank and the tops of the bluffs, providing many fine views of the river. The route is unblazed, but easy to follow. It is moderate in difficulty with several ascents and descents that are somewhat steep but none that are terribly long.

canoeing/kayaking: The Flint is a nice paddling river, most popular with canoeists, and Sprewell Bluff is the put-in for a 5-mi float to the Flint River Outdoor Center at the GA-36 crossing. 3 lively Class-II rapids are scattered through a run predominated by simple ledges. The river winds beneath high bluffs, all part of the Pine Mtn range, and is very scenic, although any decent rain will turn the water red. Other floats are possible, but access points are private. The Flint River Outdoor Center (706/647-2633) charges $3/vehicle for parking and $1/canoe to take out a boat. They also offer shuttles and rental canoes for a variety of Flint River trips, plus camping, which is not permitted in the park.

lodging: The Mountain Top Inn (800/544-6376) sets atop Pine Mtn near the mid-point of the *Pine Mtn Trail* and offers lodge rooms, cottages and chalets. Many units have hot tubs and rocking chair porches with views off the edge of the mountain. Rooms cost $55–125/night. Cabins and Chalets cost $85–145/night.

Panola Mountain State Conservation Park

Panola Mountain, an undisturbed granite monadnock that rises 220 feet above the surrounding Piedmont landscape, is the centerpiece of 766-acre Panola Mountain State Conservation Park. A designated National Natural Landmark, the mountain and much of the forest around it is included in a nature preserve that is open to the public only on guided tours. A 3.5-mile trail through the nature preserve accesses the mountain, and ranger-led hikes are offered regularly. This portion of the park is also used for scientific research. The part open to the public includes 2 nature trails, a fitness trail and a large picnic area in a fairly open mixed forest of pines and hardwoods. Having vast fields and forests on the edge of the Atlanta metro area, Panola Mountain attracts a good variety of songbirds. The park is open for day-use only.

Snapfinger (N) is the nearest town.

contact: Superintendent, Panola Mountain State Conservation Park, 2600 Highway 155 SW, Stockbridge, GA 30281; 770/389-7801; www.gastateparks.org

getting there: From the jct of I-20 and I-285 on the E side of Atlanta drive E on I-20 1.8 mi to Exit 36 (Wesley Chapel Rd/Snapfinger Rd). Turn R at the bottom of the ramp and then L at the first light onto Snapfinger Rd. Drive 7.1 mi to the park entrance on the L.

topography: Part of the park consists of gentle Piedmont terrain, but Panola Mountain, a granite monadnock, covers 100 acres. Mixed pine/hardwood forests are found throughout the park, except on the mtn, which supports only scattered trees various lichen communities. Elevations are approximately 900 ft. **maps:** USGS Stockbridge, Redan, Kelleytown.

starting out: The park office and nature center, open 9 AM to 5 PM Tu–F and 12 to 5 PM on weekends, has nice interpretive displays. Maps and information are available. There are restrooms, a water fountain and drink machines. The park is open 7 AM to dark.

Pets must be on a leash and are not permitted on park trails. All intoxicants are prohibited.

activities: Hiking.

hiking: The moderate to strenuous Panola Mtn hike is 3.5 mi long, with roughly 1 mi of that on the mountain. The interpretive journey, which begins with a slide show and includes several stops along the way, provides a close-up look at rock outcrop communities and great overviews from the mountain. Mountain hikes are generally available Tu–Su at 2:30 PM from Labor Day through Memorial Day and at 10 AM from Memorial Day through Labor Day. Hikes require a minimum of 5 participants but are limited to 25 and are contingent on favorable weather and park staff availability. Reservations must be made at least 24 hours in advance. Special hikes can also be arranged for organized groups. The mountain hike takes 2.5 to 3 hours and is not recommended for kids under 8 years old.

The publicly accessible potion of the park has 2 nature trails, the 0.75-mi *Rock Outcrop Trail* and the 1.25-mi *Microwatershed Trail*. The *Rock Outcrop Trail* begins in a pine-dominated forest, moves through a stand of mix hardwoods, and then climbs across the edge of a rock outcrop, providing a glimpse of the type habitat that is atop Panola Mtn, plus views of both Panola Mtn and Stone Mtn. There are interpretive signs along the route. The *Microwatershed Trail* cuts across a network of spring creeks and erosion ditches, which join to form the head of a small stream. Both trails are easy to moderate and easy to follow, beginning and ending at the nature center. Neither trail is blazed, but the *Microwatershed Trail* is marked with occasional yellow directional arrows on signs or trees. The park also has a 1-mi fitness trail.

Indian Springs State Park

The mineral spring at Indian Spring State Park has been open to the public since 1825, making this the oldest state park in the nation. Georgia's official state park system was developed in 1926 with the official creation of Indian Springs and Vogel parks. The springs and their reported healing waters supported several thriving resorts in the mid 1800s, and visitors can still step into the old springhouse and get a cup or a jug of the "healing waters." The park covers 523 acres that surround 105-acre Chief McIntosh Lake, named for the Indian chief who led the signing of a treaty that resulted in state ownership of the springs. Backcountry opportunities are minimal at Indian Springs, but fishing, camping and hiking are possible. The park is popular with picnickers, especially during the summer, and has a swimming beach, miniature golf course and museum that focuses on the history of the springs, the Creek Indians, the resorts, and Civilian Conservation Corps involvement in the development of the park. The park also has a large group camp with cottages, dorms, a craft building and a dining hall. Deer are abundant.

Jackson (NW) is the nearest town.

contact: Superintendent, Indian Springs State Park, 678 Lake Clark Road, Flovilla, GA 30216; (770) 503-227; www.gastateparks.org.

getting there: From Jackson, Drive S on GA-42 5.8 mi to the hamlet of Flovilla and the park entrance on the R.

topography: The park consists of gentle Piedmont terrain around a 105-acre lake. Forests are mixed, with pines predominant. **maps:** USGS Indian Springs, Jackson.

starting out: The park office, housed in an early 20th Century, two story New South style home, is open 8 AM to 5 PM, with longer afternoon hours in the summer. The office may be closed for lunch from 12 to 1 PM. Maps and information are available. A pay phone is located outside. Restrooms are located in picnic areas, near the spring and at the swimming beach. The park is open daily 7 AM to 10 PM.

Pets must be on a leash throughout the park and are prohibited in the cottage area. Alcoholic beverages are prohibited in all pubic-use areas.

activities: Camping, Fishing, Hiking.

camping: A developed campground, divided into 2 areas, includes 91 sites, each with picnic table, grill and tent pad, plus water and electricity. Sites, built with landscaping ties and poured dirt and pea-gravel, are small to medium-sized, with average isolation. The forest is mixed, but pines are dominant. Portions of the campground are very flat; others are more rolling. Some sites toward the backs of the loops look over the lake. Camping costs $12/night for tents or $14/night for RVs. Senior citizens get a 20 percent discount. The campground is open year round.

The pioneer camping area includes 4 group-type sites, each with pit toilets, a fire ring and picnic tables. The pioneer campsites are close together in a forest opening, with little isolation from one another. Pioneer camping costs $1/person, with a $15 nightly minimum.

fishing: Most fishing is done on 105-acre Chief McIntosh Lake, although limited fishing is possible in a short stretch of creek on park property, downstream of the lake. The lake and creek have bass, bream and catfish. The lake has a boat ramp, and private boats are allowed, with a 10 hp limit. Fishing boats can be rented for $4/hour, $10 for 4 hours or $14 for 8 hours. All boats must be off the lake by dark. The lake's shores are wooded, but the woods are quite open so bank-fishing access is good.

hiking: Though the park has only a single short trail, the 0.75-mi *Overland Nature Trail* is a great hike, winding through one the oldest forests in middle Georgia. The Creek Indians considered the springs and some areas around them sacred, and much of this forest has never been logged. Some oaks along the trail are more than 200 years old, but there are also big pines, hickories, beeches and one massive tulip poplar. The trail is yellow-blazed, and direction signs are also posted at several turns, making the trail easy to follow. Although a few climbs are moderate, the hike is generally easy. Interpretive stops, to be matched to a brochure that will be available at the visitor center, are being developed.

lodging: 10 2-bedroom cottages are nicely situated along a peninsula, with a few right on the water. The cottages have wood siding exteriors and paneled interiors, giving them a natural appearance. They are fully furnished, including a fireplace, television, microwave, heating and air. Cottages cost $60–75/night. A 2-day minimum stay is required for reservations. Cottages can be rented for one night on an as-available basis. For reservations, call 800/864-7275.

High Falls State Park

High Falls, which is a series of steep shoals, rather than a sheer drop, is nonetheless extremely impressive, plummeting more than 100 feet, with much of the fall contained in a single large and powerful slide. Upstream of the falls, the Towaliga River is spanned by GA-18 and impounded by High Falls Lake. Downstream, the river flattens out. High Falls State Park covers 980 acres of land, plus 650 acres of water. The park's land area surrounds the lower end of the lake and roughly 2 miles of river. The area around the falls, known as Unionville in the early 1800s and High Falls or High Shoals today, has long been a center of activity in this part of Georgia. The power of the river has been harnessed to power various plants and mills through the years. The old dam sluice and ruins from various mill and powerhouse buildings remain along the river. The park provides good fishing and nice opportunities for hiking, and has a large developed campground. Picnicking is popular around the lake, where there is also a swimming pool and miniature golf course. Deer and turkeys, plus various wading birds, are common wildlife species. Jackson (NE) is the nearest town.

contact: Superintendent, High Falls State Park, 75 High Falls Park Drive, Jackson, GA 30233; 912/933-3053; www.gastateparks.org.

getting there: From I-75, 40 mi S of Atlanta, take Exit 60, (GA-18), and drive E 2 mi to the park, which is on both sides of the road. The park office is just inside the first entrance on the L.

topography: Except around the falls, where the river drops dramatically more than 100 ft and creates a bit of a gorge, the park is made up of gentle Piedmont terrain with mixed forests of pines and hardwoods. The Towaliga River and the lake that impounds it are the area's defining features. **maps:** USGS High Falls

starting out: The park office, which doubles as a visitor center, is open 8 AM to 10 PM daily, except M–Tu from Oct to Apr, when it closes at 5 PM. Maps and information are available inside. Restrooms and a pay phone are located at the picnic area, across the river from the office.

Alcoholic beverages are prohibited in public areas. Pets must be on a leash of 6 ft or less.

activities: Fishing, Hiking, Camping.

fishing: Although park lands border only the lower end of 650-acre High Falls Lake, they provide a fair amount of shoreline for anglers to fish from, plus an access point to fish the entire lake by boat. The lake is quite varied in its offerings to anglers, with the bass, bream, crappie and channel catfish that are common in most Georgia lakes, plus big flathead catfish and hybrid bass. The lake has a 10-horsepower maximum, and all boats must be off the water by dark. Fishing boats and canoes are available for $4/hour, $20 for 4 hours or $14 for 8 hours. Some anglers also work the banks of the Towaliga River, downstream of the falls, fishing some for bass but mostly for catfish. The park has a small gravel parking area and bank-fishing access along the river.

hiking: Many park visitors use only the first portion of 2 trails to access overviews of the falls, but 3 different trails at High Falls cover more than 4 mi and provide good opportunities for day hikes. The *Falls Trail*, as its name suggests, leads to several good views of High Falls from the river's E bank and then loops back, just up the ridge from the river. The *History Trail*, across the river from the *Falls Trail*, leads to another good overview of the waterfall and goes past the mill sluice and the powerhouse ruins. The *Non-Game Nature Trail*, a 2.5 mi loop, circles though a fairly dense, mixed Piedmont forest. All trails are accessible near the park's entrance. The *Falls Trail* is sporadically blazed, and both white and yellow blazes can be found. Along the way there are many signs warning to stay behind fences and away from the falls. The *History Trail* is unblazed but signed at its trailhead. The *Non-Game Nature Trail* is well marked with double yellow blazes. All trails are well beaten and generally easy to follow and easy to moderate in difficulty.

camping: The park's 102 campsites are split into 2 areas, but only 23 of the sites are in camping area 2, which is on High Falls Lake. Of those sites, only a handful are lakefront, but all are convenient to the water. The forest of mixed pines and hardwoods is fairly open in camping area 2, providing only average isolation. 99 sties are located in camping area 1, a nice, heavily wooded area along the Towaliga River that is well isolated from the rest of the park and protected by a combination-coded gate. 13 of those sites are on the river. Each site has a picnic table, lantern post, tent pad and fire ring/grill, plus water and electricity. Restrooms have hot showers and flush toilets, plus laundry facilities. Camping is available year round, although area 2 may be closed seasonally, according to use. Sites cost $14/night, except prime sites (mostly those on the water), which cost $17/night.

A pioneer camp, also well isolated from the park's day-use areas, has picnic tables, water and electricity. The pioneer camp costs $40/night and can accommodate 24 people.

Fort Yargo State Park

Named for a well-preserved log blockhouse built in 1792 to protect settlers against Creek and Cherokee Indians, Fort Yargo State Park covers 1,850 acres and centers around a 260-acre lake, Marbury Creek Watershed. The park is quite developed, with a campground, numerous picnic areas, cottages, and the Will-A-Way Recreation Area, an extensive day-use area and group camp specially designed for used by persons with disabilities. Despite the development, the park's natural offerings are very nice, between the lake, the marshy backwaters at the head of the lake, and the mixed pine and hardwood forest that covers most of the park. Good opportunities exist for hiking, fishing and camping, and mountain biking is permitted on some of the park's trails. Beyond the deer, turkeys, songbirds and squirrels that are common in Piedmont forests, the park provides a home to marsh wildlife, including wading birds, beavers, bullfrogs and raccoons.

Winder (N) is the closest town.

contact: Superintendent, P.O. Box 764, Winder, GA 30680; 770/867-3489; www.gastateparks.org.

getting there: The main entrance to Fort Yargo SP is within the Winder city limits. From the jct of GA-53 and GA-81 in town, drive S 0.8 mi to the park entrance on the L. Entrances B and C, which access other parts of the park and are not connected by internal roads, are 2.0 and 2.9 mi, respectively, from the same point.

topography: The Piedmont terrain through this park is very gentle and most of the land is quite flat. Marbury Creek and the lake that backs it up are the main defining features. Mixed forests are generally dominated by pines, except around creek bottoms, where oaks are prevalent. **maps:** USGS Winder South.

starting out: The park office, located just inside the main entrance, doubles as a visitor center and is open 8 AM to 5 PM daily. Information and maps are available, along with restrooms, a water fountain, pay phone and drink machine. The park also has a nature center in the Will-A-Way Rec Area, open on Saturdays from 1 PM to 5 PM.

Swimming is permitted only at the designated beach. Alcoholic beverages are not permitted in public areas. Pets must be on a leash.

activities: Fishing, Camping, Hiking/Mountain Biking.

fishing: Crappie are the main attraction with local anglers, but

Marbury Creek Watershed also supports a good population of bass, bream and catfish. Fishing is popular from the banks and from boats, with most crappie fishermen choosing to work from the banks. Good shoreline access is available within the day-use part of Will-A-Way, in an established fishing area along an elongated point, and around the boat ramps and footbridge at Parking Area B. Bank-fishing is permitted from 7 AM to 9:45 PM; boating is permitted from 7 AM to sunset. No boat motor over 10 horsepower may be operated. Only rod and reel fishing is permitted. Rental boats are also available, and rates range from $3 for 1 hour in a canoe or fishing boat rental to $35 for 8 hours in a jonboat with a motor.

camping: 40 car camping sites on 2 loops are generally small, but a young mixed forest with dense undergrowth helps provide good privacy. Some sites are waterfront. Each site has a picnic table and grill, plus water and electricity. Restrooms for both loops have flush toilets and hot showers, plus pay phones outside. 7 walk-in sites on a wooded peninsula near the back of the second loop have a picnic table, tent pad and grill. The walk is quite short from the parking area. Campground restrooms are convenient. Drive-in sites cost $10/night for tents; $12/night for RVs. Walk-in sites cost $8/night. The campground is open year round.

A pioneer camping area, nicely isolated from other park activity, sets in a wooded bottom with all undergrowth cleared. The area has 3-sided concrete shelters, a picnic shelter and gill, a large fire ring, running water, pit toilets and posts for playing horseshoes. The camp costs $20/night for up to 20 people, plus $1 per extra person, up to $50. There's no official maximum group size. Reservations should be made through the park office.

hiking/mountain biking: 3 trails, the *Bird Berry*, *Woodfern* and *Old Fort* trails provide nice opportunities for easy day hikes in Fort Yargo SP, and mountain bikes are permitted on the *Woodfern* and *Old Fort* trails. *Bird Berry* is a 0.5-mi nature trail that begins beside the lake cuts through a nice section of marsh. It has interpretive signs showing common plants and animals, plus benches for wildlife observation. The trail is unmarked, except at its trailhead, but easy to follow, because it is paved. *Wood Fern* and *Old Fort* trails both follow the lakeshore over closed roads, with the *Wood Fern Trail* being the longest route in the park at 2.6 mi, and the *Old Fort Trail*, a 1 mi route, leading to Fort Yargo, as its name suggests. The trails are not blazed but marked with occasional color-coded posts. *Wood Fern* is red. *Old Fort* is blue.

Both trails are easy to walk or ride and easy to follow. A fourth trail, the *Pine Beetle Loop*, is listed in the park's trail brochure, but the trail amounts to little more than a short, connecting path between picnic areas in an open pine forest. The trail shows pine beetle damage, but the same can be seen from a car in many places through the park.

lodging: 3 cottages, built fully accessible as part of the Will-A-Way Rec Area, set together in a mature pine forest within sight of the lake. The cottages, natural in appearance with brown wood siding, have fireplaces and are fully furnished, including linens and cookware. They have 2 bedrooms, each with 2 double beds, a shower and 2 half baths. Cottages cost $55/night, Su–Th; $65/night, F–Sa. For senior citizens and persons with disabilities, the rate is $40/night, all nights. A 2-day minimum stay applies, but 1-night stays are granted, according to availability, on a day-by-day basis, with a $15 surcharge. For reservations, call 800/864-7275.

Hard Labor Creek State Park

The hard labor of Civilian Conservation Corps workers in the 1930s—building dikes, planting pines, constructing roads and clearing lake bottoms—created what today is Hard Labor State Park out of what was once very marginal farmland, but the creek's name far precedes those efforts and was assigned by the indians. Despite being one of Georgia's largest state parks at 5,805 acres, Hard Labor Creek offers only modest appeal to backcountry travelers. A golf course, 22 miles of horse trails, and two huge group camp facilities, each complete with a dining hall and sleeping cabins, take up a lot of the land. The park does have two nice lakes, Brantley and Rutledge, which provide good opportunities for fishing. Hiking trails, though limited, are also quite nice. Car camping and pioneer camping are both available. The park supports a large deer herd, along with plenty of wild turkeys. Beavers make good use of the upper end of Lake Brantley, and their work creates good habitat for wading birds and other marsh critters. Picnic areas in the park include both individual tables and group shelters, plus a large barbecue grill.

Rutledge (S) is the nearest town.

contact: Superintendent, Hard Labor Creek State Park, P.O. box 247, Rutledge, GA 30663; 706/557-3001; www.gastateparks.org.

getting there: From I-20, take Exit 49 (Newborn Rd) and drive N 2.4 mi to Rutledge. In Rutledge, follow signs through a L, R and L turn, all within a quarter mi, and then drive 0.9 mi into the park's main entrance.

topography: The Piedmont terrain is rolling through the park and covered with mixed forests that are dominated by pines, except in creek bottoms, where hardwoods are prevalent. Lakes Brantley and Rutledge are the two most significant features, and both are on Hard Labor Creek, which flows E toward the Apalachee River and then the Oconee River. **maps:** USGS Rutledge North.

starting out: The park office and trading post, which also serves as a visitor center, is officially open 8 AM to 5 PM daily, but typically the office stays open much later through the summer and fall. Information and maps are available, and there is a pay phone outside. Restrooms are located near the picnic area.

No alcoholic beverages are permitted in public areas. Pets must be on a leash.

activities: Fishing, Camping, Hiking.

fishing: Bass, catfish, bluegills and shellcrackers are stocked into lakes Brantley and Rutledge, and Lake Rutledge, the larger of the 2 lakes at 275 acres, also supports a good crappie population. Both lakes can be fished from the bank or by boat, but only Lake Rutledge has a boat ramp on it. Banks of both lakes are steep and heavily wooded in places, but both have plenty of room for shoreline anglers to work from. Bank fishing is permitted from 7 AM to 10 PM. Boating is permitted from 7 AM to sunset. A 10-horsepower motor restriction applies. Canoes and fishing boats are available for rent in the park. Boats cost $5 for 1 hour, $10 for 4 hours or $15 for 8 hours.

camping: 51 campsites are generally large but vary considerably in setting and in the amount of privacy they offer. Some are nicely isolated from one another in densely wooded areas while others are in much more open piney woods. Some also set over either Lake Brantley's main body or a beaver pond on a small feeder creek near the lake's headwaters. All sites have a tend pad, lantern post, fire ring/grill and picnic table. 4 restrooms have hot showers and flush toilets, and laundry facilities are available at 2 of those. Sites cost $14/night for tents and $16/night for RVs. The campground is open year round.

4 pioneer camps, each consisting of a clearing, pit toilets, picnic tables and basic open shelters, are available to groups. No water is available. Pioneer camps cost $15/night for up to 15 people, plus $1/person extra, up to $25. Pioneer camp reservations should be made through the park office.

hiking: Two interconnected loops, the *Lake Brantley Trail* and the *Beaver Pond Trail*, cover 2.5 mi, beginning near the entrance to the park campground. Defying its name, the *Lake Brantley Trail* never comes within site of the lake, but it's a beautiful hike through a fairly steep-sided hardwood bottom. The *Beaver Pond Trail* is listed as 1.5 mi long, but because it is accessed from the other trail, halfway through the loop, the hike takes in the entire 2.5 mi of trail. The trails are generally easy to follow, with footbridges at crossings and signs at major junctures, although blazes become quite infrequent on the back side of the *Lake Brantley Trail*. Grades are moderate.

lodging: 20 cabins sort of form a village in a hilly, forested area of the park, and some set directly up the hill from Lake Brantley. Natural in appearance with brown wood siding, the cottages have rocking chair screen porches, and most have fireplaces. All cottages are fully furnished, including linens and cookware, and have heat and air conditioning. Cottages cost $65–80/night, depending on season and day of week. A 2-night minimum (longer during peak periods) applies to reservations but 1-night stays are permitted on an as-available basis. For reservations, call 800/864-7275.

Oconee National Forest

A patchwork of tracts along the Ocmulgee, Little and Oconee rivers, the Oconee National Forest covers roughly 115,500 acres in eight Piedmont counties. The forest, made up of both planted pine stands and mixed pine/hardwood forests, is intermingled with private timberlands and rural communities. Significant backcountry is scarce, as road systems are extensive. Streams that drain the national forest range from tiny creeks to fairly large rivers, and portions of the forest border two large impoundments on the Oconee River, Lake Oconee and Lake Sinclair. Fishing is very popular on the lakes, which cover 19,050 acres and 14,750 acres, respectively. Hunting is easily the most popular recreational use of the forest itself. Camping is permitted almost everywhere in the national forest, and trails provide opportunities for hiking. The forest's larger rivers lend themselves nicely to paddling. Beyond forest species, like deer and turkeys, waterfowl and wading birds make good use of the rivers and lakes of the Oconee National Forest.

Monticello, Eatonton and Greensboro are all adjacent to portions of the forest.

contact: Oconee National Forest, 1199 Madison Road, Eatonton, GA 31024; 706/485-7110; www.fs.fed.us/conf/.

getting there: GA-15, GA-212, GA-213, GA-83, US-129 and US-279 all crisscross sizable tracts of the NF, but most individual areas are accessed by an extensive network of county and FS roads. The RS is located 6.7 mi N of Eatonton on US-129/441.

topography: The low Piedmont landscape ranges from flat to moderately hilly, with the highpoint in the forest being the top of Burgess Mountain at 654 ft. The Ocmulgee, Little and Oconee rivers, plus the network of smaller streams that feed them and the lakes that impound the Oconee, are the landscape's major defining features. Forests are of mixed pines and hardwoods, planted pines, and hardwood stands in creek and river bottoms. **maps:** See below under individual areas.

starting out: Though maps show the RS in downtown Monticello, a new RS was opened N of Eatonton in late 1998. The RS is open M–F 8 AM to 4:30 PM, plus limited weekend hours during hunting seasons. Annual parking passes, maps, brochures, and other information are available, along with restrooms and a water fountain.

activities: Fishing, Camping, Canoeing/Kayaking, Hiking.

fishing: Most fishing is concentrated on the two major lakes and occurs from boats, with bass, hybrids and crappie the 3 most popular species. Though less popular, the rivers and creeks also offer good prospects and can be fished by floating, walking their banks or wading. The streams, like the lakes, produce good bass fishing, but bream and catfish offer the best prospects in the moving water.

camping: The Oconee NF has only 2 developed campgrounds, but there are more than 20 hunt camps, and backcountry camping is permitted throughout the forest, except where posted. Hunt camps, simply openings in the forest understory established as a service to hunters, are open to anyone and are very lightly used through most of the year.

canoeing/kayaking: The Ocmulgee and Oconee rivers are both large rivers well suited for paddling, especially for canoeing. The rivers are mostly flat, with stretches of Class II whitewater. Surrounding land is a mix of forest and farmland. Strainers present the biggest hazard. Little River and Murder Creek can also be paddled, but both streams are notably smaller than the Ocmulgee and Oconee and dependent on fairly high water.

hiking: 8 Hiking trails in the NF total 14 mi, creating a mix of opportunities for easy hikes along creeks and rivers, through piney woods and hardwood stands, and to select points of interest. Only day-hikes are practical, as the longest route is just 4.5 mi long. All trails are white blazed, marked at their trailheads and easy to walk. Blaze orange clothing is advisable during hunting seasons.

Oconee River Area

Fishing on Lake Oconee is the main attraction through the northern portion of the Oconee National Forest, but good opportunities for backcountry exploration are also available along the river that lends the lake and forest their name and within the forest itself. The flat to gently rolling terrain is mostly wooded with mixed stands of hardwoods and pines, but numerous small creeks form swampy hardwood bottoms. The upper end of the lake, which is the portion that the national forest borders, is generally shallow and is loaded with standing timber. Along the Oconee River, at Scull Shoals, ruins of several buildings from a mill village that hit its heyday in the 1850s remain in surprisingly good condition,

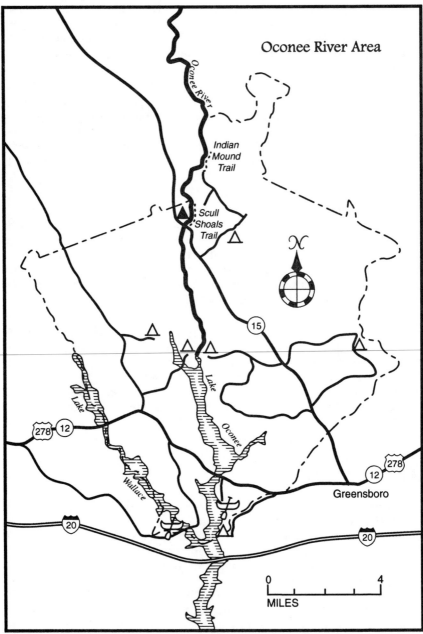

and two hiking trails connect with Scull Shoals.

Though divided by private holdings and extensive road systems, which limits wilderness qualities, this area around the Oconee River has a few nice hiking trails and plenty of room to camp. The river, meanwhile, is a fine stream to paddle and offers good prospects for fishing. Beyond deer and turkeys and other typical forest species, wetland wildlife species, like waterfowl and wading birds, can be spotted on the river and its feeders, on Lake Oconee, and especially in the Dyer Pasture area, where an observation deck overlooks a 60-acre waterfowl impoundment. Lake Oconee RA and two boating access points on Lake Oconee also have picnic areas.

Greensboro (SE) is the nearest town.

getting there: US-278 and GA-15, which meet in Greensboro, are the main arteries through the Oconee River area. To access the Oconee River RA from Greensboro, drive NW on GA-15 12.2 mi to the sign for the RA on the R. Turn R and drive 1.0 mi.

topography: The Oconee River and the upper end of Lake Oconee are the defining features of this gentle Piedmont landscape. Forests consist of planted pines, mixed pines and hardwoods and bottomland hardwoods. **maps:** USGS Greshamville, Penfield, Buckhead, Greensboro, Barnett Shoals, Apalachee, Maxeys.

starting out: Pit toilets at the Oconee Rec Area serve campers and day-users. The Dyer Pasture Area also has pit toilets. Information boards are located at scattered points. A $2 daily or $30 annual parking fee is required at the Oconee Rec Area, Scull Shoals Area, Redlands Boat Ramp, Swords Boat Ramp and Dyer Pasture Area.

Pets must be on a leash. Houseboats or other boats with a head or sleeping quarters are not permitted on Lake Oconee.

activities: Fishing, Camping, Canoeing/Kayaking, Hiking.

fishing: Largemouth bass, hybrids and crappie are the most sought-after species on 19,050-acre Lake Oconee, and fishing for all 3 species is good. The lake also supports good numbers of white bass, bream and catfish. While some bank access to the lake is possible, especially around the boat ramps, most fishing is done from boats. Lake Oconee is loaded with flooded timber and free-floating logs are common, so caution while running is essential. Lake Oconee is managed with a slot limit, so all bass under 6 inches or between 11 and 14 inches long must be released.

The Oconee River offers good fishing for bass in its far lower reaches, catfish in its slack holes and bream pretty much anywhere along its banks. White bass also run up the river in the spring. Because the banks are heavily forested and the river is generally too swift and deep to wade, most fishing is done from either jonboats or canoes. Scattered small streams offer limited wade-fishing, but access is limited to bridge crossings, and private holdings limit the distance fishermen can travel up or down most of these streams.

camping: The campground at the Oconee River RA is small and simple, with 5 medium-sized, nicely spaced sites, each tucked in the woods, along a loop just up the bank from the river. Each site has a picnic table, lantern post and fire ring/grill. The campground has a pump for water and pit toilets. Camping costs $5/night. The campground is open year-round.

Backcountry camping is permitted throughout the NF, except where posted as prohibited; areas having such restrictions include the Oconee River RA outside of designated campsites and the 2 boat ramps. 6 hunt camps, which are basically just clearings in the forest understory with space available for parking, are scattered through the district, with one at Dyer Pasture, which is also the best take-out for canoeing/kayaking.

canoeing/kayaking: A large river, the Oconee is a nice stream to paddle, and canoeing is the most popular form of boating. The river cuts through a mix of forest and farmland and is quite scenic, except that it turns muddy very quickly when it rains and stays dirty for several days after. The river is mostly flat, with a couple borderline Class II shoals. Strainers present the biggest potential hazard, as currents are fairly swift, but the river is large enough that most trees can be avoided. Access is good at the Oconee River RA and at Dyer Pasture, approximately 6 mi apart.

hiking: 3 trails along the Oconee River all lead to historical areas, as evidenced by their names: the *Scull Shoals Trail*, the *Boarding House Trail* and the *Indian Mounds Trail*. The trails are short, with Boarding House only 0.2 mi long and the other 2 each 1 mi long, but they are close enough to one another that all could be hiked in a single day. All 3 trails follow flat terrain and are easy to walk. However, in places the eroded banks of the Oconee River leave the *Scull Shoals Trail*, which runs directly riverside, somewhat narrow. The trails are lightly traveled, but frequent white blazes make them easy to follow. Footbridges are provided where needed. The *Scull Shoals Trail* leads from the Oconee River RA to Scull Shoals, the *Boarding House Trail* begins as Scull Shoals, and the *Indian Mounds Trail* begins at the end of FS-1231A, less than 2 mi from Scull Shoals.

Ocmulgee River Area

Tumbling through strings of shoals, with steep banks surrounding it, the Ocmulgee River resembles a large mountain stream in places. The shoals are modest, however, and just upstream and downstream, the same stream will flow lazily for long stretches between flat pine forests. It is a pretty river throughout, running through mostly forested land in this area and retaining clear water more often than most other Piedmont streams of its size. The national forest in this area is made up of numerous tracts, which are separated primarily by private timberlands. Except along the river itself, a nice stream for floating and fishing, opportunities for backcountry travel are fairly limited. A few trails provide opportunities for hiking in this part of the forest, and backcountry camping is permitted almost everywhere. The most southerly tract of the Oconee National Forest, which fronts the river and is surrounded by the Piedmont National Wildlife Refuge, makes up the Hitchiti Experimental Forest, where an assortment of very specific forestry practices are used on individual plots for experimentation and demonstration purposes. White-tailed deer and wild turkeys are abundant throughout the national forest, and waterfowl and wading birds are apt to be seen along the river.

Monticello (NE) is the nearest town.

getting there: GA-83 out of Monticello runs NE to SW 13.8 mi to the Ocmulgee River and splits this portion of the forest. A network of county and forest service roads provide direct access to individual areas.

topography: Terrain is flat to gently rolling, and forests are of mixed pines and hardwoods and of planted pines. Hardwoods are prevalent along creek and river drainages. The Ocmulgee River, which runs N to S along the western border of the area, is the landscape's main defining feature. **maps:** USGS Hillsboro, Berner, Lloyd Shoals Dam, Monticello, Dames Ferry.

starting out: Except for parking areas at trailheads, information boards and undeveloped hunt camps, there are no facilities in this part of the forest. Likewise no fees are required.

Pets must be on a leash. Some roads in the Hitchiti Experimental Forest are closed to public use.

activities: Canoeing/Kayaking, Camping, Fishing, Hiking.

canoeing/kayaking: The Ocmulgee River is the most popular paddling destination on the Oconee NF, and for good reason. Along with being very scenic, it is easy to paddle, with no major obstacles, and floatable at any river level. Scattered shoals, none exceeding borderline Class II ratings, are just lively enough to add to the already nice scenery, along with providing a bit of extra paddling fun. There are 3 popular access points for floating this part of the Ocmulgee, although only the middle access, Wise Creek, is actually part of the NF. The upper access point is on the river's E bank, just downstream of Lake Jackson and accessible off GA-16. The lower access is at the GA-83 bridge, 13.8 mi from Monticello on the L. From the dam access to Wise Creek is roughly 5.5 mi. From Wise Creek to GA-83 is 8 mi. Overnight trips are possible, as most of the land along the river's E bank from Wise Creek downstream is owned by the USFS and open to camping.

camping: Backcountry camping is permitted throughout the NF. There are no developed campgrounds in this area, but 8 hunt camps offer convenient sites to set up camp. The hunt camps, which are simply clearings with established parking areas, are lightly used outside of fall hunting seasons, and most have fire rings already in place from past campers.

fishing: Only the Ocmulgee River is large enough to provide significant opportunities for fishing on this part of the NF. Its offerings are very good, however, especially for largemouth bass and for catfish. While power boats can go a short distance in either direction from the GA-83 ramp, most fishing is done via one-way floats by canoe or jonboat. Bank-fishing areas that can be accessed by car are limited, but catfishermen will often use a boat to find a good hole, and then set up to fish overnight from the banks.

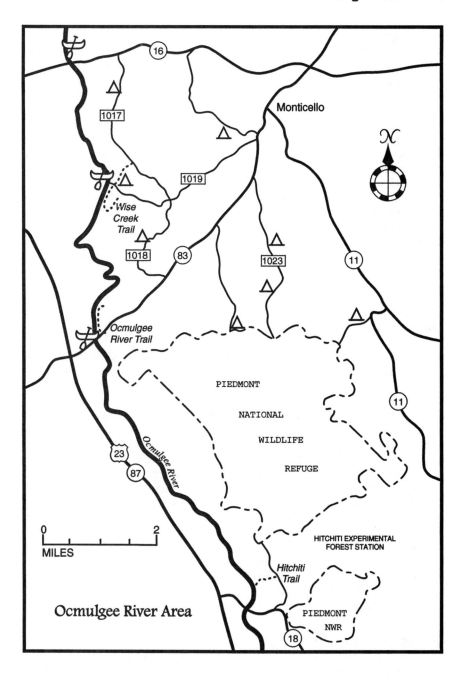

Ocmulgee River Area

hiking: 3 hiking trails in the Ocmulgee River area, all close to the river, total 9.5 mi. The 2.5-mi *Ocmulgee River Trail* and 4.5-mi *Wise Creek Trail* both wind along the river through flat piney woods and hardwood bottoms upstream of the GA-83 bridge. The *Ocmulgee River Trail* begins at the Ocmulgee Flats Hunt Camp. The *Wise Creek Trail* begins at the Wise Creek Hunt Camp. The *Hitchiti Nature Trail* follows Falling Creek, a tumbling tributary, 2.5 mi down to the Ocmulgee within the Hitchiti Experimental Forest. Numbered signs along the route correspond to an interpretive brochure. From Macon, drive N on US-23 16 mi to GA-18 and turn R. Drive 3 mi to Juliette Rd and turn L. Drive 1 mi to Jarrell Plantation Rd. The trailhead is on Jarrell Plantation Rd, at the jct, and is marked with a brown sign. A parking area is directly across the road. All trails are marked at their trailheads, white blazed and easy to walk. Like many trails on the Oconee NF, however, they get light use overall and can be difficult to follow in places.

Lake Sinclair Area

While only a single tract of the Oconee National Forest borders 15,330-acre Lake Sinclair itself, that tract contains the most popular and most developed recreation area in the national forest. Making Sinclair even more of a focal point in the national forest, all the creeks and rivers that drain its southeastern section flow toward the lake. Most recreational activity, other than hunting, is concentrated around the Lake Sinclair Recreational Area and to a lesser extent the Hillsboro Lake area. Open seasonally, Lake Sinclair has a large campground, hiking trail, boat ramp, picnic area and swimming beach. Hillsboro Lake, a small, remote lake, has numerous picnic tables and a handful of campsites around it. Most of the forest in the Lake Sinclair area is lightly traveled, but numerous county and forest service roads provide good access for folks who do want to explore. Fishing is popular on the lake and possible on several streams, and paddling is sometimes possible on the Little River. Camping is permitted throughout the forest, and 2 trails provide limited opportunity for hiking.

Eatonton (E) is the nearest town.

getting there: US-129 runs N to S out of Eatonton and borders most of this area to the E, but runs just W of the Lake Sinclair Rec Area. From Eatonton, drive S 9.8 mi to GA-212 and turn L. Drive 0.9 mi

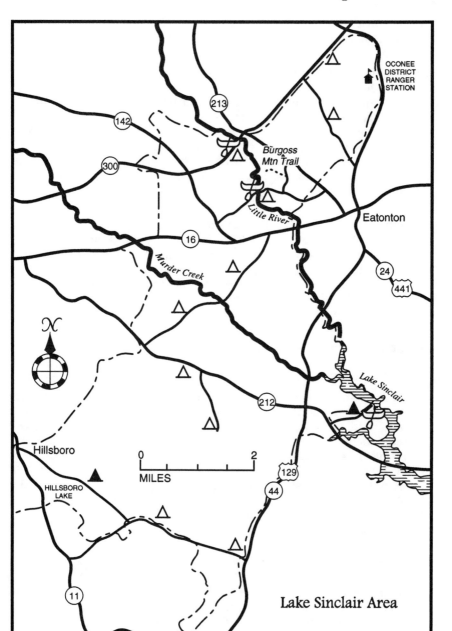

OCONEE
DISTRICT
RANGER
STATION

Burgoss
Mtn Trail

Little River

Eatonton

Murder Creek

Lake Sinclair

Hillsboro

HILLSBORO
LAKE

0   2
MILES

Lake Sinclair Area

and turn L on Double Bridge Rd. Drive 1.2 mi to the area entrance on the L. All turns are marked with signs.

topography: Little River, Murder Creek and Big Cedar Creek, along with the network of streams that feed them, all of which flow into Lake Sinclair define this area of the Oconee NF. This area contains the highest point in the Oconee NF, 645-ft Burgess Mtn, but all slopes are still quite modest and much of the forest is flat. Forest types include planted pines, mixed pine/hardwood stands and hardwood forests. **maps:** USGS Stanfordville, Resseaus Crossing, Eatonton, Smithboro, Rock Eagle Lake, Shady Dale, Hancock, Gray, Hillsboro.

starting out: The only facilities in the district are at Lake Sinclair Rec Area and Hillsboro Lake. The former has restrooms with flush toilets and water fountains in its day-use area; the latter has only pit toilets. A $2 daily or $30 annual parking pass is required. The Lake Sinclair Rec Area is open from Memorial Day to Labor Day. Hillsboro Lake is open year round.

Pets must be kept on a leash throughout the NF.

activities: Fishing, Camping, Hiking

fishing: Lake Sinclair is a popular fishing lake, especially for largemouth bass, crappie and hybrids. The lake's banks are heavily developed, and boat docks provide important cover for bass and crappie. Hybrids follow baitfish schools in the lake's main body. 2-acre Hillsboro Lake, which has no boat ramp, is primarily a bank-fishing destination, and bream, crappie, bass and catfish can all be caught. Only rod-and-reel fishing is permitted, and fishermen are restricted to 2 poles. Most of the streams that drain this area provide good prospects for bass, bream and/or catfish, with most fishing done from the banks or by wading. Fishing pressure is light in the streams.

camping: The Lake Sinclair Rec Area has the only large, developed campground in the Oconee NF, with 44 sites and bathrooms with flush toilets and hot showers. The sites are split into 3 loops, with a fourth loop reserved for group camping. The name Lake Sinclair is a little deceptive as only a few sites actually back up to or offer decent views of the lake, but most sites are nice and offer decent privacy. The sites have a picnic table, tent pad and some form of grill. Some also have a lantern post and fire ring/grill. Sites cost

$7/night. The group camp, which has no separate facilities but is convenient to the main restrooms, costs $30/night. The entire area is open from Memorial Day to Labor Day. Hillsboro also has 5 small sites, each with a picnic table, fire ring and tent pad, which are set just up the hill from the lake. Pit toilets are available near the picnic area, across the lake. There's no charge for these sites, and the area remains open year round.

Backcountry camping is permitted throughout the NF, except where posted as prohibited, and there are 11 hunt camps in this area. The hunt camps have no facilities, but are simply areas where the forest understory has been cleared to facilitate easy camping.

hiking: 2 hiking trails total just over 2 mi, with most of that mileage along the 1.8-mi *Twin Bridges Trail*, which winds through mixed pines and hardwoods at the Lake Sinclair Rec Area and follows the lakeshore. The other trail is a quarter-mi spur that follows an old road to Burgess Mtn, the highest point in the forest. The trails are white blazed and easy to follow and walk. The *Twin Bridges Trail* has 30 interpretive stops along it, newly developed in 1999. It begins in the campground. The *Burgess Mountain Trail* begins off FS-1120, NW of Eatonton.

Piedmont National Wildlife Refuge

When the Piedmont National Wildlife Refuge was established in 1939 most of the land had been badly over-farmed, and little forestland existed. Today the 35,000-acre refuge has come so far that it is known for its colonies of endangered red-cockaded woodpeckers, which require mature pine stands. Laced with clear creeks, some backed by beaver ponds, and made up of a mix of managed pine forests, bottomland hardwoods and clearings, the refuge supports abundant wildlife, including 200 species of birds confirmed as having been seen. Recreation is a secondary objective on all national wildlife refuges, so much of the refuge contains no hiking access, but 4 trails in the Allison Lake area offer good opportunities for day hikes. Several ponds and small streams offer seasonal fishing on the refuge, and mountain biking is possible on the access roads that course the refuge. Bird-watching is also popular, especially around ponds and the edges of clearings.

Juliette (W) and Round Oak (E) are the closest towns.

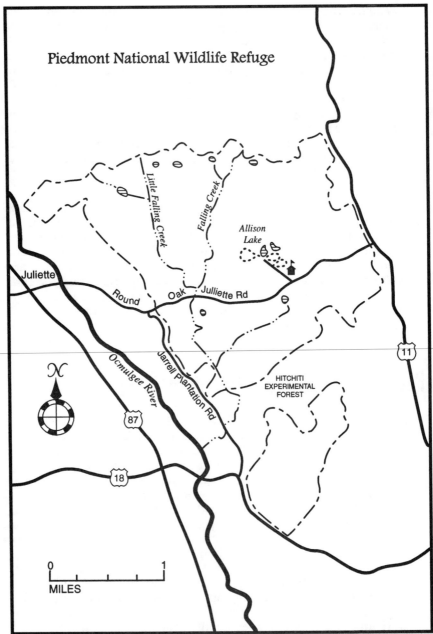

Piedmont National Wildlife Refuge

contact: Piedmont National Wildlife Refuge, Route 1, Box 670, Round Oak, GA 31038; 912/986-5441; www.fws.gov/~r4eao.

getting there: From I-75, take Exit 61 (Juliette Rd) at Forsyth. Drive E on Juliette Rd 18 mi to the sign for the visitor center and Allison Lake Rec Area and turn L.

topography: The lower Piedmont terrain consists of gentle hills divided by clear, rocky streams, all tributaries of the Ocmulgee River. Actively managed pine forests dominate the landscape, but forests along creek bottoms are made up mostly of hardwoods. **maps:** USGS James Ferry, Hillsboro, Gray, Berner, East Juliette, Macon NW.

starting out: The refuge visitor center, open 8 AM to 4:30 PM Monday to Friday, and 9 AM to 5 PM on weekends, has maps, information and several interactive interpretive displays. There are restrooms and a water fountain. The refuge is open daily during daylight hours.

Needlessly disturbing any wildlife species is not permitted on the refuge. Pets must be on a leash and closely supervised. Refuge visitors are advised to use a strong repellent against ticks and chiggers and check themselves regularly for ticks.

activities: Hiking, Fishing, Mountain Biking.

hiking: 4 trials, which total 5 mi, offer a variety of opportunities for day-hikes on the refuge. Each of the trails, which are interconnected, offers a different experience. The *Creek Trail* follows a tiny headwaters stream, the *Pine Trail* runs along a ridge, the *Allison Lake Trail* follows the shores of the lake, and the *Red-Cockaded Woodpecker Trail* winds through the woods to an active woodpecker nesting colony. All trails are easy to follow, with either white blazes or directional arrows on brown posts marking the way. Most trails are easy, with scattered moderate climbs, but the red-cockaded woodpecker trail has strenuous sections. Trailheads, at the visitor center and Allison Lake Rec Area, are clearly marked. A map, which is available in the visitor center, shows all trail routes.

fishing: Half a dozen ponds and a network of small streams provide opportunities for fishing on the refuge from May 1 to Sep 30. Ponds and streams contain natural populations of bass, bream and catfish. Streams are quite small and lend themselves best to wading. Most fishing takes place in ponds. The ponds are generally shallow and have a good mix of vegetation and downed trees to provide cover. Boats operated by paddles or electric motors may be put on Allison Lake and pond 2A. Only bank-fishing is permitted around the other ponds. Pond 21A is open to fishing for children only. Some refuge ponds are closed to fishing. A regulations brochure includes a map that shows which are open. The limit on bass is 5, with a minimum size of 12 inches, on all refuge waters. Minnows or other fish may not be used as bait. Only rod and reel fishing is permitted. Fishermen are required to stay 30 ft from wood duck boxes.

mountain biking: 45 mi of roads that lace the refuge are open for mountain biking. Most roads are gravel and lightly traveled by vehicles. Riding is generally easy, with only modest grades and roads that are suitable for passenger vehicles. Scenery includes a complete cross section of the refuge's forest types, ponds and streams.

Watson Mill Bridge State Park

The 229-foot-long covered bridge that spans the South Fork River and forms the centerpiece of Watson Mills Bridge State Park is Georgia's longest remaining covered bridge. More than 100 years old, the bridge was constructed near the site of Gabriel Watson's grist mill, which operated during the late 1800s but of which no pieces remain. Still visible, however, are the remnants of an old power plant built in 1905. The dam and raceway that were part of the power plant and the millpond formed by the dam are still intact.

Although small, covering just 785 acres, the park has nice trails for short day hikes and a couple different options for campers and for fishermen. Picnic areas are nice, with some by the pond, others in the woods and still others at riverside, and the shoals below the dam combine with the covered bridge to create as pretty a spot as any in Georgia's Piedmont. Deer, turkeys and squirrels, plus ducks around the pond, can all be seen.

Comer (NW) and Carlton (NE) are the nearest towns.

contact: Superintendent, Watson Mill Bridge State Park, Route 1, Box 190, Comer, GA 30629; 706/783-5349; www.gastateparks.org.

getting there: From Comer, drive E on GA-72 4.5 mi to a spur road on the R, which crosses a set of railroad tracks and immediately dead ends at S Railroad Ave. Turn R on the spur road, marked with a brown sign for the park, and R again onto S Railroad Ave, also well marked. The park entrance is 1.5 mi ahead.

topography: Most of the park is fairly flat, but the South Fork River, which defines the park's landscape, plunges over a long set of significant shoals beneath steep banks that enclose the lower end of the shoals. Forests are pine-dominated, although hardwoods become prevalent around the river and a few small creeks that feed it. **maps:** USGS Carlton.

starting out: The park office, which doubles as a visitors center, is typically open daily from 8 AM to 5 PM, but being a small park, Watson Mill Bridge has a small staff, and sometimes the office is closed while the workers are on the grounds. Brochures and maps are available inside. Restrooms are located near the park's N entrance. Caution around the shoals is essential. Signs caution that water levels are subject to rapid rises, that rocks are slippery and that currents are strong.

Pets must be on a leash within the park. No alcoholic beverages are permitted.

activities: Camping, Hiking, Fishing.

camping: 3 pioneer camping areas, each a short walk from any parking area, are available for individuals and for groups. Each pioneer camp has a shelter and water, plus access to pit toilets. All 3 areas are wooded and near Big Clouds Creek, with the largest camp located at its confluence with the South Fork River. Groups may reserve a pioneer camp for $1/person, with a $15 minimum. Primitive camping by individuals is permitted when the areas are not reserved. Cost is $3/night.

Camping is also available in a developed campground, which has 21 medium to large gravel sites. The area is wooded and mostly flat, providing average privacy. Each site has a fire ring, standing grill, picnic table, tent pad, water and electricity. Restrooms have flush toilets and hot showers. Sites cost

$8–10/night for tent campers. The campground is open year round.

hiking: The tumbling shoals of the South Fork River and the ruins of the powerhouse that once harnessed the river's energy are two of the highlights of the network of easy trails that wind through the park. The trails, which total roughly 4 mi, consist of the 1.5-mi *Beaver Creek Trail*, the 0.75 mi *Ridge Loop* and a network of unnamed, interconnected nature trails along the S shore of the river, up the ridge from the river, and along Big Clouds Creek. The trails are unblazed, but easy to follow. The 2 named trails begin at the parking loop just N of the covered bridge. The others can be picked up just S of the bridge, along the spur road to the L that leads to the campground.

fishing: Fishing is possible in the lake's 5-acre mill pond and in the 0.75 mi of river downstream of the dam. Most fishermen target either largemouth bass, channel catfish or bream in the pond, fishing from the easily-walked banks or from rental canoes. Canoe costs range from $5 for one hour to $20 for all day. Coosa redeye bass are the main attraction in the river, which is fairly difficult to fish, whether from the banks or by wading. The shoals are steep, broad and swift, runs downstream are generally deep, and banks are steep and densely wooded. Fishing pressure is light and very localized, but redeyes are abundant.

A.H. Stephens State Historic Park

As its name suggests, A.H. Stephens State Historic Park is first and foremost a historic park, and its primary appeal to many visitors is Liberty Hall, the home of A.H. Stephens, Vice President of the Confederacy and Governor of Georgia during the war. The park's Confederate Museum is said to house one of the best collections of confederate artifacts in Georgia. While the park covers 1,200 acres, those acres house a historic home, a museum, 12 miles of horse trails, a Junior Olympic pool, a picnic area with a barbecue shelter and a vast group camp that has a dining hall, sports fields and several camp cabins. That leaves little room for backcountry travel, but the park does have some offerings for fishing, camping and hiking. Deer are very abundant in the park.

Crawfordville (S) is the nearest town.

contact: Superintendent, A.H. Stephens State Historic Park, P.O. Box 283, Crawfordville, GA 30631; 706/456-2602; www.gastate-parks.org.

getting there: From downtown Crawfordville, Drive N on Commerce St 0.2 mi to a T-intersection and turn L. Drive less than 0.1 mi and turn R into the park. Turns are well-marked with brown state park signs.

topography: The park's lower Piedmont terrain is very gentle. Forests are mixed but dominated by pines. The 3 lakes are all built on tributaries of Little River, which flows toward the Savannah River. **maps:** USGS Crawfordville.

starting out: The park office, which doubles as an visitor center, is open 8 AM to 5 PM daily. The park is open from 7 AM to 10 PM. Brochures and maps are available. The office has restrooms with flush toilets.

Alcoholic beverages are not permitted in public areas. All pets must be on a leash.

activities: Fishing, Camping, Hiking.

fishing: Lake Liberty, behind the park office, is stocked annually with catfish and is open from mid-spring through the end of Oct, at which time it is re-stocked. Fishing is from the banks, which are cleared and mowed, making for easy access. The fishing season kicks off with a kids' fishing derby each spring. The opening day varies.

Lake Buncombe, which covers 18 acres, is managed for bass, bream and crappie, and fishing is good, especially for bass. It sets in a depression and is isolated by woods from the rest of the park, but its immediate banks are mostly cleared, making for easy bank-fishing. A fisherman's trail circles the lake. Aquatic vegetation that grows in the shallow water along the edges makes any sinking lure with exposed hooks impractical to fish from the bank through summer and fall. Private boats are allowed, but only electric motors may be used. The launch area is dirt and very primitive. The park also rents fishing boats for $5/hour, $10 for 4 hours or $15 for 8 hours. Fishing is not permitted on Federal Lake.

camping: The park campground has 25 sites, each with a picnic table, fire ring, stand-up grill, and tend pad, plus water and electricity. The campground is open and flat, with planted grass under a sparse pine stand. Most sites are small and gravel, with little shade or isolation. Restrooms have flush toilets and hot showers. Laundry facilities and a pay phone are in the same area. Sites cost $12–14/night. The campground is open year round.

A pioneer camping area, tucked away in the woods between Federal and Buncombe lakes, can be reserved for a minimum of $20/night, plus $2/person over 30 people.

hiking: 4 nature trails that total 2.6 mi lend themselves to easy walks through the woods but not really to serious hiking. The longest trail in the park, the *Lake Buncombe Trail*, is 1 mi long, running from the lake to the campground. The routes are not blazed but they are easy to follow and well-marked at trailheads. While not prohibited, hiking is discouraged on the horse trails, which are unappealing as footpaths anyway.

Lake Richard B. Russell State Park

Covering 26,500 acres, Lake Richard B. Russell is the second of three major impoundments along the Savannah River. The lake was named for a former Georgia governor and U.S. Senator—the youngest person ever elected to a Senate seat. The state park that bears the same name covers 2,700 acres on a large wooded peninsula between two major creek arms on the lake.

Lake Russell offers excellent fishing, and is a nice big-water paddling destination. Although most popular with vacationers and picnickers, the park also offers limited opportunities for camping, hiking and mountain biking. In addition there are three boat ramps, a disc golf course (played with a flying disc) and facilities for competitive rowing. Opened in 1990, Russell SP is a relatively new park that's still in development. Deer and wild turkeys are both common around the Savannah River lakes; deer especially are commonly seen along park roads and trails.

Elberton (SW) is the nearest town.

contact: Superintendent, Lake Richard B. Russell State Park, 2650 Russell Park Drive, Elberton, GA 30645; 706/213-2045; www.gastateparks.org.

getting there: From the jct of GA-72 and GA-77 in Elberton, drive N on GA-77 1.3 mi to Ruckersville Rd, which slants off to the R. Drive 7.9 mi on Ruckersville Rd to the park entrance on the R.

topography: The park covers most of the peninsula between Coldwater and Van creeks, with a portion of the peninsula fronting Lake Russell's main body. The Piedmont landscape, flat to rolling, is covered by a young but dense forest of mixed hardwoods and pines. Normal lake elevation is approximately 475 ft. **maps:** USGS Rock Branch, Lowdensville.

starting out: The park office, which also serves as a visitors center, is open 8 AM to 5 PM daily, with maps and brochures available inside. A pay phone, drink machine and ice machine are outside. Bathrooms are located in the picnic area near the swimming beach and at the boat ramp.

Pets must be on a leash, and alcoholic beverages are not permitted in public areas.

activities: Fishing, Camping, Hiking/Mountain Biking, Canoeing /Kayaking.

fishing: Largemouth bass and crappie are the main attractions on Lake Russell, and fishing is very good for both. Most bass fishermen work from boats, focusing on stands of flooded timber, on trees fallen into the lake along its shores and on the poles that mark channel edges. Crappie fishing is popular by boat and from the banks. The park offers extensive shoreline access for fishing, and most banks, although wooded, are fairly easy to walk along and fish from. Rental canoes are also available. GA and SC have a reciprocal licensing agreement, so a proper license from either state covers the entire lake, which straddles the state border.

camping: A 28-site developed campground offers the only camping opportunity. The sites are of medium size and generally offer limited privacy, but most are right on the lake, and all are within a few steps of it. The sites are built flat with landscaping ties and poured gravel, and each has a picnic table, double lantern post, fire ring/grill and tent pad, plus water and electricity. Restrooms have hot showers and flush toilets. A pay phone, laundry room, drink machine, private boat ramp, fish-cleaning station and area for parking boat trailers are also available. Sites cost $10–14 /night. The campground is open year round.

hiking/mountain   biking: 158 ft long and 18 ft wide, Brackwell Bridge is the largest remaining steel truss bridge in Elbert County. Built in 1917, the bridge that highlights the 2.2-mi *Brackwell Bridge Trail* has been moved from its original site on nearby Beaverdam Creek. This loop trail, which winds first along the lake shore, then over a narrow cut in the lake via the bridge, and then back through the woods, is by far the park's best path for hiking. It is unblazed but easy to follow, well-marked at its trailhead with a wooden arch, and open only to foot traffic. 3 routes under development, which total 3.4 mi, are being built of gravel and will be open to hikers and bikers. All trails in the park are easy.

canoeing/kayaking: Although fishermen in bass boats sometimes open it up when running from spot to spot, Lake Russell gets very little use by water skiers and other pleasure boaters, even through summer. This, combined with 540 mi of undeveloped shoreline, make it a nice destination for flat-water paddling. The water is clear, and the banks are heavily wooded. Rental canoes are available near the swimming beach for $3/hour, $8/half-day or $12/day

lodging: 10 cottages, all lakeside, provide a nice alternative to camping within the park. Siding that simulates log-cabin construction, big brick chimneys, and screened-in porches give the cottages a nice appearance. Each cottage has two bedrooms and is fully furnished, including everything needed for cooking, a television and a fireplace. Cottages cost $55 to $65/night. Call 800/864-7275 for reservations.

Bobby Brown State Park

Remnants of Petersburg, Georgia's third largest Colonial town in the 1790s, lie flooded under Clark Hill Lake, just down the point of the peninsula that now holds Bobby Brown State Park. The town was long gone by the time the lake was built in the 1950s, but foundational pieces from some of its buildings remain. The park is named in memory of Lt. Robert T. Brown, who gave his life in WW II while serving in the U.S. Navy. The state park covers

665 mostly wooded acres at the confluence of the Broad and Savannah rivers. The lake, which spreads over 78,000 acres, is the park's main attraction, and almost all activity centers around it, even if the activity is sometimes simply a lake-side picnic. Clark Hill Lake is popular with fishermen, and the park offers access both to boating and bank-fishing anglers. The park also offers camping and one trail for hiking, plus several picnic areas. Deer and wild turkeys are abundant.

Elberton (NW) is the nearest town.

contact: Superintendent, Bobby Brown State Park, 2509 Bobby Brown State Park Road, Elberton, GA 30635; www.gastate-parks.org.

getting there: From the jct of GA-17 and GA-72E at the S end of Elberton, Drive E on GA-72 12.5 mi to Bobby Brown Park Rd. Turn R and drive 6.8 mi to the park.

topography: The park covers the tip of the peninsula between the Broad and Savannah rivers along Clark Hill Lake. Most of the park is wooded, with forests of mixed pines and hardwoods most common but some stands of almost all hardwoods. The terrain ranges from flat to hilly, but none of the slopes are long or steep. Normal lake elevation is 330 ft. **maps:** USGS Chennault.

starting out: The park office and camp registration area is open 10 AM to 6 PM M–Tu, and 12 to 8 PM, F–Su. W–Th hours vary. The park itself is open 7 AM to 10 PM daily. The office has park brochures and maps. Restrooms are available near the pool.

No artifacts may be removed from the park or from the town of Petersburg, buried by the lake.

activities: Fishing, Hiking, Camping.

fishing: Striped bass and striped/white bass hybrids are the most talked-about species on Clark Hill, but the lake also offers good fishing for bass, crappie and bream. Most fishing is from boats, especially for stripers and hybrids, which are open-water species. The park does offer limited bank-fishing access, however, and fishermen working from the shores often do well with bream and crappie, especially around trees fallen into the water. Fishermen are allowed to work from the banks throughout the park, but in places the thickness of the woods or the slope of the bank eliminates practical access. One area is designated specifically for bank-fishing, and the park also has a short fishing pier.

hiking: The park's one trail, the 1.9-mi *History Nature Trail*, winds through the forest in places, but also offers good views of the lake, going almost out to the main point of the peninsula. The trail also passes a historical marker that recognizes the old town of Petersburg. When the lake is low, foundations of the town can be seen. The trail is well-trodden and easy to walk, with only modest ups and downs. The trail can be accessed from the day-use area, near the playground and pool, or from the end of the main road through the park.

camping: Two pioneer camping areas have simple structures and pit toilets but no water or electricity. Both areas front the lake on the Broad River side and are separated from other parts of the park. These areas can accommodate up to 100 campers and cost $25/night. Reservations must be made through the park office.

The park also has 2 developed camping areas, which together offer 61 sites. Each area has a restroom with hot showers and flush toilets, plus laundry facilities. All sites have a tent pad, lantern post, fire ring, stand-up grill and picnic table. Sites cost $12 to $14. Area #1, with 22 sites, is heavily forested and somewhat hilly and offers good isolation, despite the sites being small and fairly close together. About half the sites are right on the water. Others set up the hill and offer nice views out over the lake. This area has its own boat ramp and parking area for boat trailers. It is closed from Nov–Mar. Area #2, open year-round, is flatter and set in a more open pine forest. Sites are less isolated and much less attractive. Facilities include a pay phone, playground and fish cleaning station. 8 sites are lakefront.

Mistletoe State Park

Named for Mistletoe Junction, an area locals used to visit in search of abundant mistletoe each Christmas, Mistletoe State Park is set on the banks of Clark Hill Lake, which covers 78,000 acres on the Savannah River. The 1,920-acre park fronts several small creeks and coves on the Little River arm of the lake, providing public access to a long area of shoreline. The majority of the park is wooded and undeveloped, with most facilities for camping and day-use concentrated on a couple major points. Clark Hill Lake provides good fishing, and many campers and cabin-users in the park come to fish the lake. The park also has a good network of hiking trails and nice lakeside picnic area. Deer and wild turkeys are abundant in the park, along with a mix of songbirds. Various ruins from past settlements, ranging from chimneys to grave sites to a moonshine still, are scattered through the park, but no trails lead to specific ruins, and the park does not publicize their whereabouts.

Thomson (SW) and Lincolnton (NW) are the nearest towns.

contact: Superintendent, Mistletoe State Park, Route 1, Box 335, Appling, GA 30802; 706/541-0321; www.gastateparks.org.

getting there: From I-20, just E of Thomson, take Exit 60 (GA-150). Drive E on GA-150 7.2 mi to Mistletoe Rd. Turn L and drive 3 mi to the park entrance. All turns, beginning at the interstate, are well marked.

topography: Flat to gently rolling Piedmont terrain is covered by mixed forests of pines and hardwoods within the park. Normal lake elevation is 330 ft. **maps:** USGS Woodlawn.

starting out: Brochures and maps are available both at a nature center and at the park office, which also handles registration for campsites and cabins. The office is open from 8 AM to 5 PM daily. Nature center hours vary. Public restrooms are available in 3 different picnic areas.

Alcoholic beverages are not permitted in public areas. All dogs must be on a leash of no more than 6 ft.

activities: Fishing, Camping, Hiking.

fishing: Striped bass and striped/white bass hybrids are the most popular species on Clark Hill Lake, but it also offers good fishing for bass, crappie and bream. Most fishing is from boats, especially for stripers and hybrids, which are open-water species. The park does offer bank-fishing access, however, and fishermen working from the shores can do well with bream and crappie, especially around trees fallen into the water. The park actually has a lot of lake frontage, but large areas have no easy access and are difficult to fish from because the banks are steep and the woods are dense.

camping: One backcountry campsite is being established along the *Rock Dam Trail*. Reservations will not be needed, once the site is open, and there will be no charge to camp there. The site will be about 3 mi down the trail.

A pioneer camping area is set in a pine forest opening, where the otherwise dense underbrush has been cleared but trees have been left standing. Just far enough from the road to provide nice isolation, the pioneer camp has a pit toilet and a few picnic tables, but no other facilities. It can accommodate groups of 75 campers. Cost is $15/night for up to 15 people, plus $1/person, up to $25. Pioneer camp reservations must be made through the park office.

The park also has a large developed campground with 102 campsites, most of which are on the lake or within site of it. Because of the campground's size and the fact that it is spread over several loops and spurs, sites vary substantially in their appeal. Some are small and set in flat, open pine forests, offering very little isolation. Others are larger, farther from one another and better isolated by modest hills or by underbrush. All sites, except 4 walk-in sites, have a tent pad, picnic table, fire ring/grill and lantern post, plus water and electricity. 3 bathrooms in the campground have flush toilets and hot showers. The walk-in sites, which require a minimum walk of a couple hundred yards, are simple but very nice. They set on an isolated point, well back in the woods, and a couple are near the end of the point, at water's edge. Each site has just a picnic table and lantern post. Rock fire rings have been established and a pit toilet is available. Except on mid-summer weekends, campers usually have plenty of sites to pick from. Reservations are accepted for 10 sites. The others are offered first-come, first-served. No individual sites can be reserved. Campsites cost $12–14/night.

hiking: A good network of trails wind through the undeveloped parts of Mistletoe SP, and connecting different parts of the park. While the trails have no outstanding highlights beyond views of the lake, they offer nice hikes of up to 8 mi along the lake, across small creeks and through interior forests, with good opportunities to see wildlife, especially deer, turkeys and squirrels. Trails total 12.7 mi and include the 1.9-mi, yellow-blazed *Twin Oaks Long Trail*, the 0.3-mi, yellow-blazed *Cabin Area Spur Trail*, the 2.5-mi, white-blazed *Cliatt Creek Nature Trail*, and the newly established, 8-mi *Rock Dam Trail*, which had not yet been blazed when this was written. Trails are easy to walk and easy to follow. Footbridges are provided where needed. A state park trail guide is available from the office or nature center.

lodging: 10 cabins in the park are divided into 2 groups. 5 cottage-style cabins are contemporary in design but have wood siding that gives them a natural appearance. 5 others are log-cabin designs, with rocking chair porches and loft-style bedrooms. All cabins are lakefront, have fireplaces and sleep up to 8 people. They are fully furnished and have central heating and air conditioning. Cabins cost $65–75/night, depending on the season and the day of the week. A 2-night minimum stay is required. For reservations, call 800/864-7275.

The Coastal Plain

Coastal Plain Region Key Map

1. Providence Canyon SP
2. Georgia Veterans SP
3. Kolomoki Mounds SHP
4. Reed Bingham SP
5. Magnolia Springs SP
6. Hamburg SP
7. George L. Smith SP
8. Ohoopee Dunes NA
9. Little Ocmulgee SP
10. General Coffee SP
11. Banks Lake NWR
12. Stephen C. Foster SP
13. Suwanee Canal Rec Area
14. Skidaway Island SP
15. Fort McAllister SHP
16. Wassaw NWR
17. Harris Neck NWR
18. Blackbeard Island NWR
19. Melon Bluff
20. Cumberland Island NS
21. Crooked River SP

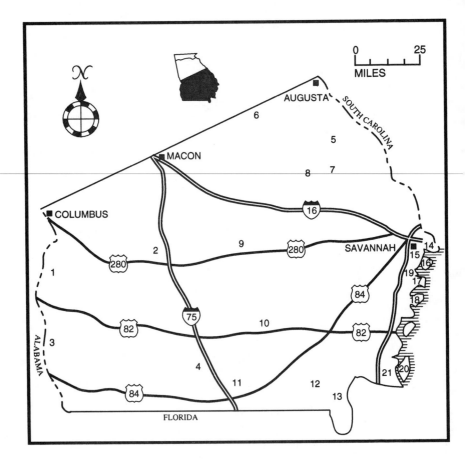

Weather & Climate Readings at Savannah

Month	Avg High F°	Avg Low F°	Precipitation (Inches)	Snowfall (Inches)
Jan	60	38	3.7	0.1
Feb	63	41	3.3	0.3
Mar	71	48	3.6	0
Apr	78	54	3.2	0
May	84	63	3.9	0
Jun	89	69	5.5	0
Jul	92	72	6.3	0
Aug	90	72	7.0	0
Sep	86	68	4.5	0
Oct	78	56	2.1	0
Nov	71	48	2.2	0
Dec	62	40	2.9	0.1

Introduction

From the Fall Line to the ocean side of Georgia's barrier islands, the Coastal Plain is easily Georgia's largest physiographic region, covering roughly half of the state. The region is made up of numerous distinctive habitats, among them sandhills, swamps, inter-tidal marshes, maritime forests, dune communities and beaches. Top elevations in the upper Coastal Plain are in the 600-foot range, with the landscape sloping gradually downward all the way to the ocean. The Eastern Continental Divide splits the region, running northwest to southeast. The most easterly head of a major river that flows toward the Gulf of Mexico is the Suwannee, which forms in Okefenokee Swamp.

The upper Coastal Plain has the most productive soils in Georgia, and for that reason the region has been farmed extensively. Through the lower Coastal Plain, which has poor, sandy soils, lands are used for the production of pulp, instead of corn, peanuts or other crops. The coastal mainland is flanked by broad marshes and a string of barrier islands commonly known as the Golden Isles. The Coastal Plain is mostly rural, with its towns small and scattered. Savannah and Albany are the two largest population centers. Even the actual coast and its beautiful islands are largely undeveloped, with only areas around Savannah and Brunswick having been built up significantly. To some extent the Coastal Plain is defined by the rivers that drain it. Major rivers include the Savannah, Ogeechee, Altamaha, Satilla, Suwannee, and St Marys. Upper portions of coastal rivers are bounded by swamps; lower portions are bounded by marsh.

A striking feature throughout the Coastal Plain is that habitat types vary radically with very minor elevation changes. A rise of only a few feet can quickly change the landscape from a cypress swamp to a very dry sandhill community. On barrier islands, ecosystems also change abruptly in very short distances, going from beaches to dune communities to maritime forests within only a few steps. The variance caused by every hint of a hill is evidenced in the fact that while the land and mostly flat, dozens of place names throughout the Coastal Plain include words like hill, mount and bluff. Common trees in various habitat types include slash pines, longleaf pines, pin oaks, live oaks, southern magnolias, bald cypress, tupelos and cabbage palmettos.

Across much of the Coastal Plain, backcountry areas are small and scattered, similar to those that are found in the Piedmont. Most are state parks that are built on lakes or rivers or that surround a specific unique natural feature or areas of historical significance. Examples are Providence Canyon, a spectacular series of canyons that are actually the result of over-farming in the early part of the century, and Kolomoki Mounds, a major group of Indian mounds. The Coastal Plain also includes some of Georgia's most remote backcountry areas, however, including the 396,000-acre Okefenokee National Wildlife Refuge and remote barrier islands like Blackbeard, Wassaw and Cumberland, which are accessible only by boat. Wassaw Island, among the least developed barrier islands along the entire Atlantic Coast, looks much like most of the Georgia Coast did when European settlers first arrived. Several of Georgia's remote barrier islands, such as Sapelo, St. Simons, St. Catherines and Ossabaw, are either closed to the public or open only for very restricted use.

For canoeists and sea kayakers, trip possibilities are outstanding and widely varied across the Coastal Plain. Okefenokee Swamp offers an unparalleled opportunities canoe camping in a vast swamp wilderness. Tidal waters, meanwhile, offer a seemingly limitless array of possibilities for exploration with a sea kayak. Anglers find good places to fish for bass, bream, catfish and other freshwater species in rivers and lakes. Nevertheless, saltwater fishing tends to steal the show, and areas that offer good prospects include tidal creeks, bays, the island surf and the open ocean. Opportunities for hiking and biking range from developed trail systems in state parks to miles of beaches and maintenance roads on barrier islands that are unmarked and often abandoned. Camping possibilities are likewise varied and range from developed car campgrounds to backcountry sites that require a long paddle through Okefenokee Swamp or hike across Cumberland Island just to get to them.

Like the landscapes they inhabit, wildlife species are quite varied throughout the Coastal Plain. Among the most celebrated species are gopher tortoises, loggerhead sea turtles, American alligators, indigo snakes, wood storks, and red-cockaded woodpeckers, all threatened or endangered. Eastern diamondback rattlesnakes, abundant in gopher tortoise areas and on all of Georgia's barrier islands, also receive a fair amount of attention. Large fauna include black bears, wild boars and white-tailed deer. Wading birds are common in swamps and in tidal rivers, while neotropical migrants make heavy use of coastal forests through spring and fall. Shorebirds are abundant and widely varied on beaches.

Providence Canyon State Park

Providence Canyon doesn't look like it belongs in the Coastal Plain of South Georgia, what with its colorful walls, some sheer and 150 feet high. The canyon is actually a network of 16 interconnected canyons at the head of Turner Creek. Erosion ditches gone wild, the canyons are the result of poor farming practices in the early and mid-1800s that broke through the erosion-resistant top layer of clay and allowed water to begin to work on the soft, sandy soils below. The canyons have reached their current form in only 150 years, and every major rain changes the landscape a bit. They aren't getting measurably deeper, having hit still another layer that is quite erosion resistant, but walls between canyons and along their edges continue to wash away. Efforts to curtail the erosion date back to the 1930s, when Civilian Conservation Corps workers planted kudzu and pine trees. Forest communities that have become re-established have significantly slowed the process.

Providence Canyon State Park, which covers 1,108 acres and has been in place since 1971, takes in all the canyons, with the most dramatic scenery in 9 canyons closest to the day use area. Hiking is the most popular activity in the park, with some hikers toting packs and hiking the backcountry trail to camp. Only backcountry and pioneer camping are available in the park. Wildflowers and wildlife abound; the former include the world's largest concentration of plumleaf azaleas. Wildlife includes deer, turkeys and armadillos. Outside the canyon, picnic areas are convenient to several nice overlooks.

Lumpkin (E) is the nearest town.

contact: Superintendent, Providence Canyon State Park, Route 1, Box 58, Lumpkin, GA 31815; 912/838-6202; www.gastateparks.org.

getting there: From Lumpkin, Drive W on GA-39 Connector 6.9 mi to the park entrance on the L.

topography: 16 interconnected canyons define the park's terrain, creating sheer drops in the typically flat Coastal Plain. Even the land outside the canyons is hillier than much nearby farmland, however, which also contributed to the initial formation of the canyons. Forests are of mixed pines and hardwoods outside the canyons while pines prevail inside the canyons. Wildflowers are diverse and abundant throughout the park. **maps:** USGS Lumpkin SW

starting   out: The visitor center, open 8 AM to 5 PM daily, has information and maps. A 13-minute slide show, shown on request, provides a good primer on the park and the formation of the canyons. Restrooms, a water fountain and pay phone are also available at the visitor center. All climbing, rappelling and rock collecting is strictly prohibited. Because canyon rims continue to erode, crossing fences for a "better view" is illegal and extremely dangerous. The park is open from 7 AM to 9 PM Apr 15 to Sep 14, 7 AM to 6 PM Sep 15 to Apr 14.

Pets must be on a leash of no more than 6 ft. Alcoholic beverages are prohibited.

activities: Hiking, Camping.

hiking: the park has 2 hiking trails and both access some of the canyons. The 3-mile *Canyon Loop* is for day-use only and provides access to the most impressive canyons from above and below. The *Backcountry Loop* is open for day-use but is designed for backpacking and has 6 designated campsites along it. The Canyon Loop provides access for hiking in 9 of the canyons, which is permitted as long as hikers do not climb any canyon walls. The *Backcountry Trail* runs along the edges of some canyons not visible from the day-use area. Both lead to numerous overlooks, each of which is remarkably different from the rest. Hiking is moderate to strenuous on either trail. The *Canyon Loop* is white-blazed and easy to follow. The *Backcountry Trail* is red-blazed and usually easy to follow. One section follows the creekbed inside the canyons and can be confusing. A permit is required for hiking the red trail, whether for day-use or backpacking.

camping: Backcountry camping is limited to 6 sites spread along the *Backcountry Trail*. The closest site is 2.5 mi down the trail. The campsites, which are available to groups of up to 10 people, consist of just a fire ring and a clearing large enough for a few tents. Campfires are permitted in fire rings only, and campers are required to stay close to designated sites after dark. Individual sites are selected on a first-come first-served basis, but a reservation (800/864-7275) guarantees a site. Camping costs $3/person, per night.

The park also has 2 pioneer camping areas, each with pit toilets, picnic tables, an Adirondack shelter and a large fire ring. The sites, surrounded by woods and nicely isolated from other parts of the park, can handle up to 50 campers. Each has a spur trail connecting it with the *Backcountry Loop*. Pioneer sites cost $30.

lodging: Florence Marina State Park (800/864-252 for reservations; 912/838-6870 for information) is a converted private marina and resort located 11 mi W of Providence Canyon. The park has 10 cottages on Lake Walter F George, each fully furnished and complete with cooking utensils, color TV and central heating and air. Cottages cost $40–80/night.

Georgia Veterans Memorial State Park

Established as a permanent memorial to U.S. veterans, Georgia Veterans Memorial State Park has a military museum and a large outdoor display of airplanes, cannons and tanks from World War I through the Vietnam War. Located on Lake Blackshear, a 7,000-acre impoundment on the Flint River, the park is a first-rate fishing destination. Backcountry is quite limited, however, as an 18-hole golf course, conference retreat center and swimming pool share space with a large picnic area, 3 developed camping areas, and the museum and airplane and armament displays. Most of the park's 1,322 acres are made up of either open fields of mowed grass or pine trees planted in straight rows. The park does have two short nature trails, both through forested areas. Common wildlife species include deer and fox squirrels.

Cordele (E) is the nearest town.

contact: Superintendent, Georgia Veterans Memorial State Park, 2459-A Highway 280 West, Cordele, GA 31015; 912/276-2371; www.gastateparks.org.

getting there: From the jct of US-41 and US-280 in Cordele, drive W on US-280 8.3 mi to the park entrance on the L.

topography: Lake Blackshear, which the park borders, is the only defining feature of this flat coastal plain habitat. Most of the park is landscaped, but natural habitats that remain include cypress backwaters and dry oak/pine forests. **maps:** USGS Cobb.

starting out: The park office, which serves as its visitor center, is open 8 AM to 5 PM daily. Information and maps are available inside and there are restrooms, water fountain and pay phone. The park is open from 7 AM to 10 PM.

Pets must be on a leash of no longer than 6 ft. Alcoholic beverages are prohibited in public areas. Georgia resident disabled veterans receive a 25 percent discount on campsites and cottages.

activities: Fishing, Camping, Hiking.

fishing: Lake Blackshear offers excellent fishing for bass, bream, crappie, stripers, hybrids and catfish. The shallow lake has plenty of vegetation and cypress trees to provide good cover for the fish. With 3 launch ramps, the park is a popular access point for boating anglers. It also offers extensive bank-fishing access, plus 4 fishing piers. Most shoreline fishermen target crappie, for which the lake is well known. Largemouth bass must be at least 14 inches to be kept.

camping: 3 camping areas contain 77 sites, with 2 of the areas side by side along the lake. Area 3, which has 24 sites, is in an open pine forest away from the water. These sites are quite basic, consisting of just a fire ring and picnic table. Sites in areas 1 and 2 are more defined, and each has an established tent pad, lantern post, fire ring/grill and picnic table. 25 sites are on the lakefront. All sites have water and electricity. Campsites are average size, and none of the camping areas offer much privacy, as the forest understory is open and sites are close together. Camping costs $14/night; $17/night for waterfront sites. The campground is open year round.

2 pioneer camping areas are nicely isolated from the rest of the park and from each other. Facilities are limited to pit toilets, and the sites are just clearings in the forest understory for tents. Pioneer camping costs $15/night.

hiking: 2 short nature trails total just over 1 mi. While signs for each say simply, "Nature Trail," a park brochure names them the *Yucca Nature Trail* and *Lakeshore Nature Trail*. The former, which cuts through a dry sandhills forest and then a stand of planted pines, has interpretive signs along the way and an accompanying brochure, which provides additional information. The trail is unblazed but wide and easy to follow. The trailhead, along the road to the conference retreat center and campgrounds, sets among several massive cork oak trees brought from Portugal or Spain 300 to 400 years ago. The *Lakeshore Trail* has a few interpretive signs along it, but the short trail is quickly lost to a maze of fishermen's trails in a very dense, somewhat swampy area. There is less then 0.25 mi of maintained and recognizable trail. The area is quite pretty though, and birds are abundant between the backwaters and the thicket beside them.

lodging: 10 2-bedroom cottages are set in a row along the lake and even have a fishing pier behind them. The cottages are natural in appearance with brown wood siding, are fully furnished, and all have central heating and air, fireplaces and screened porches overlooking the lake. Cottages cost $60-$75/night, with a 2- to 5-night minimum stay required for reservations, depending on the season. For reservations, call 800/864-7275.

Kolomoki Mounds State Historic Park

Although established as a historic park and centered around the 7 namesake ancient Indian mounds, Kolomoki Mounds State Historic Park also has great recreational value within its 1,293 acres, which contain 2 lakes that together cover more than 100 acres. The mounds, built during the 12th and 13th centuries by the Swift Creek and Weeden Island Indians, include a temple mound, two burial mounds and four ceremonial mounds. The park has a museum that interprets the mounds and culture of the Indians who built them, plus interpretive signs around the mounds. Portions of the park have a county park appearance, with planted grass among scattered pine trees, picnic shelters, a swimming pool and a miniature golf course. Other portions are densely forested, with a good mix of Coastal Plain habitats represented. The park has two developed campgrounds, two pioneer camping areas, two lakes for fishing and two hiking trails, with a third trail being built. Wildlife species commonly seen include deer and alligators.

Bluffton (N) and Blakely (S) are the nearest towns.

contact: Superintendent, Kolomoki Mounds State Historic Park, Route

1, Box 114, Blakely, GA 31723; 912/723-5296; www.gastate-parks.org.

getting there: From Bluffton, Drive S on Kolomoki Rd 5.4 mi to the park entrance on the R.

topography: Kolomoki Creek and the 2 impoundments on it are the defining features of this Coastal Plain landscape. The lakes back into cypress swamps but are surrounded by dense and varied forests. Oaks, pines and magnolias are abundant. **maps:** USGS Blakely North.

starting out: The park office, which doubles as a visitor center, is open 8 AM to 5 PM daily. The park is open from 7 AM to 10 PM. Information, including maps of the park, is available. There are restrooms inside. Restrooms, water fountains, pay phones and drink machines are also found near picnic areas.

Alcoholic beverages are prohibited in public areas. All pets must be on a leash of no more than 6 ft.

activities: Fishing, Hiking, Camping.

fishing: Fishing is available in 35-acre Lake Yohola, 70-acre Lake Kolomoki, and Kolomoki Creek, downstream of the lakes. The lakes have bass, bream, crappie and catfish; the catfish are heavily stocked but only lightly pressured by local anglers. Submerged, emerging and floating vegetation are plentiful in park waters, providing good cover for the fish. Both lakes have boat ramps, and private boats are permitted with a 10-horsepower limit. Canoe and jonboat rentals are available for $4 for the first hour and $1 for each additional hour, up to $12. All boats must be off the water before dark. Lake Yohola has a fishing pier, but its banks are largely inaccessible. Lake Kolomoki offers better access for bank-fishing. Fishing in the creek is primarily for bass and done exclusively from the banks.

hiking: The park has 2 nature trails, each 1.5 mi long, and another 2 mi route that will connect those trails currently in place is being developed. The white-blazed trail begins near the Indian mounds, while the yellow-blazed trail begins near the picnic area on Lake Kolomoki. Both trails provide easy walking as they wind through dense forests of large pines, oaks and magnolias. They are generally easy to follow, although a couple shortcut routes along the white-blazed trail can cause confusion. Footbridges and boardwalks are provided for crossing creeks and swampy areas.

camping: The park has 2 campgrounds, with 18 sites in the Rustic Campground and 25 sites in the more modern Lakeside Campground. Each site has a picnic table and fire ring/grill, plus electricity and water, and most sites in the Lakeside Campground also have a lantern post. The Rustic Campground is set in a large grassy area, with very scattered trees. Sites are average sized but close together, providing very little privacy. Individual sites are defined only by placement of facilities and worn areas in the grass. The much newer Lakeside Campground has nice sites built of landscaping ties and poured sand and gravel. Several sites are in fact lakefront, and a forest of young oaks provides decent privacy, despite some sites being close together. Both campgrounds have modern restrooms, with flush toilets, hot showers and laundry facilities. Campgrounds are open year round. Sites cost $12/night for tents or $14/night for RVs.

The park also has 2 pioneer camping areas, each with picnic tables, grills and a fire ring. 1 has water available. 1 has a 3-sided shelter. Both are set in small clearings in the woods and isolated from other parts of the park. Pioneer camping costs $1/person per night, with a $15 minimum and a $25 maximum.

lodging: George T. Bagby State Park (800/864-7275), 18 mi from Kolomoki Mounds, has 5 waterfront cottages and a 30-room lodge on Lake Walter F. George. The lodge has modern, hotel-type rooms and a restaurant. The cottages, each with 2 bedrooms, are fully furnished, with fully equipped kitchens, air conditioning and heat. Lodge rooms cost $42–75/night. Cottages cost $65–80/night.

Reed Bingham State Park

The land that today makes up Reed Bingham State Park used to operate as two separate recreation areas in Colquitt and Cook counties, with the Little River not only forming the county line but prohibiting direct access from one side to the other. Today a bridge spans the river, just downstream of the dam that forms the park's 375-acre lake, and brings all 1,620 acres into a single state park. The park is named for Reed Bingham, who did much of the original survey work around the Little River and who devoted significant energy to helping get the state park established. The lower end of the park lake has open banks, with scattered pines and mowed grass. The upper end is enclosed by cypress swamps. Most of the park's backcountry surrounds the upper end of the lake and the moving waters of the river that flow into it. Three miles of river upstream of the lake flow through park property. Fishing is popular in the lake, and camping is available at a developed campground and pioneer camp. A 3.5-mi trail system provides opportunities for hiking, while the park's 3 mi of river lend themselves to a short but scenic canoe trip. The park also has picnic areas, a miniature golf course and two butterfly and hummingbird gardens. Endangered gopher tortoises and indigo snakes inhabit the park's dry sand ridges, while deer are apt to be seen in forested areas.

Adel (SE) is the nearest town.

contact: Superintendent, Reed Bingham State Park, Box 394 B-1, Route 2, Adel, GA 31620; 912/896-3551; www.gastateparks.org.

getting there: From I-75 at Adel, take Exit 12, which is GA-37. Drive W on GA-37 5.7 mi to Reed Bingham Rd on the R. Follow signs 0.7 mi into the park.

topography: Little River and the lake that impounds it are the defining features of this coastal plain area that offers a wide variety of habitats including longleaf pine/wire grass communities, mixed hardwood forests, pocosins and cypress swamps. **maps:** USGS Ellenton.

starting out: The park office and visitor center, located just inside the main entrance, is open 8 AM to 5 PM daily. Information and maps, including a trail map with good interpretive information, are available. Restrooms, drinking fountains and pay phones are in the picnic area. The park is open 7 AM to 10 PM.

Alcoholic beverages are prohibited. All pets must be on a leash of 6 ft or less.

activities: Fishing, Hiking, Camping, Canoeing.

fishing: The 375-acre park lake has bass, bream, crappie and catfish; fishing is popular from boats and from the banks. The park has 2 boat ramps, and private boats are permitted on the lake from 7 AM until sunset. Bank-fishing is permitted until 10 PM. The best bank-fishing access is around the open lower end. Fishing for all the same species is also possible in the Little River, but most anglers concentrate their efforts on the lake. The river is narrow and winding and is bounded by a swamp. All fishing access is by boat, either from the lake or from a boat ramp that is upstream of the main area of the park.

hiking: Although no single trail at Reed Bingham is more than 0.9 mi long, together 5 short routes cover 3.5 mi and course a great mix of coastal plain habitats. All but the 0.5-mi *Gopher Tortoise Nature Trail* are interconnected and begin at a common trailhead near the upper end of the lake on the Cook County side. These trails, collectively known as the *Coastal Plains Nature Trails*, pass through a dozen different habitat types, all of which are discussed on the back of a trail map. The trails are wide and easy to follow. They are color-coded but infrequently blazed. The *Little River* and *Boardwalk* trails, both of which follow boardwalks much of the way, were closed in late 1998 and were being refurbished. The *Gopher Tortoise Nature Trail*, which begins near the campground, is an easy interpretive route well-suited for family hikes. Several signs along the way interpret longleaf pine/wire grass communities, which offer ideal habitat for gopher tortoises. Several unofficial paths make the trail easy to loose, but the area is sufficiently small and open that finding it again is generally simple.

camping: 46 dirt campsites are located in a very open forest of scattered mature oaks. Sites are average sized but offer very little privacy because the area is so open. Each site has a picnic table, fire ring/grill and tent pad, plus water and electricity. Restrooms have hot showers, flush toilets, and laundry facilities. The campground is open year round. Sites cost $14/night for tents or $16/night for RVs.

2 pioneer camping areas are tucked away in a dense hardwood forest near the upper end of the lake and are nicely isolated from the rest of the park. Each site has an open area for tents, picnic tables, pit toilets, a grill and a large fire ring. Pioneer camping costs $15/night.

canoeing: The Little River's dark, clear waters wind lazily through cypress swamps for 3 mi before backing into the lake. Alligators and an assortment of wading birds may be seen and paddling is easy on the slow-moving river. Downed trees present the only potential hazard, as the river averages only about 30 ft wide. The put-in, though part of the park, must be driven to from outside the park. From Reed Bingham Rd, facing GA-37, turn L on Evergreen Church Rd and drive 2.8 mi to Roundtree Bridge Rd. Turn L and be prepared to turn L again almost immediately to access the boat ramp. Evergreen Church Road is dirt and initially looks like a private drive to a farm. Canoeists can take out at either of 2 ramps on the lake, but both are toward the lake's lower end, so a bit of flat-water paddling is necessary.

Magnolia Springs State Park

Named for its natural springs, which pump out an estimated 9 million gallons of water per day, Magnolia Springs State Park also preserves the remnants of Camp Lawton, a Civil War prison camp. The stockade, which held a total of 10,200 Federal prisoners of war, was located north of Millen because of the water provided by the springs. The park's 948 acres are mostly forested and include a 28-acre lake. A good system of trails is open to mountain biking and hiking. Fishing and camping are also popular activities. The park has an aquarium of native Georgia species, which gets its water from directly from the springs, as well as a large group camp that has a dining hall and swimming pool. Picnic areas are close to the spring and the small pond it bubbles up into. Various fish, reptiles and amphibians are easy to spot around the spring because the water is ultra-clear. Larger wildlife species that use the park include deer, alligators, raccoons and bobcats.

Millen (S) is the nearest town.

contact: Magnolia Springs State Park, 1053 Magnolia Springs Drive, Millen, GA 30442; 912/982-1660; www.gastateparks.org.

getting there: From the jct of GA-17 and US-25/GA-121 in Millen, Drive N on US-25/GA-121 5.1 mi to the park entrance on the R.

topography: The park's landscape is made up of very gentle hills with dry sandy soils. Most forests are mixed pines and oaks. The 28-acre lake and small pool that the springs rise to form are the major defining features of the landscape. **maps:** USGS Perkins.

starting out: The park office and visitor center is open 8 AM to 5 PM daily. Information and maps are available inside. There is a drink machine and an information board outside. Restrooms and a water fountain are nearby in the picnic area.

Alcoholic beverages are prohibited. Pets must be kept on a leash.

activities: Mountain Biking/Hiking, Fishing, Camping.

mountain biking/hiking: Magnolia Springs is different from most state parks in the fact that bicycles are permitted on trails. In fact, an entire network of trails in the park was developed with mountain bikers in mind. The most popular route, a 5 mi loop, is marked with directional arrows, but additional loops and connecting roads more than double the total trail mileage and allow the trails to be ridden in many different combinations. Made up of single-track, old roads and fire breaks, the trail system is generally easy to ride. The only technical section is a sink hole, which is sandy and steep, but it can be avoided. The mountain biking trails begin between the spring and the cottages, on the opposite side of the road. There is a large sign with a map at the trailhead. Maps are also available form the office.

The park's other 2 trails, the 1.2-mi *Beaver Nature Trail* and the *Woodpecker Woods Nature Trail*, which is less than 0.5 mi, are better suited for foot travel. The *Beaver Nature Trail* winds along the banks of the lake and leads to an observation platform over the water. The *Woodpecker Woods Nature Trail* begins at the spring on an interpretive boardwalk and then circles through a mixed forest. Both trails are easy. No trails in the park are blazed, but all are well maintained and easy to follow.

fishing: Fishing in the park's 28-acre lake is popular from the banks and from boats, but only the lower end of the lake has open banks, so a boat offers access to much more of the lake. The lake is stocked with bass, bream, crappie and catfish. Weeds along the lake's edges provide good cover. The lake has a boat ramp and fishing pier. Rental canoes and fishing boats are available for $3/hour, $8 for 4 hours or $12 for 8 hours. There is a 10-horsepower limit for boating on the lake, except from 10 AM to 6 PM, and not more than 2 boats with motors exceeding 10 horsepower are permitted on the lake at one time. All boats must be off the water by dark. No fishing is permitted around the spring.

camping: 26 campsites are located in an open forest of large pines. Sites are average sized but well spaced, providing decent privacy despite the openness of the forest. Each has a picnic table, fire ring/grill and tent pad. Several sites are built of landscaping ties and poured gravel and sand. Except 3 walk-in tent sites, all sites have water and electricity. Restrooms have flush toilets, hot showers and laundry facilities. There is also a pay phone and drink machine. The campground is open year round. Camping costs $14/night. Walk-in sites cost $12/night.

2 pioneer camping areas, well separated from the rest of the park, are in grassy clearings surrounded by forest. Each area has a pit toilet, picnic tables, a 3-sided shelter and a fire ring/grill. Pioneer camping costs $15/night for up to 15 people, plus $1 for each extra person.

lodging: The park has 6 cottages, all fully furnished, that have rocking chair screen porches in front and picnic tables and grills out back. The cottages, which have brown wood siding, aren't quite lakefront, but they set close enough to the lake to provide views of the water. 2- and 3-bedroom cottages, all with central heating and air, are available. Cottages cost $50/ to $75/night, with a 2-night minimum stay, except in July when the minimum stay is 5 nights. For reservations, call 800/864-7275.

Hamburg State Park

A grist mill built by George Gillmore in 1921 on the Little Ogheechee River is still fully functional. In fact, the mill and the pond that was built to power it are the main attractions at Hamburg State Park, and corn meal ground in the mill can be bought from the park's country store. Covering 750 acres in Washington County, the park attracts a lot of visitors who come simply to tour the working mill and a museum that showcases agricultural tools once commonly used in Georgia. The park also draws fishermen, however, as Hamburg Millpond has earned a reputation as one of the top spots in the entire state for yielding hefty largemouths. The millpond also provides a nice backdrop for a developed campground, a short hiking trail and a large picnic area. There are also pleasant spots for picnicking downstream of the mill, both along the rocky run immediately below the dam and farther downstream, where the placid stream cuts between the woods and a grassy opening. Wildlife includes deer, wild turkeys and alligators.

Warthen (S) is the nearest town.

contact: Superintendent, Hamburg State Park, Route 1, Box 233, Mitchell, GA 30820; 912/552-2393; www.gastateparks.org.

getting there: From Warthen, Drive E on GA-102 1.6 mi to Hamburg State Park Rd and veer L. Drive 6 mi to the park, which is on both sides of the road. The park office is reached by the second turn to the L.

topography: Hamburg Millpond and the Little Ogheechee River are the central features of this upper coastal plain habitat that features very gentle hills and mixed hardwood/pine forests. **maps:** USGS Warthen NE.

starting out: The park office, next to the dam and mill, is open from 8 AM to 5 PM, except around mid-day, when it may close for lunch. Information and maps are available inside. A water fountain, drink machine and pay phone are also there. Restrooms are nearby in the picnic area. The park is open from 7 AM to 10 PM.

Alcoholic beverages are prohibited in public areas. Pets must be on a leash of 6 ft or less.

activities: Fishing, Camping, Hiking, Canoeing.

fishing: Hamburg Millpond, which covers 225 acres, is well known for the huge bass it sometimes yields. An old pond that still holds an abundance of flooded timber, the millpond has produced numerous fish breaking the 10-pound barrier, including some 12- and 13-pound monsters. Even beyond the trophy fish, however, bass fishing is good overall, and there are also bream, crappie and catfish. Along with the flooded timber, rocky banks that are steep in places provide good cover for the fish. Most fishing is done from boats, but the park offers good bank access to the lower end of the pond. Rental canoes and fishing boats are available. Private boats are permitted, with a 10-hp limit. There are 2 boat ramps. Channel catfish are the main attraction downstream of the dam, where there is a fishing pier.

camping: 30 campsites set in a fairly open mixed forest across Hamburg Millpond from the day-use areas, isolating them from the rest of the park. Some campsites are quite large and well spaced, and many are on or very near the water. Each site has a picnic table, grill, fire ring, tent pad, water and electricity. Restrooms have flush toilets and hot showers, plus laundry facilities. The campground is open year 'round. Camping costs $12/night for tents, $14/night for RVs.

hiking: The park has 1 trail, which is 1.5 mi long. It begins behind the office, winds along the banks of the pond, and then loops away from the water, up a hardwood ridge. The first part of the white-blazed route passes through the park's picnic grounds and a very open pine forest, but eventually the trail winds away from areas of activity and disappears into denser woods. The trail is easy to walk and easy to follow. Footbridges are provided for crossing wet, low-lying areas.

canoeing: With steep wooded banks and scenic stands of flooded timber, the millpond is a nice canoeing destination. Rental canoes are available, and there are 2 boat ramps for launching private boats.

George L. Smith State Park

Cypress, black tupelo, eastern redbud and water oak are only a sampling of trees that grow in and around Parish Pond, a beautiful 412-acre mill pond built in 1880. Watson Mill, which consists of a covered bridge and mill house, is still intact and operational, and in fact the mill remained in active duty until 1973. The bridge is open to foot traffic during the day and is set up as a museum. The park, named for a Georgia legislator, covers 1,700 acres around the mill, the pond and the creek downstream of the dam. A network of marked canoe trails through the trees makes Parish Pond an excellent paddling destination. The park also offers good opportunities for fishing, hiking and camping. Picnic areas look over the lake. The pond's vast shallow flats and many trees create outstanding wildlife habitat, especially for birds. Wading birds are abundant, as are waterfowl during the winter. Other wildlife species in the park include alligators, otters, deer and both red and grey foxes.

Twin City (NW) is the nearest town.

contact: Superintendent, George L. Smith State Park, P.O. Box 57, Twin City, GA 30471; 912/763-2759; www.gastateparks.org.

getting there: From Twin City, drive S on GA-23 7 mi to George L. Smith Park Rd on the L, which leads into the park.

topography: The 412-acre mill pond and 15-Mile Creek, which it impounds, are the major defining features of this upper coastal plain landscape. The terrain is flat to gently rolling and supports forests dominated by pines and oaks. **maps:** USGS Twin City SE, Twin City.

starting out: The park office, which serves as a visitor center, is open 8 AM to 5 PM daily. Maps and information are available inside. There is a pay phone in front of the office and restrooms nearby. The covered bridge is open from 8 AM to 5 PM. The park is open from 7 AM to 10 PM.

Alcoholic beverages are prohibited. Pets must be on a leash of 6 ft or less.

activities: Canoeing, Fishing, Hiking, Camping.

canoeing: 10 mi of canoe trails follow 3 main routes through the tupelos and cypresses of 412-acre Parish Pond. The trails are blazed with painted blocks on trees and are very easy to follow. 1 route goes up the center of the pond, while the others wind along opposite sides. The upper end of the pond is quite riverine and the canopy is dense. Birding opportunities are outstanding. Rental canoes are available.

fishing: Bass, bream and chain pickerel are the most sought-after fish species in Parish Pond. The trees, plus vegetation in the shallow upper end and along its edges, provide the main cover. Some bank-fishing is possible around the lower end of the lake, but most serious fishing is done from boats. Private boats are permitted on the lake, but no motors over 10 horsepower may be operated. A permit is required to launch any boat that has a motor over 10 horsepower. All boats must be off the water by sunset. Fishing for the same species is also possible from the banks of the creek, downstream of the mill pond.

hiking: The park's main hiking trail, a 3-mi loop that has a 0.7-mi cut-off route through the middle of it, is open 8 AM to 5 PM only, because reaching it requires crossing the covered bridge, which is locked every afternoon at 5. The trail, unblazed but broad and easy to follow, leads through a variety of coastal habitats, passing tupelo swamps along the lake's edge and cutting through everything from hardwood forests to pine barrens. The trail, which has scattered interpretive signs along it, passes gopher tortoise holes, and crosses the broken dam of an old pond. On the more developed side of the park is a 0.5-mi trail that passes through a forest of mixed pines and hardwoods and connects a small picnic area with the campground. The trail is straight, broad and flat.

camping: Most of the campground's 25 sites back up to the lake and offer outstanding views through the cypress trees. Sites are average sized and offer decent privacy, as most are tucked back into the woods. They have recently been refurbished with landscaping ties and poured gravel. Each site has a picnic table, grill and fire ring, plus water and electricity. The central part of the loop, where restrooms, laundry facilities and a pay phone are located, is fairly open. Restrooms have hot showers and flush toilets. There is also a fish-cleaning station. Sites cost $12/night for tents, $14/night for RVs. The campground is open year round.

lodging: Four 2-bedroom cottages with log-cabin-type exteriors and wood-paneled interiors are nicely isolated from the rest of the park. All cottages are fully furnished, with fireplaces, rocking chair porches and central heating and air. Cottages cost $50 to $60/night, with a 2-night minimum stay. For reservations, call 800/864-7275.

Ohoopee Dunes Natural Area

Established to protect a series of 40- to 80-foot-high dune-like sandhills along the Little Ohoopee River, the Ohoopee Dunes Natural Area is not managed with recreational use in mind. The state-owned area is open to the public during daylight hours, however, and both hiking and fishing are possible. The natural area is divide into three tracts of 1,017, 791 and 693 acres, each bordered to the west by the Little Ohoopee River and all similar in character. The sandhills provide excellent habitat for gopher tortoises and in turn for indigo snakes, which use the tortoise's holes. Wood ducks, beavers and wading birds make use of the river and cypress sloughs along it.

Swainsboro (E) is the nearest town.

contact: Georgia Department of Natural Resources, 1773-A Bowens Mill Highway, Fitzgerald, GA 31750; 912/426-5267; www. ganet.org/dnr.

getting there: All 3 tracts are best accessed from Swainsboro, and directions are given from the jct of US-1 and US-80. There are no large signs marking any of the tracts, but area borders are designated by fluorescent orange natural area signs on trees. Tract 1: Drive W on US-80 4.7 mi to Kemp Rd and turn L. Drive 1.1 mi to Halls Bridge Rd and turn R. Drive 2.6 mi to the natural area, which is on both sides. There is an information board and limited parking space to the R. • Tract 2: Drive W on US-80 6 mi to the area entrance on the R. The turn-in is unmarked and very rough. • Tract 3: Drive W on US-80 3.5 mi to Old McLeod Bridge Rd and turn R. The natural area begins 2 mi ahead on both sides of the road, continues for the next mi, and ends at the river. Parking is possible at various points.

topography: All 3 tracts are characterized by dune-like sandhills 40 to 80 ft high, interspersed by swampy creeks and bordering a blackwater stream. Scrub oak/longleaf pine forests, bottomland hardwoods and bay swamps make up 90 percent of the landscape. **maps:** USGS Norristown.

starting out: There are no facilities at the natural area, and most access to interior areas is by foot only. Only day-use is permitted. ATVs and horses are prohibited. Maps and information sheets are sometimes available at information boards.

activities: Hiking, Fishing.

hiking: The natural area has no measured or marked trails, but an extensive system of sandy maintenance roads that are closed to vehicular traffic allow hikers to explore all 3 tracts. Soft sand makes walking tough in places, and some roads may be overgrown. Most routes are through scrub-oak/longleaf pine sandhill communities. Although the largest single tract is barely more than 1,000 acres, the Ohoopee Dunes Natural Area is very remote and completely undeveloped. A map, compass and hiking companion are recommended.

fishing: The Little Ohoopee River forms the western border of all 3 tracts, which together provide 4.6 mi of river access. Fishing for bass, catfish and an assortment of sunfish is possible, but only bank-fishing is permitted. No trails run riverside and much of the stream is bordered by swampy sloughs, so access to much of the river is difficult.

Little Ocmulgee State Park

Established in 1940 on properties donated by local landowners, Little Ocmulgee State Park was developed by Civilian Conservation Corps and National Parks Service workers. Building the park's lake, which impounds 265 acres on the Little Ocmulgee River, was part of the development process. The state park, which covers 1,397 acres, is quite developed, so legitimate backcountry is somewhat limited. There is an 18-hole golf course, lodge and conference center, 75-person group camp, tennis courts and a pool. Nevertheless, some good opportunities for backcountry activities do exist. The park's sandhill communities provide habitat for endangered gopher tortoises, and a nice hiking trail winds through the sandhills and along the lake. The lake, meanwhile, offers good fishing prospects, and the park's campground is quite nice. The park also has a beach, a miniature golf course and a lakeside picnic area. Along with the tortoises, wildlife includes alligators and white-tailed deer.

McRae (S) is the nearest town.

contact: Superintendent, Little Ocmulgee State Park, P.O. Drawer 149, McRae, GA 31055; 912/868-7474; www.gastateparks.org.

getting there: From McRae, Drive N on US-280/US-319 1.6 mi to the fork in the road. Veer L onto US-441/US-319 and drive 0.6 mi to the park entrance on the L.

topography: The park's upper coastal plain terrain is flat to slightly rolling. Much of the park is developed, but forested portions include oak forests, mixed hardwoods and pines and sandhill communities dominated by pines. **maps:** USGS McRae.

starting out: The park office is open from 11:30 AM to 7 PM, W–Su, Mar 15 to Oct 31. When the office is closed, whether for the season or the day, information and maps are available in the lodge lobby. There are restrooms, water fountains and pay phones at the lodge and around the picnic area. The park is open 7 AM to 10 PM.

Alcoholic beverages are prohibited in public areas. Pets must be on a leash of no more than 6 ft.

activities: Fishing, Camping, Hiking, Canoeing.

fishing: Bass, bream, crappie and catfish are all part of the normal offerings in the park's 265-acre lake, but a breached dam had much of the shallow lake's bottom exposed as of late 1998. Signs noted that repair plans were underway, but no projected completion dates were included. Under normal conditions, the park offers some access for bank-fishing, plus a nice fishing pier, but the best way to fish the lake is by boat. Canoe rentals are available for $3/hour, but only when the park office is open. Private boats are permitted on the lake, with no motor restrictions, and there is a ramp near the dam (closed until the dam is repaired.)

camping: A nice developed campground with 58 sites is set in a forest of young, moss-draped oaks. Most of the understory has been cleared, but the trees provide decent privacy. Most sites are formed with landscaping ties and are average in size. Some sites toward the back of the campground are less developed but more widely spaced. Each site has a picnic table, lantern post, fire ring/grill and tend pad. Restrooms have flush toilets and hot showers, plus laundry facilities. The campground is open year round. Campsites cost $12/night.

hiking: The *Oak Ridge Trail* winds through the only noteworthy backcountry in the park, forming a 2.3-mi loop along the edge of the lake. A cut-off trail part way through makes a 1.7 mi loop also possible. Hiking is easy, and footbridges are provided as needed. Numerous interpretive signs explain changes in forest type and point out common flora and fauna. Sandhills communities, which provide habitat for gopher tortoises, are prevalent, but the habitat changes continually along the route. The trail is well marked, with red blazes along the main route and yellow blazes marking the cut-off. The trailhead, which is located near the back of the picnic area, is well marked.

canoeing: Paddling is possible when the lake level is at normal pool. Canoe rentals are available for $3/hour when the park office is open. Private boats can be launched at the boat ramp, near the dam. The lake has a long, narrow profile and is surrounded by a mix of wooded banks and swampy backwaters.

lodging: The park has a 30-room lodge and 10 cottages. The lodge, which offers basic motel-type accommodations with a restaurant and conference center, backs up to the golf course. The cottages set in a row along the edge of the lake. Each has a big picture window and a deck overlooking the water. Cottages are fully furnished, including cookware and linens. Lodge rooms cost $50 to $75/night. Cottages cost $60 to $70/night. For reservations, call 800/864-7275.

General Coffee State Park

Historical and natural resources are both part of the appeal of General Coffee State Park, which covers 1,510 acres on both sides of Seventeen-Mile River. The park is named for General John Coffee, a planter, U.S. Congressman and military leader. The front part of the park centers around Heritage Farm, a living museum with an assortment of historical buildings, including an 1828 farm home, tobacco barn, chicken coop, and blacksmith shop. Behind the farm is the Bog Walk, a short interpretive boardwalk over a bog at the edge of the Fish Pond. The Fish Pond, which has picnic areas around it, has manicured grassy banks and an easy footpath around it. Several ducks make the Fish Pond home. Farther into the park, the woods are natural, and include habitats that range from river swamp to sandhills. Hiking, camping and fishing are possible in the park. Bikes and canoes are available for rent, but neither is really for backcountry use. Bikes are not permitted on hiking trails, and canoes are for paddling on 4-acre Fish Pond. There is also an archery range and a group lodge, across the river from the day-use areas, plus a swimming pool and several picnic areas. Wildlife includes gopher tortoises, indigo snakes, alligators, and deer.

Douglas (W) is the nearest town.

contact: Superintendent, General Coffee State Park, 46 John Coffee Road, Nicholls, GA 31553; 912/384-7082; www.gastateparks.org.

getting there: From Douglas, drive E on GA-32 5.7 mi to the park entrance on the L.

topography: Covering land on both sides of Seventeen-Mile River, the park includes the river's cypress-studded swamp and the low sandhills that surround it. Forests are dominated by oaks and pines. **maps:** USGS Douglas North, Nicholls.

starting out: The park office and trading post is open 8 AM to 5 PM. Maps and information are available, and there are restrooms, a pay phone and drink machines. The park is open from 7 AM to 10 PM.

Alcoholic beverages are prohibited in public area. Pets must be on leash of no more than 6 ft.

activities: Camping, Hiking, Fishing.

camping: The park campground has 51 sites around 2 loops that are nicely isolated in a forest of moss-draped oaks. Forests along the campground's edges are dense, but the middle part of each loop is open and grassy and has a playground. The sandy campsites are average sized, and each has a picnic table, fire ring/grill and tent pad. Restrooms have flush toilets and hot showers. There is also a pay phone. The campground is open year 'round. Sites cost $12/night.

Two pioneer camping sites are nicely isolated from the rest of the park down a dirt road that is closed to public travel due to extensive gopher tortoise use. Sites are in a dense forest dominated by young hardwoods. The understory is cleared for setting up tents, and there are pit toilets, picnic tables and grills. Pioneer sites cost $15/night minimum, plus $1 for each person over 16 people.

hiking: The 2-mi *River Swamp Trail* runs first through an almost jungle-like moist forest, with vines and magnolias and various hardwoods. In places the trail runs right next to the cypress swamp around Seventeen Mile River. The final section of trail goes through dry sandhills habitat, past numerous gopher tortoise holes. The trail, which begins behind picnic shelter 4, is yellow blazed and easy to follow. There are scattered interpretive signs. Boardwalks are provided where needed.

fishing: Fishing in the park is possible in the Fish Pond and Seventeen Mile River. The pond, which has bass, bream and catfish in it, has mowed banks and a couple bridges across its coves, making for simple shoreline access. Fishing is possible from canoes, but bank-fishing is the most common approach. The pond has little structure. Most river fishing is for bass or catfish. The river is narrow and winding, with dark water that often runs low. Small oxbows line its course, but they are typically inaccessible. Because most of the river is bounded by swamp through the park, however, access is quite limited. Fishing by canoe is sometimes possible, depending on water levels.

lodging: The park's 4 cottages are across the river from the day-use area and campground and separated by the forest from other facilities on that side. The cottages, which have a log-cabin appearance, are fully furnished, with linens, cookware, central heating and air. They have screened back porches and big brick fireplaces. Cottages cost $50 to $65/night.

General Coffee SP also offers one the most unique lodging opportunities in Georgia's state parks system. The Burnham Cottage is a 3-bedroom 19th-century home with Queen Ann period furnishings. The master bedroom has its own fireplace, a 4-poster, rice carved bed and separate reading room. The master bath has stone floors and a clawfoot-style bathtub. The cottage also has a television and VCR, plus a fully equipped kitchen with modern amenities. The Burnham Cottage costs $125/night. For reservations, call 800/864-7275.

Banks Lake National Wildlife Refuge

Georgia's second largest Carolina Bay, Banks Lake is part of an expansive wetland complex that extends through Grand Bay to Moody Air Force Base. The Banks Lake National Wildlife Refuge totals 4,049 acres, 1,000 or so of which are open waters of the lake. The lake itself is actually an old mill pond built over the wetland. The lake is tea colored from tannin put out by thousands of cypress trees. Much of the refuge is covered in freshwater marsh that offers no practical access. Only a small portion is uplands, including the boating access area off GA-121. Fishing is easily the most popular recreational use of the refuge. Limited hiking is possible on a very short nature trail that loops through the woods near the boat ramp. Banks Lake is also a nice place to paddle a canoe or kayak, but bass boats with big motors tend to diminish solitude. The lake and the wetlands surrounding it are havens for wildlife, especially birds. Wood ducks are commonly seen darting among the cypress trees, and sandhill cranes use wetland areas on migratory routes. Bald eagles have nested in trees over the lake, and there are nesting colonies of osprey on the refuge.

Lakeland (E) is the nearest town.

contact: Banks Lake NWR, c/o Okefenokee NWR, Route 2, Box 3330, Folkston, GA 3330; 912/496-7366; www.fws.gov/r4eo.

getting there: From Banks City, drive W on GA-121 1 mi to the access area on the L, marked by a brown sign.

topography: The lake is shallow and filled with cypress trees. Surrounding areas consist of freshwater marsh, plus limited uplands densely forested with oaks, magnolias and pines. **maps:** USGS Lakeland, Ray City.

starting out: The only facilities at the refuge are a parking area, pit toilets, a boat launching ramp and a fishing pier. A building at the access area once housed a concessions operation, but it is vacant and locked up at present. The refuge is open daily from daylight to dark. Camping, fires, and the collection of artifacts, plants or animals are prohibited. Children under 7 must be accompanied by an adult at all times.

activities: Fishing, Hiking, Canoeing/Kayaking.

fishing: Banks Lake is known as a South Georgia angling hotspot, with largemouth bass as the main attraction. Along with producing good numbers of quality fish, Banks Lake yields some real giants every year. There is a handicapped accessible fishing pier at the main access point, but most bass fishing is done from boats. There are no motor restrictions, but boaters should be aware that stumps and trees, including floating, dead trees, create a potential hazard in all parts of Banks Lake. Most bass fishermen simply focus on the trees, often using spinnerbaits and plastic worms. Banks Lake yields fabulous topwater fishing on summer nights, but night-fishing is by permit only, and only during the summer. Call the refuge office to apply for a permit. The lake also has bream and crappie, plus a limited population of catfish, but most fishermen who visit Banks Lake target largemouth bass. Bream offer the best prospects from the fishing pier.

hiking: A short nature trail with signs at both ends warning: "Watch For Snakes"—runs first along the edge of the lake's swampy backwaters and then turns back through a dense forest of live oaks, pines and magnolias and circles around, coming out right next to where it began. The trail, which is less then 0.25 mi long, is fairly broad and mostly open. There are no blazes, but the path is easy to follow. It begins at the access area, and a sign behind the parking area points to it.

canoeing/kayaking: The cypress trees that rise from Banks Lake's dark waters are intriguing to paddle among, but there are no established canoe trails through them or particular destinations to paddle to. Aquatic vegetation is too dense to make paddling practical in some areas. The biggest potential downfall of canoeing or kayaking on Banks Lake, however, is that boating activity is sometimes heavy because of the popularity of bass fishing. The best routes for paddling are among dense stands of timber, where boats can not travel fast.

Okefenokee National Wildlife Refuge

Established in 1937, the Okefenokee National Wildlife Refuge preserves 396,000 acres of the 438,000 acre swamp that bears the same name. In 1974, 353,981 acres of the swamp's interior portion were given further protection by being designated a National Wilderness Area. Forming the headwaters of the Suwannee and St Marys rivers, Okefenokee Swamp is one of the best preserved freshwater wetlands in America. The swamp extends 38 miles from north to south and 25 miles from east to west. The name Okefenokee comes from an Indian word meaning "land of the trembling earth." A massive bog, the swamp has peat deposits up to 15 feet thick covering much of its floor, so in places the trees and shrubs will literally tremble when stomped upon. The swamp is densely forested and often impenetrable, but a network of designated canoe trails cuts through a portion of it. Because Okefenokee, like all national wildlife refuges, is managed primarily for wildlife, more than half of the refuge remains closed to any public use. Recreation is an important secondary management objective, however, and the refuge offers outstanding opportunities for backcountry canoeing/kayaking, camping and fishing. Although much more limited, some hiking opportunities also exist. Rules for refuge use are numerous and strictly enforced, as needed for the protection of visitors and of the swamp's fragile ecosystems.

Wildlife is abundant in the refuge, including 234 bird species, 49 mammal species, 54 reptile species, and 60 amphibian species. Among those are numerous threatened or endangered species. American alligators, the animals most closely identified with Okefenokee Swamp, number between 9,000 and 15,000. The swamp is home to five different species of poisonous snake, but neither gators nor snakes generally bother humans who don't bother them. Insects are a different story. Mosquitoes can be thick after dark, and both deer flies and yellow flies can be a menace during early summer.

Waycross (N), Fargo (W) and Folkston (E) are the nearest towns.

contact: Refuge Manager, Okefenokee National Wildlife Refuge, Route 2, Box 3330, Folkston, GA 31537; 912/496-7836; www.fws.gov /~r4eao.

getting there: Going clockwise from Waycross, US-1, GA-121, GA-94, US-441 and US-84 encircle the perimeter of the refuge, providing access to different areas. The refuge office is located within the Suwannee Canal Rec Area. From Folkston, Drive S on GA-121 (Okefenokee St) 7.8 mi to the refuge entry road, which is well marked with signs, and turn R. Drive 3 mi to the refuge office on the R.

topography: The swamp is a vast peat bog inside a huge, saucer-shaped depression and is 103 to 128 ft above sea level. Most of the swamp is shallowly flooded and forested with cypress, blackgum, bay and maple. There are also 50 islands totaling 25,000 acres, 60,000 acres of open freshwater marsh or prairie and several small lakes. **maps:** USGS Dinner Pond, Billy Island,

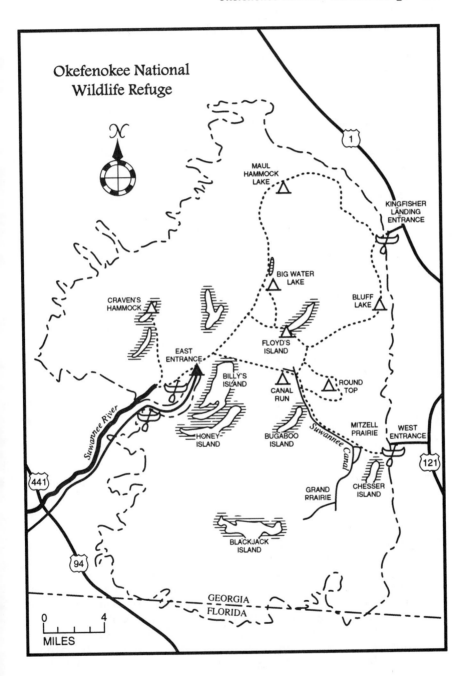

Okefenokee National
Wildlife Refuge

N

MAUL
HAMMOCK
LAKE

KINGFISHER
LANDING
ENTRANCE

BIG WATER
LAKE

CRAVEN'S
HAMMOCK

BLUFF
LAKE

FLOYD'S
ISLAND

EAST
ENTRANCE

BILLY'S
ISLAND

CANAL
RUN

ROUND
TOP

MITZELL
PRAIRIE

WEST
ENTRANCE

HONEY-
ISLAND

BUGABOO
ISLAND

Suwannee Canal

121

Suwannee River

441

GRAND
RRAIRIE

CHESSER
ISLAND

94

BLACKJACK
ISLAND

GEORGIA
FLORIDA

0   4

MILES

Blackjack Island, Cravens Island, The Pocket, Strange Island, Double Lakes, Chase Prairie, Chesser Island, Waycross SE, Waycross SW, Fort Mudge, Spooner, Colon, Fargo, Eddy, Sargent, Moniac, Toledo.

starting out: Stephen C. Foster SP and Suwannee Canal Rec Area are good starting points for swamp exploration. Each has a visitor center, with information and maps. Canoe and motorboat rental are also available in both places. Sill Landing, located off the road to Stephen C. Foster, and Kingfisher landing, located off US-1 between Waycross and Folkston, have only a boat ramp, parking area, and information board with rules and a sign-in sheet. A $5 daily entry fee is required at all entrances. Travel is restricted to established, designated routes and to designated areas during posted hours only. Hours vary by season and by entry point.

Pets must be on a leash and are not permitted in boats or public buildings. Swimming is prohibited in all refuge waters. Collecting plants and feeding or harassing wildlife are prohibited.

Okefenokee Swamp Park (912/283-0583), although listed as a swamp entrance, is not really an entry point for backcountry travel. The park uses some refuge waters based on a lease agreement with the USFWS, but boat trails are not connected with those through the rest of the refuge. Most swamp travel is on guided boat tours. The park has several animal habitats and interpretive exhibits, a pioneer homestead, a network of boardwalks, and a 90-ft observation tower overlooking the swamp. General admission is $8. 4 other admission packages that range from $12 to $20 include guided boat tours of different lengths or a canoe for individual exploration.

activities: Canoeing/Kayaking, Camping, Fishing, Hiking.

canoeing/kayaking: The only way to see much of the Okefenokee Swamp is by canoe or kayak, ideally on a multi-day outing. 120 mi of boat trails course the swamp, and half of that mileage is on trails open by permit only on paddling/camping excursions of 2 to 5 days. 62 mi of boating trail are open for day-use, and some day-use waters are accessible from every entrance. 5 major trails in the swamp cut through every kind of habitat, and each is different. Some are through open canals that are easy to paddle. Others cross broad prairies or lakes, where wind can be a major factor. Others cross long, shallow stretches where paddling can be tough or the boat may even have to be pushed because of low water levels or peat blow-ups. Open waterways are clearly marked throughout the refuge, with signs at junctures indicating directions, distances to various points and permitted uses. Major canoe trails are blazed with colored icons and mileage markers. Many day-use waterways are open to motor boats, but no motors of more than 10 hp may be operated. Boaters must sign in and out at concession area or landing.

camping: Backcountry camping is restricted to 7 designated stops in the swamp's interior that are accessible only by canoe or kayak. Stops range from an old hunting cabin on an island to a simple shelter on a platform in the middle of a prairie. Camping is allowed only with a permit on wilderness trips of 2 to 5 days, and reservations must be made for specific stops and specific nights. Only 1 group is permitted per stop, per night, so reservations, which may be made only within 2 months of the first day of a trip, can be difficult to get during the peak months of Mar and Apr. In fact, groups and individuals are limited to 1 trip per year during this period, with trip lengths limited to 2 nights. Permits cost $10/person, per night and are due within 15 days of securing a reservation. For reservation information, call 912/496-3331. A wilderness canoeing brochure includes a map, a description of each trail, listings of a dozen trips available, and much other information, including 17 regulations specific to wilderness canoeing.

Camping in Okefenokee's interior is a true backcountry experience with legitimate risks and any help a long way away in most instances. A flashlight, compass, map, portable toilet with disposable bags, and Coast Guard-approved floatation devices are required, along with a permit, and safety items like a first-aid kit, rope and quality raingear are strongly recommended. Stops are as far as 12 mi apart, and travel after dark is neither safe nor legal. Therefore, a fair assessment of conditions, routes and each person's paddling abilities are essential when planning a trip.

Camping outside the swamp but still within the refuge is possible in a developed campground in Stephen C. Foster State Park.

fishing: Fishing, which is by boat only, is popular on Okefenokee NWR. Generally speaking, small lakes that are scattered throughout the swamp provide the best opportunities. Suwannee Canal and the Suwannee River also offer good prospects, however. Pickerel (jackfish), bowfin (mudfish) and an assortment of sunfish are the most commonly targeted species in the swamp, although its dark waters also hold largemouth bass and channel catfish. Travel on refuge waters is prohibited after dark. Minnows are prohibited as bait. Trotlines may not be used.

hiking: Hiking opportunities are limited to areas around entrances, as travel within the swamp's interior is by boat only. There are 5 mi of trail at Steven C. Foster SP and Suwannee Canal Rec Area; the highlight in each area is a long, elevated boardwalk extending out across the swamp.

Stephen C. Foster State Park

Although the state park itself is among the smallest in Georgia, covering just 80 acres, Stephen C. Foster State Park is a primary access point to the 396,000-acre Okefenokee National Wildlife Refuge. In fact, 25 of miles day-use waterways through the swamp are most commonly accessed from the state park. The park sets on Jones Island, on the western side of the half-million acre swamp, and lies totally within the refuge boundaries. Access to the swamp is by a short canal that connects with the Suwanee River. While there is a campground and a hiking trail in the park, most backcountry activities occur farther out on the refuge, only beginning at Stephen C. Foster. Backcountry activities include hiking, canoeing/kayaking, camping and fishing. For less adventurous visitors who still want to see some of the swamp, motor boat rentals are available, and park naturalists lead guided boat tours 3 times a day. There is also an interpretive museum in the park. The boat basin, at the head of the canal, is the center of activity in the park. The office is beside it, the trailhead is behind it, and the museum is across the street.

Wildlife is abundant in and around Stephen C. Foster State Park. The swamp provides a home to 49 species of mammals alone, including black bears and bobcats, and more than 230 bird species use the refuge. Alligators are Okefenokee's most famous residents, and some days a visitor won't have to go beyond the edge of the state park to see plenty of gators.

Fargo (SW) is the nearest town.

contact: Superintendent, Stephen C. Foster State Park, Route 1, Box 131, Fargo, GA 31631; 912/637-5274; www.gastateparks.org.

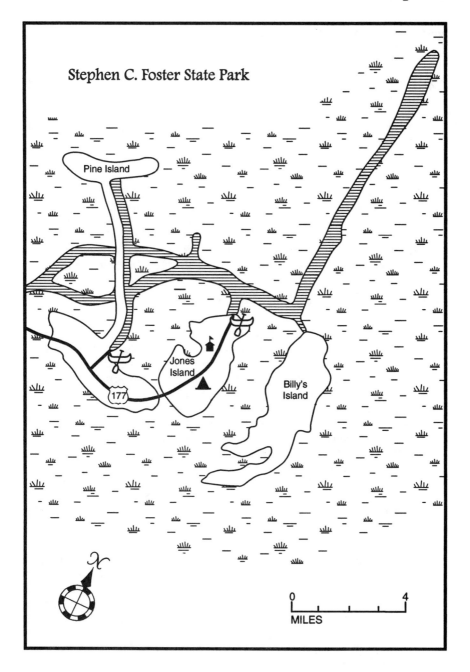

Stephen C. Foster State Park

Pine Island

Jones
Island

Billy's
Island

177

0   4

MILES

getting there: From Fargo, drive S on US-441 1 mi to GA-177. Turn L and drive 17 mi to the park office on the L.

topography: The park is located on an island, but facilities, including the boardwalk, stretch out into the swamp. The swamp is a massive peat bog. Most is shallowly flooded and densely forested with cypress, blackgum, bay and maple. There are also 50 islands totaling 25,000 acres and 60,000 acres of prairie. **maps:** USGS Billys Island, The Pocket.

starting out: The park gate is open 7 AM to 7 PM Sep 12 to Feb 28 and 6:30 AM to 8:30 PM Mar 1 to Sep 11. The park office is open 8 AM to 5 PM daily and has maps and information. Restrooms, pay phones, water fountain and drink machine are there. A $5 daily refuge entrance fee applies to the park. A $2 ParkPass, required for all other Georgia state parks, is neither needed nor honored.

activities: Canoeing/Kayaking, Camping, Fishing, Hiking.

canoeing/kayaking: Canoeing and sea kayaking opportunities range from day-trips of any distance—with 25 mi of day-use waterways to pick from—to overnight excursions of up to 5 days. Day-use waters include the Suwanee River and several small lakes and lead past various islands. Billys Island, only a couple miles from the park, is open to exploration and even has a short trail on it. Open waterways are very well marked throughout the refuge, with signs at junctures indicating directions, distances to various points and permitted uses. Major canoe trails are blazed with colored icons and mileage markers. Day-use waterways are open to motor boats, but no motors of more than 10 horsepower may be operated. Canoes rentals cost $6 for 1 hour, $11 for 4 hours, $15 for 8 hours or $26 for overnight use. A $1 launch fee is required for private boats. All boaters must sign in and sign out.

camping: Backcountry camping is allowed by permit only on overnight canoe trips of 2 to 5 days. There are 7 designated camping areas within the refuge. 8 of 12 official routes use Stephen C. Foster State Park as a possible starting or ending point. See Okefenokee NWR chapter for more on rules and permit procedures.

The park has a developed campground, with 66 sites on 2 long, narrow loops. Dense palmettos and other shrubs that are more than head high provide excellent privacy for the medium-sized sites, despite many being quite close together. Each site has a picnic table, fire ring/grill, water and electricity. The campground is open year round. Camping costs $12/night for tents from Jun 1 to the last day of Feb, and $15/night for tents from Mar 1 to May 31. RV camping costs an additional $2/night.

The pioneer camping area, a clearing in the Palmettos with pit toilets and picnic tables, is available to organized groups only. Pioneer camping costs $21/night minimum, plus $1.50/person over 15 people.

fishing: Most fishing in the swamp is for chain pickerel (jackfish), bowfin (mudfish), or various species of sunfish. Many fishermen throw small plugs, spoons or jigs and simply fish for fish, enjoying the swamp's varied offerings. All fishing is from canoes or from motorboats, which are restricted to motors of 10 hp or less. Minnows are not permitted as bait.

hiking: The *Trembling Earth Nature Trail* is highlighted by a 0.5-mi boardwalk out into the swamp. The trail also includes a 0.5-mi loop on Jones Island, so walking the boardwalk both ways and then walking the loop makes for a total hike of 1.5 mi. Several interpretive signs on the boardwalk describe habitats and the swamp's inhabitants, and most are matched with specific observation points. Opportunities to see alligators, wading birds and other wildlife are outstanding. The trail begins behind the visitor center. Because it follows a boardwalk part of the way and is broad and well maintained around the loop portion, no blazes are needed.

lodging: The park has 9 cottages, each with 2 bedrooms and complete furnishings, including kitchen-ware and linens. The cottages set along a sandy half-loop among pine trees and palmettos. They are sufficiently separated from the office, boat basin and museum to offer some privacy, but still within easy walking distance. Cottages cost $55 to $76/night. There is a $15 surcharge for 1-night stays. For reservations, call 809/864-7275.

Suwannee Canal Recreation Area

Suwannee Canal, a 12-mile-long historic canal built in 1891 in an attempt to drain Okefenokee Swamp, now serves as a major entry point into the swamp and the central feature of a U.S. Fish and Wildlife Service recreation area. Many 2- to 5-day canoe-camping excursions into the swamp begin or end at Suwannee Canal, but there are also several miles of day-use waterways accessible only from this entrance. The USFWS manages the area, which includes an interpretive driving tour, 4 short hiking trails, a picnic area and a visitor center. The trail system includes a 0.75 mi boardwalk that leads to a 50 foot observation tower. The tower overlooks a lake and prairie. A private concessionaire operates the boat basin and gift shop along the edge of the canal, and rents canoes, motor boats and camping gear, along with providing guided boat tours of the swamp.

The Suwannee Canal borders several large prairies, which are the most extensive open areas in the swamp. Fishing is excellent in this part of the Okefenokee, and the prairies offer outstanding bird-watching opportunities. The swamp is home to an incredible assortment of wildlife species. Birds, alligators and some snakes are readily viewed. Most mammals are much more reclusive, and many are mostly nocturnal. Land outside the swamp but still within the refuge and recreation area also provides habitat for a variety of species, including gopher tortoises and red-cockaded woodpeckers.

Folkston (E) is the nearest towns.

contact: Refuge Manager, Okefenokee National Wildlife Refuge, Route 2, Box 3330, Folkston, GA 31537; 912/496-7836; www.fws.gov /~r4eao. For rental information, call 912/496-7156 or 800/792-6796.

getting there: From Folkston, drive S on GA-121 (Okefenokee St) 7.8 mi to the refuge entry road, which is well marked with signs, and turn R. Drive 4.2 mi to the parking lot for the visitor center and concessionaire's outpost.

topography: The recreation area straddles the eastern edge of the swamp and includes pine forests and mixed pine/hardwood forests, along with the swamp itself. Habitats in the swamp, a giant peat bog, include shallowly flooded, dense forests dominated by cypress, islands and prairies. The area around the rec area has extensive prairie habitat. **maps:** USGS Chesser Island, Toledo.

starting out: A very nice visitor center, open 8 AM to 5 PM Sep 11 to Feb 28 and 9 AM to 5 PM Mar 1 to Sep 10, has numerous interpretive displays, plus maps and information. There are restrooms and a water fountain. Information is also available in the concession area, open throughout refuge hours, which are 8 AM to 6 PM Sep 11 to Feb 28 and 7 AM to 7:30 PM Mar 1 to Sep 10. A $5 entrance fee is charged.

Pets must be on a leash and are not permitted in public buildings or boats.

activities: Canoeing/Kayaking, Hiking, Camping, Fishing.

canoeing/kayaking: Canoeing and sea kayaking opportunities range from day-trips to overnight excursions of up to 5 days. More than 20 mi of day-use waterways accessible from the rec area include the Suwannee Canal, a handful of small lakes, and various winding water trails that cut through Grand, Buck, Mizell and Chase prairies. There are 3 picnic areas with restrooms along day-use waterways that are accessible only by boat. Open waterways are clearly marked throughout the refuge, with signs at junctures indicating directions, distances to various points and permitted uses. Major canoe trails are blazed with colored icons and mileage markers. Many day-use waterways are open to motor boats, but no motors of more than 10 hp may be operated. Canoe rental costs range from $11.25 for 1 day to $63.75 for 5 days. Launching private boats costs $2.50 per boat. All boaters must sign in and out.

hiking: By far the most popular trail in the rec area is the 0.75-mi boardwalk to the observation tower. An interpretive route keyed to a brochure available in the visitor center, the boardwalk crosses forested swamp, ponds and prairies. There are wildlife watching areas with benches along the way. 3 other short trails, each approximately 0.5 mi long, are available. The *Canal Digger's Trail* crosses the head of Suwannee Canal and interprets its history. The *Chesser Island Homestead Trail* winds through the old homestead of the family that once owned much of the swamp. The *Deerstand Trail* cuts through a dense forest to an old deerstand, which can then be climbed. All trails begin along Swamp Island Drive, and trailheads are clearly marked. Trails are unblazed, but broad and well maintained.

camping: Camping is not permitted within the rec area, which does, however, serve as the starting and ending point for 2- to 5-day paddling/camping trips into the interior of the swamp. There are 7 designated sites in the swamp and 12 possible trips, half of which can be planned to begin and/or end at Suwannee Canal. Camping is by permit only. See the Okefenokee NWR chapter for more on rules and permit procedures.

fishing: Suwannee Canal and several small lakes and gator holes around the prairies that branch off the canal provide some of the best fishing in the swamp. Most fishing is for chain pickerel (jackfish), bowfin (mudfish), or various species of sunfish. Fishing is from canoes or from motorboats, which are restricted to motors of 10 hp or less and are restricted to some day-use waterways. Minnows are not permitted as bait.

lodging: The Inn at Folkston (912/496-6256; www.innatfolkston.com) is a 1920s heart-pine bungalow in the heart of Folkston. 4 guest rooms, each unique in its decor, have private baths and feather beds. The inn has a warm, friendly feel that begins with its innkeepers and offers a nice starting or ending point for a trip into the inhospitable swamp. Rooms begin at $90/night and include a full breakfast and afternoon refreshments.

Skidaway Island State Park

Skidaway Island State Park, located on the western side of Skidaway Island, offers a nice backcountry getaway within 15 miles of downtown Savannah. Although fairly small, covering just 533 acres, the park is largely undeveloped and has a good representation of island habitats, including mature forests, freshwater ponds and saltwater marsh. The park has two interpretive hiking trails, plus a developed campground and three pioneer camps. There is also a large picnic area and a pool. Fishing and boating, including sea kayaking, are possible in waters all the way around the island, but there is no access for either within the park. A public boat ramp in Skidaway Narrows Park, across the Intracoastal Waterway from the state park, is one of several nearby access points. Wildlife includes deer, raccoons, and a variety of wading birds.

Savannah (NW) is the closest city.

contact: Superintendent, Skidaway Island State Park, 52 Diamond Causeway, Savannah, GA 31411; 912/598-2300 or 912/598-2301; www.gastateparks.org.

getting there: From I-16 in Savannah take Exit 34 (I-516). Drive 4.6 mi E on I-516, which becomes DeRenne Avenue. Turn right on GA-204 and drive 2.5 mi to Montgomery Crossroads. Turn L and drive 1.3 mi to Waters Ave. Turn R and drive 5.6 mi to the park entrance on the L, just past the bridge over the Intracoastal Waterway.

topography: Skidaway Island is a secondary barrier island, separated from the mainland by the Intracoastal Waterway, but sheltered from the open ocean by Wassaw Island. The park is on the interior side of the island and consists of marsh, hammocks, small ponds and high ground covered by maritime forest. **maps:** USGS Isle of Hope.

starting out: The park office, located just inside the main entrance on the R, has trail maps and information. The park also has a visitor center with interpretive displays, but it may be closed if the interpretive ranger is not on duty or if special programs are going on, making the office a better starting point for basic information. There are telephones and public restrooms near the visitor center and adjacent picnic area. The park is open from 7 AM to 10 PM.

Alcoholic beverages are prohibited in public area. Pets must be on a leash of 6 ft or less.

activities: Hiking, Camping.

hiking: 2 excellent hiking trails course most of the habitats typical of Georgia's barrier islands; they also provide a peek into the area's history. The *Big Ferry Interpretive Trail* is a 3-mi loop, but it can be shortened to 2 mi. Along the way is a 3-story wooden tower built over the marsh that provides a good view. The trail also leads past freshwater and saltwater sloughs. The trail begins 0.1 mi or so behind a gate near the campground, just past a split in the road that leads L to the Pioneer Camp. The *Sandlapper Trail*, which begins behind the visitor center, begins by crossing the marsh on a boardwalk that leads to a hammock. The 1-mi route is dominated by marshes and salt flats. Both trails lead to remnants of stills and confederate earthworks, the latter built to help defend Savannah from the Federal naval blockade. Neither trail is blazed, but both are wide and well maintained, making them easy to follow. Both have interpretive signs along the way and accompanying brochures that provide additional information.

camping: 88 campsites in a fairly open forest are divided into 4 loops. All sites are sandy half-loops off a paved road, each with a tent pad, picnic table, fire ring/grill, water and electricity. Sites are medium sized. Some offer average privacy, while others offer almost none. Restrooms have hot showers, flush toilets and laundry facilities. The campground is open year round, although 1 or more loops may be closed seasonally, according to occupancy. Camping costs $15/night Nov 1 to Feb 28, $17/night Mar 1 to Oct 31.

3 large pioneer camping areas are located near the *Big Ferry Interpretive Trail* and are isolated both from the rest of the park and from each other. Pioneer areas have pit toilets, a fire-ring grill, campfire ring with benches, picnic tables, a 3-sided shelter and plenty of cleared ground for tents.

Fort McAllister State Park

Established to protect an earthen Confederate fort on the Ogeechee River, Fort McAllister State Historic Park includes 1,700 acres of salt marsh and forest dominated by hardwoods, including huge live oaks along the river. A state historic site, the fort and a museum that helps interpret the fort are located at the back of the park, separated from other facilities. Built of sand and marsh mud as a defense for Savannah, Fort McAllister was attacked seven times during the Civil War, but did not fall until it was captured by General Sherman on December 13, 1864 on his march from Atlanta to the sea. The park provides access to the Ogeechee River and smaller Red Bird Creek for fishing or sea kayaking, and has a fishing pier on the river. It also has two hiking trails, a campground and a pioneer camping area. There is a large picnic area under the live oaks and overlooking the river. The marsh supports a variety of wading birds, while the most common forest wildlife species are deer and squirrels.

Richmond Hill (W) is the nearest town.

contact: Superintendent, Fort McAllister State Park, 3894 Fort McAllister Rd, Richmond Hill, GA, 31324; 912/727-2339; www.gastateparks.org

getting there: From the jct of I-95 and GA-144 in Richmond Hill, drive W on GA-144 6.7 mi to GA-144-Spur. Turn L and drive 3 mi to the park.

topography: Marsh and uplands along the Ogeechee River comprise the park. Forests are dominated by large oaks, pines and magnolias. **maps:** USGS Richmond Hill.

starting out: The park museum, open 9 AM to 5 PM Tu to Sa and 2 PM to 5:30 PM on Su, serves as an information center and has maps and brochures. The park is open from 7 AM to 10 PM. To explore the museum and fort, a separate fee from the regular ParkPass is charged. Visitors paying the historic site fee do not need to purchase a ParkPass, however. The fee is $2/adult, $1/youth. Kids 5 and under are free.

Alcoholic beverages are prohibited in public areas. Pets must be on a leash of no more than 6 ft.

activities: Hiking, Camping, Fishing, Kayaking.

hiking: The park has 2 hiking trails, both winding through the woods but along the edge of the marsh. The trails cover close to 5 mi, with 3 mi included in a newly developed route that had not yet been named or signed by early 1999. The trail, which follows old roads part of the way and includes boardwalk where it crosses the marsh, is white blazed, well established and easy to follow. The trail begins along the short gated road to the group shelter and is recognizable by a white double blaze on a tree along the right side of the road. The *Magnolia Nature Trail*, which begins in the campground, is unblazed but marked at its trailhead with a sign and is wide and easy to follow. The *Pioneer Trail*, a spur off the *Magnolia Nature Trail* of a half mile or so, runs right along the edge of the marsh.

camping: 63 sites in a developed campground are surrounded by marsh and set in a mixed forest of pines, oaks and magnolias. Palmetto underbrush is fairly dense between sites, providing decent privacy. Each of the sites, which are medium-sized and sandy, include a picnic table, grill, water and electricity. Restroom have hot showers and flush toilets. The campground has a boat ramp and fishing pier on Red Bird Creek that are available to campers only. Camping costs $12/night. The campground is open year-round.

2 pioneer campsites have pit toilets, fire rings with benches around them, and 3-sided shelters. The pioneer area is in a mixed forest, with the understory of palmettos cleared around the sites.

fishing: The Ogeechee River and Red Bird Creek offer good fishing prospects for red drum, speckled trout, whiting, flounder and a host of other species. Good fishing is possible from the pier in the park's day-use area. Most fishing is done by boat, and there is a launch ramp on the Ogeechee River near the park's entrance. Bank-fishing is not practical because a wide marsh borders the river, prohibiting direct access. Campers have direct access to Red Bird Creek by a ramp and pier. Otherwise it is accessible from the river via the Intracoastal Waterway. The river is brackish while the creek is pure salt water.

kayaking: For registered campers, Red Bird Creek is an excellent sea kayaking destination. Other park visitors are only permitted to use the ramp on the Ogeechee River, which is much larger and has more boating traffic but is still a nice place to paddle. Tidal currents, especially on ebb tides, are strong on all waters near the park. The creek is narrow and winding and bounded by expansive salt marsh . Boating traffic is very light, and opportunities to view wading birds are excellent.

Savannah Coastal Refuges

Seven national wildlife refuges along the South Carolina and Georgia coast cover 54,077 acres and are known collectively as the Savannah Coastal Refuges. Though the refuges are often grouped together and are managed out of a single office, they are spread across roughly 100 miles of coast, and each refuge is unique. Of them, Pinckney Island lies completely in South Carolina, and the Savannah Refuge is divided by the state line. While close to half of this 26,349-acre refuge lies within Georgia's borders, there are neither developed trails, other facilities, nor any automobile access on the Georgia side. Made up largely of hardwood bottoms along the Savannah River, this part of the refuge varies dramatically in character and accessibility according to river levels. Two other refuges, 100-acre Tybee NWR and 5,123-acre Wolf Island NWR are closed to public use, except in their saltwater areas for uses such as fishing.

That leaves only three of seven refuges as destinations for Georgia backcountry exploration. All three offer very good opportunities, however. The Wassaw and Blackbeard refuges are both located on primary barrier islands that are accessible only by boat. Both are completely undeveloped, but laced with maintenance roads, which, along with their beaches, serve as trail systems for hiking and mountain biking. Fishing is possible in the Atlantic surf and in the marshes on the interior side of each island. Sea kayaking is also possible around the islands, although day-tripping to either refuge by kayak demands a good degree of skill and plenty of careful planning. Harris Neck NWR is the only coastal refuge in Georgia that is accessible by car. The refuge has many miles of footpaths and roads that can be hiked. Fishing and sea kayaking are also possible in the tidal creeks that border the refuge.

The Savannah Coastal Refuges provide outstanding habitat for wildlife that ranges from endangered wood storks to abundant eastern diamondback rattlesnakes. Hundreds of alligators use the canals and impoundments at the Savannah NWR, and loggerhead sea turtles come ashore on Blackbeard Island to lay their eggs on summer nights. Wading birds are always abundant on all the coastal refuges, and during winter, waterfowl flock to impoundments on the Savannah and Harris Neck refuges.

The refuges are spread from Hilton Head, SC to Darien, GA. Savannah is the nearest city.

contact: Savannah Coastal Refuges, Parkway Business Center, Suite 10, 1000 Business Center Drive, Savannah, GA 31405; 912/652-4415; www.fws.gov/~r4eao.

getting there: Some refuges are accessible by highway; others can be reached only by boat. Refuge headquarters is located in Savannah, off I-16. Take Exit 33-A (Chatham Parkway) and drive 1 mi S to the Parkway Business Center on the L. The office is in Suite 10.

topography: Covering more that 54,000 acres on 7 separate tracts, the Savannah Coastal Refuges take in a broad range of coastal habitats. Representative habitats include hardwood bottoms, managed impoundments, saltwater and freshwater marshes, freshwater ponds, maritime forests, dune environments and beaches. **maps:** See below under individual areas.

starting out: Individual refuges have no visitor centers and limited facilities of any kind. Only Savannah and Harris Neck have restrooms. The refuge headquarters, in Savannah, can provide maps and information. A visit or call to headquarters is a good first step for any exploration on the Savannah Coastal Refuges. Headquarters is open weekdays from 8 AM to 4:30 PM.

Pets, camping, campfires, and collecting artifacts, plants or animals are prohibited. During winter, it is important to check on hunt dates, as most refuge tracts are closed to other public uses during scheduled hunts. Portions of all refuges may be closed at any time to protect wildlife.

activities: Hiking/Mountain Biking, Fishing, Kayaking.

hiking/mountain biking: There are no named trails on any of the refuges, but more than 70 miles of roads, rough trails and dike-tops criss-cross Pinckney Island, Savannah, Wassaw, Blackbeard and Harris Neck, providing great opportunities for hiking and mountain biking. The terrain is flat, and most routes are wide and well-packed, but hiking can be challenging simply because of the remoteness and lack of markings. A map is essential, and carrying a compass is a good idea. Trails cut through every kind of habitat present on the refuges.

fishing: Fishing is permitted in freshwater impoundments on the Savannah NWR with some restrictions and seasonal limitations (a South Carolina freshwater license is required). Beyond that, however, all fishing is for saltwater species. Most is done from boats in tidal creeks and rivers: flounder, redfish and speckled trout are the most commonly targeted species. Surf-fishing is also possible on the ocean side of Blackbeard and Wassaw islands.

kayaking: Sea Kayaking is possible around most of the refuges, but Harris Neck and Wassaw offer the most manageable paddling prospects. The Savannah River is large and very powerful, with plentiful sandbars and strong downstream currents that often battle with tides. Blackbeard NWR is accessible only by a very long journey. Camping is prohibited, so paddlers must travel both ways in a day, which must be timed in conjunction with outgoing and incoming tides to even be possible. An alternative for either is to shuttle a sea kayak out in a motorized boat and spend the day exploring around the island, instead of trying to first paddle there and back.

Wassaw National Wildlife Refuge

Said to be the most primitive of Georgia's Golden Isles, Wassaw Island has never been affected by significant development or management activities. The refuge that surrounds Wassaw and bears its name also includes Little Wassaw and Pine islands, Flora Hammock and broad expanses of open marsh. The refuge, which is accessible only by boat, covers 10,070 acres. The only facilities are a single dock and a network of trails. The trails are open to hiking and mountain biking. Fishing is good from the beach and in tidal creeks that wind through the refuge. Sea kayaking is also possible, both as a means of reaching the island and of exploring the waters around it. Wassaw Island's uplands are forested with slash pines and giant live oaks that run to the edges of the unspoiled dunes. 7 miles of beach are usually abandoned. In fact, it's not uncommon for backcountry travelers to spend an entire day on Wassaw Island and see no one else. The downfall of such isolation is there may be no one around to help when a hiker or paddler gets into trouble. Biting insects and poisonous snakes are part of the environment on the island. In truth, however, wind, sun, sandbars and tides, combined with poor planning, are more likely causes of most problems.

Wildlife is abundant on the refuge, and birding opportunities are outstanding. Numerous shorebirds can be spotted along the beach on any given day, and forests are used by populations of various warblers and vereos, especially during spring and fall migrations. Wading birds are also abundant, and the island supports rookeries for herons and egrets. The island has a large population of small-bodied white-tailed deer and plenty of raccoons. Loggerhead sea turtles lay eggs on Wassaw's beaches on summer nights. Like most islands along the Georgia coast, Wassaw also provides a home to some champion-caliber Eastern diamondback rattlesnakes. The rattlers don't present problems as long as visitors stay on trails and be certain they can always see where they are stepping.

Savannah (NW) is the nearest city.

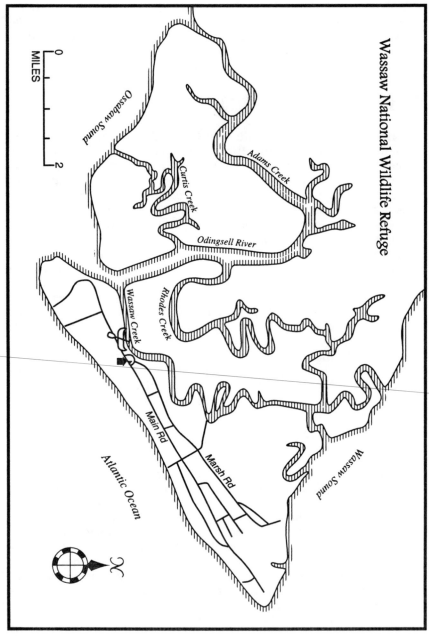

Wassaw National Wildlife Refuge

MILES

0

2

Ossabaw Sound

Adams Creek

Curtis Creek

Odingsell River

Rhodes Creek

Wassaw Creek

Main Rd

Marsh Rd

Atlantic Ocean

Wassaw Sound

getting there: Access is by boat only, with no public ferry available. Several routes are possible, and the best way to get to the island varies according to watercraft type and tidal stages. Most trips begin around Skidaway Island. Headquarters has a list of access points, both public and private, and of charter captains who run shuttles to the refuge.

topography: The refuge consists of beaches that have well preserved dunes, maritime forests, and vast salt marshes broken by the Odingsell River and numerous creeks. **maps:** USGS Isle of Hope, Wassaw Sound.

starting out: There are no facilities at Wassaw NWR except a landing dock on Wassaw Creek, which may be used only for the loading and unloading of gear. Boats may be moored or beached, but beaching is a risky proposition because of large tidal swings. A shuttle boat is kept on the island. Call the refuge office for details about using it. Wassaw Island and Pine Island are open from sunrise to sunset. Other upland areas are closed to all public use.

Pets, camping, campfires, and collecting artifacts, plants or animals are prohibited. Check on scheduled hunt dates with headquarters during fall and winter. The refuge is closed to other uses during managed hunts.

activities: Hiking/Mountain Biking, Fishing, Kayaking.

hiking/mountain biking: 20 mi of trails and 7 mi of beach provide outstanding opportunities to hike or ride a bike on a completely undeveloped barrier island. Some trails overlook the marsh or lead past small freshwater ponds, but most routes are through ancient maritime forests dominated by massive live oaks. Unspoiled beaches, meanwhile, are alive with shorebirds and loaded with seashells. The trails are actually maintenance roads, so they are broad, well packed and not overgrown. The trails have no markings of any kind, but a map showing all routes is available from headquarters. Both hiking and bike riding have their appeal. Hiking allows for closer looks at habitats along specific trails and the best opportunity to see wildlife. Mountain biking provides the means to see more of the island in a day and to get to its most remote areas.

fishing: Most fishing is done in the waterways that wind through Wassaw's marshes and along the edges of Ossabaw Sound and Wassaw Sound. Fishing in tidal creeks is exclusively by boat. The species most commonly targeted are red drum, speckled trout and flounder, with live bait and artificial lures both popular among anglers. Grubs on leadheads are popular offerings, especially for red drum and trout. On the other side of the island, surf-fishing is possible in the Atlantic Ocean, and catches range from red drum to whiting to small sharks.

kayaking: Wassaw Island is an intriguing sea kayaking destination for ambitious and experienced paddlers. Because no camping is permitted on the refuge, however, the trip out and back must be completed in the same day. No route involves less than 10 mi of paddling, and very strong tides make it essential to time trips out and back so they coincide with the direction of the tide. Along with a tidal range of 7 to 8 ft, open-water conditions can create hazards along most routes. It's 5.5 mi, one-way, from a primitive boat ramp on Wassaw Island. The route is down the Wilmington River and along the edge of Wassaw Sound to the beaches on the ocean side of the island. Refuge officials stress that anyone considering a sea kayaking trip to Wassaw NWR should be very certain of their abilities, go with at least one other paddler and plan very carefully. An alternative plan for exploring the refuge in a sea kayak is to shuttle a boat out to the island in a motorized watercraft and spend most of the day exploring the miles of waterways around the islands.

Harris Neck National Wildlife Refuge

Established in 1962, Harris Neck National Wildlife Refuge is located at the site of an abandoned WW II Army airfield. The runway system still forms a large triangle near the heart of the 2,762-acre refuge, and broad upland areas remain unforested. Despite its unusual origins, Harris Neck attracts extensive wildlife because of very diverse habitats and is a fascinating place to explore. Salt marsh surrounds Harris Neck Island, a secondary barrier island between St Catherines Island and Georgia's mainland. Uplands are a mix of natural fields, croplands and seven freshwater ponds. The ponds get heavy winter use by waterfowl, including 10 different kind of ducks. The most celebrated summer visitors are endangered wood storks, which

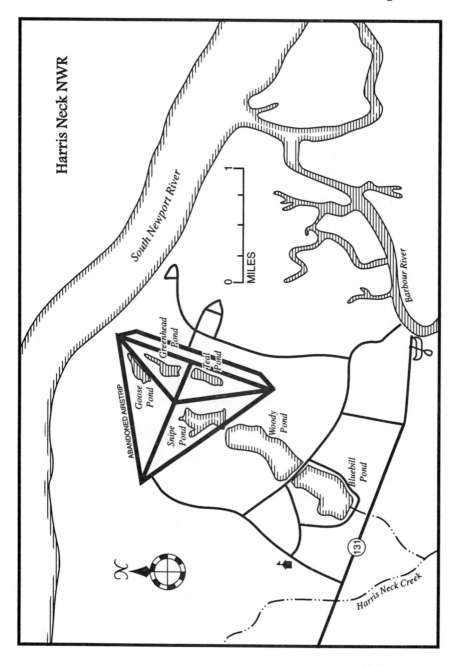

nest extensively on the refuge, taking advantage of unusual nesting structures that were crafted with the big birds in mind. 225 different species of bird have been seen at Harris Neck NWR. Larger fauna include deer and alligators.

Harris Neck is easily the most accessible of the Savannah Coastal Refuges in Georgia, since it's the only one that can be reached by car. There is a 4-mi driving tour, marked with directional arrows, which passes through a nice cross-section of the refuge's habitats. Roads that can be driven on also offer easy access to various points along trails and to wildlife viewing areas. Hiking, usually for the purpose of wildlife watching, is popular on the refuge's roads and trails. The refuge serves as a good starting point for fishing trips or sea kayaking excursions in tidal creeks and rivers. Fishing is also possible from 2 small piers on Harris Neck Creek, but most angling outings only begin and end at the refuge.

Midway (NW) is the nearest town.

getting there: From I-75, between Savannah and Darien, take Exit 12 (US-17). Drive S 1.5 mi to GA-131 (Harris Neck Rd) on the L. A brown directional sign is before the turn. Drive 6.4 mi to the main refuge entrance, which is on the L, just past a bridge over Harris Neck Creek. The boat landing is at the end of the road, less than 1 mi past the main entrance.

topography: The refuge, which covers the northern end of Harris Neck Island, consists of saltwater marsh, grasslands, mixed deciduous woods, cropland and freshwater ponds. **maps:** USGS Saint Catherines Island.

starting out: An information board near the main entrance has large area maps, descriptions of wildlife and habitats, and listings of restrictions and allowable refuge uses. Maps and brochures are also available here. Pit toilets are nearby. The refuge is open daily from sunrise to sunset. A boat ramp on the Barbour River is open from 4 AM to midnight.

Pets, camping, fires, and gathering artifacts, plants or animals are prohibited. Some portions of the refuge may be closed seasonally to protect wildlife from human disturbance. Check hunt dates with headquarters before visiting during fall and winter. The refuge is closed to other public use on days of managed hunts.

activities: Hiking, Fishing, Kayaking:

hiking: 15 mi of interconnected roads and trails crisscross the entire refuge and provide excellent opportunities for hiking. Because of the diversity of habitats on the refuge, trails offer a great variety of scenery, as well as outstanding birding prospects. Some routes cut through forests and fields that are filled with songbirds during spring and fall migrations. Others follow dikes between ponds or lead to overviews of the marsh, providing the best opportunities to see ducks during winter and wading birds throughout summer. Trails are accessible at many points along the driving tour. Individual trails are not named, nor are lengths listed. Some trails are marked at entry points with signs that either mark them as hiking trails or state that vehicles are prohibited. Most trails follow internal roads, used for refuge maintenance, so they are broad and open. All routes are easy to follow without blazes.

fishing: The Harris Neck Creek Fishing Area, which consists of 2 fishing piers and a primitive boat ramp on a small tidal creek, is open from sunrise to sunset. The piers are most popular with cast netters and crabbers, however, because they are not in very productive fishing spots. Better fishing is found in tidal waters accessible from Barbour River Landing. Red drum, speckled trout and flounder are the most commonly sought species in the network of tidal creeks and rivers that the Barbour River connects with.

kayaking: Barbour River Landing is a good starting point for kayak explorations because the river connects with an entire network of tidal waterways between St Catherines Island and the mainland. Routes wind through open marsh and past numerous hammocks. Birding opportunities are outstanding. The rivers connect with much more open water in Sapelo Sound. Tidal currents can be strong, especially in large waterways like the South Newport River, and boating traffic can be heavy on the main river and the sound. Because the tidal range is 7 to 8 ft, it is also important to study charts before venturing up any small creek.

Blackbeard Island National Wildlife Refuge

First acquired as a source of live oak timber for Naval ships in 1800, Blackbeard Island was established as a national wildlife refuge in 1940. The refuge covers 5,618 acres, more than half of which was also declared a national wilderness in 1975. A primary barrier island that can be reached only by boat, Blackbeard is located adjacent to Sapelo Island, and is the second most southerly of the Savannah Coastal Refuges. Although Blackbeard Island has been logged and impoundments were once created for wildlife management purposes, the island remains undeveloped and very primitive in character. Facilities are limited to a loading dock and a network of maintenance roads that serve as the refuge's trail system. The trails, along with 7 miles of beach-front, are used for both hiking and biking. Opportunities for fishing and sea kayaking are also available. The island's remoteness offers tremendous isolation, but it also adds risk to any backcountry excursion. If a hiker or boater gets in trouble on the island, there may be no one nearby to help or even know that help is needed. The refuge has its share of insects, alligators and poisonous snakes, but sun, sandbars, tidal currents and summer storms are more apt to cause serious problems.

Wildlife viewing opportunities are outstanding on the refuge. Shorebirds and wading birds are abundant year round, and songbirds flock to the forests during spring and fall migrations. Winter fills the marshes and freshwater ponds with waterfowl. The island has large populations of deer and raccoons. Alligators and eastern diamondback rattlesnakes are also abundant on the island.

Shellman Bluff (NW) and Darien (SW) are the nearest towns.

getting there: Access is by private boat only. Several routes are possible, and the best way to get to the island varies according to watercraft type and tidal stages. Most trips begin at private marinas in the Shellman Bluff area or at Barbour River Landing at Harris Neck NWR. Headquarters has a list of access points, both public and private, and of charter captains who run shuttles to the refuge.

topography: The refuge consists of freshwater and saltwater marsh, freshwater ponds, maritime forest, sand dune communities and beaches. **maps:** USGS Sapelo Sound, Cabretta Inlet.

starting out: There are no facilities at Blackbeard NWR except a landing dock on the marsh side, which may be used only for loading and unloading of gear. Boats may be moored or beached, but beaching is a risky proposition because of large tidal swings. A shuttle boat is kept on the island. Call the refuge office for

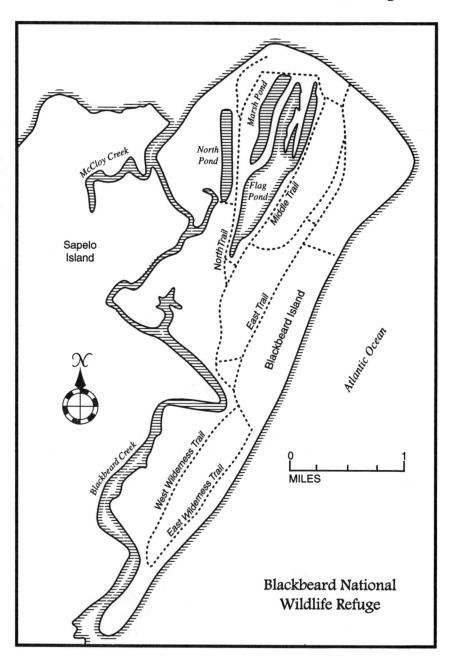

Blackbeard National
Wildlife Refuge

details about using it. Blackbeard Island is open from sunrise to sunset.

Pets, camping, fires, and collecting artifacts, plants or animals are prohibited. Check dates of scheduled hunts with headquarters before visiting during fall and winter. The refuge is closed to other uses during managed hunts.

activities: Hiking/Mountain Biking, Fishing, Kayaking.

hiking/mountain biking: 20 mi of trail and 7 mi of beach provide outstanding opportunities to hike or ride a bike on a largely undeveloped barrier island. Some trails cut through maritime forest, while others run close to the beach or the marsh. Still others wrap around the ponds at the N end of the island. The beach along the northern end of the island also has a beautiful and extensive "boneyard" of driftwood trees. The trails are actually the refuge's maintenance roads, so they are broad, well packed and not overgrown. The trails have no markings of any kind, but a map showing all routes is available from headquarters. Both hiking and bike riding have their appeal. Hiking allows for closer looks at trailside habitats and the best opportunity to see wildlife. Mountain biking provides the means to see more of the island in a day and to get to its most remote areas.

fishing: Most fishing at Blackbeard NWR is in the estuarine waters between Sapelo and Blackbeard islands or in the surf off the beach on the ocean side. Fishing is permitted in the freshwater ponds, but fish populations are modest and alligator numbers are enormous. The ponds are also very marshy, making for difficult access. Only non-motorized boats (electric motors allowed) are permitted in freshwater ponds. Red drum, trout and flounder are the most sought-after species in tidal creeks and Sapelo Sound. The island surf yields a wide variety of species. Many anglers will put out fresh cut bait and fish for whatever bites.

kayaking: Blackbeard Island is not a viable destination for reaching by kayak. The trip is too long and difficult to make paddling out to the island and back in a single day practical for most kayakers, and no camping is permitted. Plus tidal currents are very strong, and any route would require significant open water paddling amidst heavy boat traffic. That said, the refuge is a terrific place to explore by kayak for any paddler who is willing to shuttle a boat out in a motorized watercraft. A sea kayak is ideal for birding on the tidal creeks on the island's W side. On calm days, the open-ocean side offers nice beachfront paddling.

lodging: Open Gates Bed & Breakfast (912/437-6985) occupies a 2-story 1878 home on Darien's Vernon Square. Modern amenities include air conditioning and a pool. The innkeeper loves to tell guests about the coastal rivers, and barrier islands, and their history, and she even leads sea kayaking trips with some guests. Rooms cost $58 to $68/night and include a hearty breakfast.

Melon Bluff Nature and Heritage Preserve

Established to protect land along the North Newport River from development, Melon Bluff Nature and Heritage Preserve is used regularly for educational programs and historical and environmental research. The 3,000-acre private preserve is also open to day use, however, and more than 20 miles of trails wind through its woodlands and run along the edge of the marsh that bounds the river. All trails are open to hiking, and a large portion of the trail system is also open to mountain biking and horseback riding. There are also picnic areas, some of which are accessible only by trail. The long, narrow tract of land that the preserve occupies has a rich history that includes very early occupation by Spanish explorers. Melon Bluff was deeply entrenched in the rice culture prior to the Civil War, and old dikes are still evident around former ricefields that have since been reforested. Most of the property is still recovering from heavy logging in the past. Giant live oaks along the edge of the marsh give testimony to what the forest once looked like—and what it someday will look like again

Beyond the main preserve, Melon Bluff also operates three historic bed and breakfasts, and guests of two of the inns enjoy use of a vast network of private trails, plus direct access to tidal creeks that are well suited for recreational sea kayaking. These trails and waterways are also used for guide-led educational tours, which Melon Bluff regularly conducts. Wildlife is abundant, with deer, wild turkey and many species of songbirds common in forested areas. 309 bird species have been identified on Melon Bluff, including wood storks, white pelicans, painted buntings and spoonbills.

Midway (NW) is the nearest town.

contact: Melon Bluff Nature and Heritage Preserve, 2999 Islands Highway, Midway, GA 31320; 888/246-8188; www.melo nbluff.com.

getting there: From I-95, between Savannah and Brunswick, take Exit 14, which is Islands Highway. Drive E 3 mi to a large wooden building on the R, which is the preserve's nature center. Melon Bluff is written on a large green-and-white mailbox, but there is no sign at present.

topography: A long narrow tract along the North Newport River, the preserve consists of pine uplands, mixed pine/hardwood forests, old ricefields, swamp and salt marsh. **maps:** USGS Seabrook, Riceboro, Limerick SE.

starting out: The nature center is the starting point for all exploration at Melon Bluff. Trail maps and information, including route recommendations, are available. Posted hours are Tu to Su 10 AM to 4 PM, but actual closing time is typically much later, especially during the long days of summer. Daily admission is $5. Pets are prohibited.

activities: Hiking, Mountain Biking, Kayaking.

hiking: 20 mi of well marked trails at Melon Bluff wind through a broad range of habitats. The trail system is made up of more than a dozen main trails, plus numerous short connectors. All routes are interconnected, beginning at the nature center, so hikes of nearly any length and description are possible. Trails wind through forests in many stages of succession. Some lead to marsh overviews, wind along the edges of swamps or lead to areas opened up for wildlife watching. Trails are not blazed, but they are marked with directional signs at junctures. Most are wide, well-packed and easy to follow. A few narrow paths through swampy areas are open only during the winter, when snakes are not a significant concern. Numerous interpretive signs along several different routes describe the forests at Melon Bluff, the property's history, wildlife use, and wildlife management practices that are actively employed, like controlled burning.

mountain biking: Many trails are open to mountain bike use. Specific routes open and closed vary, and riders may be directed away from trails that hikers or horseback riders are known to be using any given day (or vice versa). There are always many miles of open trail available, however. The scenery is great, and riding is easy. Mountain bikes are available for rent at the visitor center.

kayaking: Sea kayaking is possible only on guided tours or on a rental basis to bed and breakfast guests. Melon Bluff typically offers 1 or 2 planned excursions per month, usually with a theme, like a sunrise paddle followed by brunch, a trip to a hammock for lunch, or a birding excursion when wood storks or some other species are most abundant. Private tours can be arranged. Paddling routes beginning on Palmyra Plantation, beside the bed and breakfasts, are generally fairly easy, and birding is outstanding. The North Newport River in the area around Melon Bluff has very strong tidal currents, but some trips for experienced paddlers do begin at the preserve.

lodging: 3 historic bed & breakfasts operated by Melon Bluff are housed in a restored barn, an 1830s plantation cottage and a 70-year-old farmhouse. Palmyra Barn and Palmyra Plantation Guesthouse set over a bluff on a tidal creek and are surrounded by massive live oaks. The barn's corncrib has been converted into a dining room, and stalls are now guest rooms. The cottage is furnished with period antiques and reproductions, but the kitchen is modern. Ripley Farm sets at the edge of Melon Bluff Preserve. Many idiosyncrasies of the "make do" building that once characterized tiny farmhouses have been left in their original state. Rates range from $75/night for a guest room at Ripley Farm to $290/night to rent the entire Palmyra Plantation Guesthouse. All rates include a full breakfast and afternoon tea, and free admission into the preserve.

Cumberland Island National Seashore

The most southerly of Georgia's barrier islands, Cumberland Island is also the largest. Although human history on the island is long and some stately private estates are still maintained, most of the island's uplands are completely undeveloped and unchanged over the past century. Dense maritime forests are dominated by huge, sprawling live oaks, with cabbage palmetto blanketing the ground. More than half the island's uplands, beginning 4 miles

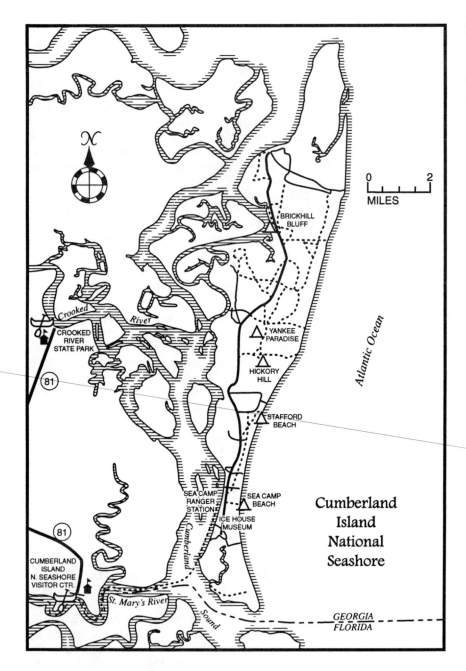

Cumberland
Island
National
Seashore

north of the Sea Island Boat Dock, are designated as federal wilderness. The island is 17.5 miles long and covers 33,900 acres, about half of which is marsh, mud flats and tidal creeks. A remote beach runs along the eastern side of the island and wraps around its southern tip.

Cumberland Island is best known for shell-covered beaches, wild horses and the ruins of the historic Dungeness mansion. The island offers backcountry travelers more than 50 miles of trail, beach and dirt road to hike. Camping opportunities are terrific, both in a developed campground and at four backcountry areas. Fishing is good in the surf and in the sound, and sea kayaks can be used both for getting to the island and for exploring its marshes. The southern end of Cumberland Island is beautiful and its habitats are representative of what is found from tip to tip. Nevertheless, the island offers far too much to take on in a day, and it warrants at the very least an overnight stay.

Wildlife is abundant on Cumberland, with birds providing the best opportunities for observation. Shorebirds abound on the island's east side, and loggerhead sea turtles come ashore on summer nights to lay eggs. Wading birds fill marshes to the west, while freshwater ponds have their own mix of avian species, plus big and abundant alligators. Forests support armadillos, raccoons and deer, plus a terrific variety of songbirds, especially during spring and fall migrations. Songbirds also make good use of vegetation in dune communities between the forest the beach. Snakes, including Eastern diamondback rattlesnakes, are also numerous.

St Marys (W) is the nearest town.

contact: Cumberland Island National Seashore, P.O. Box 806, St Marys GA, 31558; 912/ 882-4336 (information); 912/882-4335 (reservations); www.nps.gov.

getting there: Access is by boat only, with trips typically beginning either in St Marys or from the boat ramp at Crooked River SP. The most practical access for most visitors is by the public ferry, which leaves out of the Cumberland Island visitor center in St Marys. From I-95, take Exit 2, (GA-40). Drive E 9.3 mi to the end of the road in St Marys. The visitor center is across the street, just to the R.

topography: Cumberland Island NS is made up of marsh, mud flats, tidal creeks, maritime forest, freshwater ponds and beach and dune communities. Forests are dominated by massive live oaks. **maps:** USGS Cumberland Island South, Cumberland Island North, Fernandina Beach; NOAA 11489

starting out: The visitor center at St Marys is open daily from 8:15 AM to 4:30 PM. It has maps, guidebooks and other information and is the starting point for ferry trips. The ferry, operated by a private concessionaire, runs 2 to 3 times daily from Mar to Sep and twice per day W to Sa from Oct to Feb (no ferries on M or Tu during winter months). The ferry costs $10.17, including tax, for adults. It does not transport cars, bikes or pets. On the island, information is available at the Sea Camp Ranger Station. There are restrooms at the ranger station, the Ice House Museum, the Dungeness ruins and Sea Camp Beach, all at the S end of the Island. No supplies are available. A $4 day-use fee or nightly camping fee is required of all visitors. Visitation is limited to 300 people per day. Sand dunes may be crossed only at designated crossings, which are marked with black and white striped posts and are easy to recognize. Collection of artifacts, plants or animals is prohibited. Shells may be taken, as long as they have no living residents

activities: Hiking, Camping, Fishing, Kayaking.

hiking: The system of trails on Cumberland Island is extensive and well maintained, and routes cut through all parts of the island's uplands. The most popular trails are those on the S side of the island, which are convenient to the ferry docks. The *Dungeness Trail* and *Nightingale Trail*, for which interpretive brochures are available, are especially popular. Beyond actual trails, the beach is a popular hiking destination. The Main Road, which runs the length of the island, also gets regular use by hikers, especially those bound for the Brickhill Bluff backcountry camping area or other destinations at the N end of the island. Most routes are through maritime forests, but trails run beside ponds or the edge of the marsh or lead to a beach access crossing. Trails are not blazed, but they are signed at all junctions and are broad, well packed and easy to follow. The network of interconnected trails can be accessed from either ferry dock or from dune crossings on the ocean side.

camping: 4 backcountry camping areas have no facilities, except with water nearby, which should be treated. Each area holds up to

20 campers and has a handful of actual sites nicely isolated from one another and consisting only of clearings in the palmetto-dense understory. Backcountry sites are 3.4, 5.5, 7.4 and 10.6 mi from the Sea Camp Ranger Station, where all campers must register and pick up a required permit. All but Stafford Beach, the most southerly of the backcountry camping areas, are within the federal wilderness. Campsites are assigned at the ranger station on a first-come, first-serve basis, so all backpackers must be prepared to hike the full 10.6 mi each way if sites at the first 3 backcountry camping areas have been assigned. Fires are prohibited in the backcountry. Rope is required equipment for hanging packs, because raccoons are abundant. Backcountry camping is permitted year round and costs $2/person.

The Sea Camp Beach Campground is a very nice developed campground with 16 sites that are tucked away in the forest yet are only footsteps from the beach. The campground is 0.5 mi from the Sea Camp Dock, and all gear must be carried. Traveling light is therefore a good idea. The sites are large and well spaced, with a dense layer of palmettos providing terrific privacy. Each site has a picnic table, fire-ring/grill, lantern post, and raccoon-proof food box on a pole. There are restrooms with cold showers. The campground is open year round. Camping costs $4/person, per night. Fires are permitted in fire rings, but only dead and downed wood may be used. All camping is limited to 7 nights.

fishing: Fishing is excellent on both sides of the island. On the mainland side fishermen generally target redfish, speckled trout or flounder. Trout can be caught from the shore on grubs or plugs, but most red drum and flounder fishermen work the creeks that wind through the island's marshes. On the ocean side, fishermen use boats to work from the beaches and wade in the surf to catch a good variety of species, including red drum, bluefish, whiting and sharks.

kayaking: Cumberland Island is arguably Georgia's best destination for a paddle-driven island excursion because camping is permitted. Most barrier islands that are open to the public are open for day-trips only, making it necessary to spend the whole day just getting there and back. Sea kayak trips typically begin either in St Marys or at the boat ramp at Crooked River SP. The 7-mi St Mary's route is shortest and is best for overnight trips because it is convenient to the Sea Camp dock. It does require crossing the open waters of Cumberland Sound, however. Tidal currents are strong for any route, so it is important to time paddling trips to coincide with outgoing and incoming tides. Beyond being a means of getting to the island, a sea kayak is also ideal for exploring the rivers and creeks that break up Cumberland's marshes and for observing the abundant birds that use these marshes.

lodging: The 18-room Riverview Hotel (912/882-3242) is located on the banks of the St Marys River, close to the Cumberland Island Visitor Center. Built in 1916 and restored in 1976, the hotel has a sitting room and veranda with a row of rocking chairs. The hotel also houses Seagle's Restaurant, which specializes in seafood and char-broiled steaks and often packs picnic lunches for Cumberland Island explorers. Rooms cost $32–49/night.

The Greyfield Inn (904/261-6408) is a turn of the century mansion built by the Carnegie family on Cumberland Island. Furnished in period antiques, the inn has a dozen large rooms and suites, many with outstanding island views. Rates range from $275–450/night and include a Southern breakfast, picnic lunch, gourmet dinner, canapes at the bar, bicycles and guided island tours. Private ferry transportation is provided to and form the island from Fernandina Beach, Fla.

Crooked River State Park

Gopher tortoises in dry pine forests, and large, moss-draped live oaks overlooking a salt marsh are part of the offerings of Crooked River State Park. Although small, covering only 500 acres, the park provides easy access to Crooked River, which offers good saltwater fishing and shrimping and serves as a popular access route for sea kayakers and power boaters destined toward Cumberland Island National Seashore. Short trails for hiking, a developed campground and a pioneer camping area are all available in the park. Other attractions include a large picnic area, which overlooks the river, a swimming pool, and a miniature golf course. Wildlife is abundant and includes a large deer population, feral hogs, armadillos and a variety of shorebirds in the marsh.

Kingsland (SW) is the nearest town

contact: Superintendent, Crooked River State Park, 3092 Spur 40, St Marys, GA 31558; 912/882-5256; www.gastateparks.org.

getting there: From the jct of I-75 and GA-40 in Kingsland, drive W on GA 40 2.3 mi to Kings Bay Rd and turn L. Drive 3 mi to GA-40 Spur, turn L, and drive 3.6 mi to the park entrance on the R.

starting out: The park office and visitor center, located just inside the main entrance, is open 8 AM to 5 PM daily. Information and maps are available. A drink machine, ice machine and pay phone are there too. Restrooms are available at the picnic area. The park is open 7 AM to 10 PM.

Alcoholic beverages are prohibited in the picnic area. Pets must be on a leash.

topography: The park sets on a broad, flat bluff over the Crooked River. Slash pine/longleaf pine forests and hardwood forests dominated by big live oaks are prevalent. **maps:** USGS Harrietts Bluff.

activities: Hiking, Camping, Fishing, Kayaking.

hiking: 2 nature trails of equal length cover a total distance of 3 mi and provide nice opportunities for easy day-hikes in the park. The *Hardwood Trail* is aptly named for the massive live oaks it winds through near the edge of the marsh, but half of the trail also cuts through a forest of slash pines and longleaf pines with a dense palmetto understory. Most of the *Palmetto Trail* cuts through a pine forest and palmetto thicket. The *Hardwood Trail* begins behind the cottages and is marked by a sign. The left side of the trail route is blazed red, while the right side is blazed orange. The middle portion, which includes a shortcut and the route's beginning and end, is unblazed. The *Palmetto Trail*, which begins in the back of the picnic area, is unblazed but signed at the trailhead and easy to follow. All trails are easy to hike.

camping: A developed campground has 63 sites in 2 loops. The sites, which are defined only by worn areas in the grass, are large but offer little privacy. The forest of tall pines is quite open. Sites include a picnic table, fire ring/grill, water, and electricity. Restroom have hot showers and flush toilets. Camping costs $14/night for tents or $16/night for RVs. The campground is open year round.

3 pioneer camping areas share cold showers, pit toilets and a parking lot. The sites, well isolated from each other by dense

palmetto thickets, are set among tall pines. Each site has running water, picnic tables and an opening for tents. Pioneer camping costs $1/person with a minimum of $15/night and a maximum of $25/night.

fishing: Fishing and cast-netting for shrimp are popular from the dock at the boat ramp, but most fishing is from boats. Red drum, speckled trout and flounder are the most commonly sought-after species, but fishermen catch a host of saltwater species that sometimes even includes sharks. The river is pure salt water. Fishing for bass, bream and catfish is also possible from the banks of a small pond near the campground.

kayaking: The ramp at Crooked River SP is a popular starting place for sea kayaking trips to Cumberland Island NS (see separate chapter) 8 mi away. An easier day-trip route that offers great birding opportunities is to paddle upstream along Crooked River. For either route, it's important to consider tides. Incoming tides are moderate but ebb tides are quite strong. Paddlers going downriver should be cautious to stay out of King Bay Submarine Base waters, which are marked by signs.

lodging: 10 2- and 3-bedroom cottages, lined up in two groups along the river, are fully furnished. The cottages have fireplaces, heating and air, and big back porches with rocking chairs and swings looking over the Crooked River. Cottages cost $65–95/night. For reservations, call 800/864-7275.

Outfitters & Supply Stores

The following businesses sell gear or offer services for the outdoor activities covered in this book. These stores are arranged here geographically, by city, from northwest to southeast. Within a given city, listings are alphabetical. Fishing supply stores and bike stores have not been included; you'll find them in just about any town near a popular fishing or mountain biking area.

Key to some terms used below: camping=tents, backpacks, sleeping bags & clothes; paddling=canoes, kayaks & accessories; topos=USGS 7.5-minute topographic maps.

Calhoun

Outdoor Pleasures—117 S Wall St; 706/625-9901
M–F 10 AM–6 PM, Sa 10 AM–5 PM
Sells: camping, paddling, mountain biking

Blairsville

Mountain Crossings—9710 Gainesville Hwy; 706/745-6095
M–Su 9 AM–5 PM
Sells: camping, rock climbing, kayaks

Helen

Unicoi Outfitters—7082 S Main St; 706/878-3083
M–Sa 9 AM–5:30 PM, Su 1–5:30 PM
Sells: fly fishing; Trips: fly fishing

Woody's Mountain Bikes—19 Clayton Rd; 706/878-3715
M–Su 10 AM–dark
Sells: mountain biking; Rents: mountain biking;
Trips: mountain biking

Dahlonega

Appalachian Outfitters—24 N Park St; 706/867-6677
M–F 10 AM–7 PM, Sa 9 AM–8 PM, Su 1–7 PM
Sells: camping, rock climbing; Trips: rock climbing

Appalachian Outfitters—GA-60 S; 706/864-7117
M–F 10 AM–7 PM, Sa 9 AM–8 PM, Su 1–7 PM
Rents: paddling; Trips: paddling

Roswell

Call of the Wild—425 Market Pl; 770/992-5400
M–F 9 AM–6 PM, Sa 9 AM–5 PM
Sells: camping, rock climbing, topos; Rents: camping

Atlanta

Blue Ridge Mtn Sports—3393 Peachtree Rd NE; 404/266-8372
M–Sa 10 AM–9 PM, Su 12–6 PM
Sells: camping, rock climbing, topos; Rents: camping

High Country—4400 Ashford Dunwoody Rd; 770/391-9657
M–Sa 10 AM–9 PM, Su 12–6 PM
Sells: camping, rock climbing

High Country—3906 Roswell Rd; 404/814-0999
M–Sa 10 AM–9 PM, Su 12–6 PM
Sells: camping, rock climbing, paddling, topos;
Rents: camping, kayaks; Trips: rock climbing, paddling

Outback Outfitters & Bikes—1125 Euclid Ave NE; 404/688-4878
M–F 11 AM–7 PM, Sa 10 AM–6 PM, Su 12–6 PM
Sells: camping, mountain bikes

REI—1800 NE Expressway; 404/633-6508
M–F 10 AM–9 PM, Sa 10 AM–7 PM, Su 11 AM–6 PM
Sells: camping, rock climbing, paddling, mountain bikes, topos;
Rents: camping

REI—1165 Perimeter Ctr West; 770/901-9200
M–F 10 AM–9 PM, Sa 10 AM–7 PM, Su 11 AM–6 PM
Sells: camping, rock climbing, paddling, mountain bikes, topos
Rents: camping

Athens

Outfitters Ltd—1490 Baxter St; 706/546-7575
M–F 10 AM–6 PM, Sa 10 AM–5 PM
Sells: camping, rock climbing, topos; Rents: camping
Trips: Backpacking

Columbus

Outdoor World—3201 Macon Rd; 706/563-2113
M–F 10 AM–8 PM, Sa 10 AM–6 PM
Rents: camping, paddling; Shuttles

Savannah

Oak Bluff Outfitters—4501 Habersham St; 912/691-1115
M–Sa 10 AM–6 PM
Sells: fly fishing; Trips: fly fishing

Wilderness Outfitters—105 E Montgomery Cross Rd; 912/927-2071
M–W, Sa 10 AM–6 PM, Th–F 10 AM–8 PM, Su 1–5 PM
Sells: camping. paddling; Rents: camping

Brunswick

Southeast Adventure Outfitters—1200 Glynn Ave; 912/265-5292
Tu–F 10 AM–6 PM, Sa 10 AM–6 PM
Sells: camping, paddling, topos; Rents: camping, paddling;
Trips: paddling

St Simons Island

Bedford Sportsman South—3405 Frederica Rd; 912/638-5454
M–F 10 AM–5 PM
Sells: some camping, canoes, fly fishing; Trips: fly fishing

Southeast Adventure Outfitters—313 Mallory St; 912/638-6732
M–Su 10 AM–6 PM
Sells: camping, paddling, topos; Rents: camping, paddling;
Trips: paddling, fly fishing

Environmental Organizations

The organizations listed below are working to preserve the natural resources of Georgia. They are listed here simply to provide our readers with further sources of information, not as an endorsement of specific policies. Many of the national organizations have local chapters in which you're automatically enrolled when you join.

American Bass Association, Inc
2810 Trotters Trail
Wetumpka, AL 36092
205/567-6035

American Fisheries Society
5410 Grosvenor Ln
Suite 110
Bethesda, MD 20814
301/897-8616

American Hiking Society
P.O. Box 20160
Washington, DC 20041-2160
703/255-9304
www.outdoorlink.com

American Rivers
801 Pennsylvania Ave, SE
Washington, DC 20003
202/547-6900
www.amrivers.org

American Trails
1400 16th St, NW
Washington, DC 20036
202/483-5611

Appalachian Trail Conference
P.O. Box 807
Harper's Ferry, WV 25425
304/535-6331
www.atconf.org

Bat Conservation International
PO Box 162603
Austin, TX 78716
512/327-9721
www.batcon.org

Boy Scouts of America
PO Box 152079
1325 W. Walnut Hill Ln
Irving, TX 75015
214/580-2000
www.bsa.scouting.org

Center for Marine Conservation
1725 DeSales St., NW
Suite 500
Washington, DC 20036
202/429-5609

The Cousteau Society, Inc
870 Greenbrier Circle
Chesapeake, VA 23320
804/523-9335

Defenders of Wildlife
1101 Fourteenth St, NW
Washington, DC 20077
202/682-9400
www.defenders.org

Ducks Unlimited, Inc
906 Victorian Ave
Sparks, NV 89431
702/358-7747
www.ducksunlimited.com

Earth Island Institute
300 Broadway
San Francisco, CA 94133
415/788-3666
www.earthisland.org

Earthwatch
PO Box 403N
Watertown, MA 02272
800/776-0188
gaia.earthwatch.org

Environmental Defense Fund
275 Park Ave S
New York, NY 10010
212/505-2100
www.edf.org

Federation of Fly Fishers
502 South 19th St
Bozeman, MT 59771
406/585-7592

Girl Scouts of America
420 Fifth Ave
New York, NY 10018
212/852-8000

Greenpeace, Inc
1436 U St, NW
Washington, DC 20009
202/462-1177
www.greenpeace.org

International Game Fish Assoc
1301 E. Atlantic Blvd
Pompano Beach, FL 33060
305/941-3474

The Izaak Walton League
707 Conservation Ln
Gaithersburg, MD 20878
800/453-5463
www.iwla.org

League of Conservation Voters
1707 L St, NW
Washington, DC 20036
202/785-8683
www.lcv.org

League of Women Voters
1730 M St, NW
Washington, DC 20036
202/429-1965

National Audubon Society
700 Broadway
New York, NY 10003
212/979-3000
www.audubon.org

National Geographic Society
17th & M Sts, NW
Washington, DC 20036
202/857-7000
www.nationalgeographic.com

National Organization for River
Sports
PO Box 6847
Colorado Springs, CO 80934
719/473-2466

National Parks & Conservation
Association
1776 Massachusetts Ave, NW
Washington, DC 20036
202/223-6722
www.npca.org

National Wild Turkey
Federation
P.O Box 530
Edgefield, SC 29824
803/637-3106

National Wildlife Federation
1400 16th St, NW
Washington, DC 20036
202/797-6800
www.nwf.com

Natural Resources Defense
Council
40 W 20th St
New York, NY 10011
212/727-2700
www.nrdc.org

The Nature Conservancy
1815 N Lynn St
Arlington, VA 22209
703/841-5300
www.tnc.org

Rails-to-Trails Conservancy
1400 Sixteenth St, NW
Washington, DC 20036
202/797-5400

The Sierra Club
730 Polk St
San Francisco, CA 94109
415/776-2211
www.sierraclub.org

Southern Environmental Law
Center
201 W Main St
Suite 14
Charlottesville, VA 22902
804/977-4090

Southern Off-Road Bicycle
Association
P.O. Box 671774
Marietta, GA 30067

Trout Unlimited
1500 Wilson Blvd
Suite 310
Arlington, VA 22209
703/522-0200
xenon.proxima.com

The Wilderness Society
900 Seventeenth St, NW
Washington, DC 20006
202/833-2300
www.wilderness.org

World Wildlife Fund
1250 24th St, NW
Washington, DC 20037
202/293-4800
www.worldwildlife.org

Index